DEMOCRACY'S DESTRUCTION?

Democracy's Destruction?

CHANGING PERCEPTIONS OF THE SUPREME COURT, THE PRESIDENCY, AND THE SENATE AFTER THE 2020 ELECTION

James L. Gibson

Russell Sage Foundation NEW YORK

ROR: https://ror.org/02yh9se80
DOI: https://doi.org/10.7758/dvkr4409

LIBRARY OF CONGRESS CATALOGING-IN-PUBLICATION DATA

Library of Congress Cataloging-in-Publication Data

Names: Gibson, James L., 1951– author.
Title: Democracy's destruction? : changing perceptions of the Supreme Court, the presidency, and the Senate after the 2020 election / James L. Gibson.
Other titles: Changing perceptions of the Supreme Court, the presidency, and the Senate after the 2020 election
Description: New York : Russell Sage Foundation, [2024] | Includes bibliographical references and index. | Summary: "In Democracy's Destruction, James L. Gibson investigates the degree to which the 2020 presidential election and its aftermath did lasting damage to American national political institutions. It focuses on the U.S. Supreme Court, the presidency, and the U.S. Senate-the institutions that most observers feel were put at risk by the election and its attendant events-as well as on the legitimacy of democracy in America itself. Gibson argues that the election and its aftermath undermined confidence and faith in American political institutions-and perhaps in American democracy as well. To assess the impact of the 2020 election on American political institutions, Gibson embeds the inquiry squarely within legitimacy theory writ large and particularly in the studies of institutional legitimacy that have accumulated over the years. Consequently, the book is not just an analysis of the election of 2020 but also a more general treatise that interrogates a variety of hypotheses about levels of legitimacy and how legitimacy changes"—Provided by publisher.
Identifiers: LCCN 2023056431 (print) | LCCN 2023056432 (ebook) | ISBN 9780871548658 (paperback) | ISBN 9781610449274 (ebook)
Subjects: LCSH: United States—Politics and government—2017-2021. | United States—Politics and government—2021- | Presidents—United States—Election—2020. | Democracy—United States.
Classification: LCC E916 .G53 2024 (print) | LCC E916 (ebook) | DDC 324.973/0933—dc23/eng/20240206
LC record available at https://lccn.loc.gov/2023056431
LC ebook record available at https://lccn.loc.gov/2023056432

Text design by Linda Secondari. Front matter DOI: https://doi.org/10.7758/dvkr4409.1227

RUSSELL SAGE FOUNDATION

112 East 64th Street, New York, New York 10065

10 9 8 7 6 5 4 3 2 1

To Washington University in St. Louis, and especially its Weidenbaum Center—
Because it is difficult to imagine a university that is more supportive of social
science research

CONTENTS

ILLUSTRATIONS

Additional figures, tables, and discussion can be found in the online appendix at https://www.russellsage.org/publications/democracys -destruction.

ABOUT THE AUTHOR

JAMES L. GIBSON⑩ is the Sidney W. Souers Professor of Government at Washington University in St. Louis and Professor Extraordinary in political science at Stellenbosch University, South Africa.

PREFACE

WE LIVE IN tumultuous political times. Indeed, some if not many regard the current political situation in the United States as a battle about nothing less than the survival of democracy in the country.

Perhaps that is so, but perhaps it is not. Historians often remind us that the political history of the country is one of intense struggles over a wide variety of issues and institutional arrangements. Was the election of 2020 that much different from the election of 1876? Does anyone seriously believe that a second civil war is about to break out in the United States? Politics is always about conflict—about designing rules and institutions to gain political advantage. Politics today may be nasty, noisy, noxious, and notorious, but whether it is that much different from the politics of many past eras in American political history is unclear.

I often live in South Africa, a country with weak political institutions; they have been captured, have little legitimacy with the people, and rarely serve the interests of anyone other than privileged elites (who inevitably seek greater privilege). From my perspective, the political systems in South Africa and America differ enormously.

Perhaps I am wrong, but one possible conclusion from the 2020 election imbroglio in the United States is that the country's democratic institutions prevailed against one of the most serious threats ever. After all, Donald Trump and his Republicans won practically none of more than eighty lawsuits over the election outcome, and hundreds of insurrectionists have been prosecuted for their seditious acts. I do not wear rose-colored glasses, but at the same time, I do not join the ranks of those claiming that "the sky is falling."

And yet . . .

This book is about American democracy and the election of 2020, and about its aftermath, the insurrection and impeachment of former president Trump. It is not about the midterm elections of 2022 or the presidential election of 2024. I do not necessarily claim that what is true of the past will be true of the future. Democracy in the United States still faces very serious threats. Round two could conceivably have an outcome different from that of round one, in part owing to the exposure of the soft pressure points of American democratic institutions (for example, election administrators in the states). Specifically, this book seeks nothing more than to answer the question whether the canards of Trump, his fellow Republicans, and their fellow travelers in 2020 and early 2021 did serious damage to American political institutions. Nothing more.

My work has been stimulated to a considerable degree by a paper that Michael Nelson and I published in 2019 in which we sought to understand whether Trump's attacks on the federal judiciary in the United States undermined the legitimacy of the courts.[1] Our findings were unambiguous: Trump did little damage to the judiciary, in part because of a backlash to his attacks and in part because he had insufficient credibility to make his charges stick. We were unable to assess the myriad ways in which institutional legitimacy can be lost, but that short paper activated and reinforced my view that conclusions should not be drawn without data, and that the conclusions of social scientists are often at odds with the conclusions of pundits and casual observers.

I therefore set out to understand whether Trump and the Republicans' claims beginning in the summer of 2020 that the election would be rigged had any consequences. I had already constructed the 2020 version of my long-running Freedom and Tolerance Surveys before I gave serious attention to the democracy-damage hypothesis. As events leading up to the election (such as the Amy Coney Barrett nomination) unfolded, it became clear that my July 2020 survey could (and should) become a t_1 data point in a longitudinal research design, if only additional resources could be found to mount subsequent interviews in the time series.

That is where the Weidenbaum Center stepped in. After the National Science Foundation discouraged the submission of a quicky proposal on the matter, the Weidenbaum Center, and especially its director, Steve Faz-zari, ponied up to fill the void in my treasury. This allowed t_2 to be mounted with fieldwork initiated in December 2020.

This truly is a firehouse study—the research agenda and design evolved as events unfolded. The next important episode in the election saga was the January 6, 2021, insurrection by Trump and his followers. The December 2020 survey was still in the field as the sun rose that morning. Shortly there-after, I terminated the fieldwork and filtered the t_2 dataset to include only interviews completed by January 5, 2021. Then I set about trying to find a banker for a t_3 survey.

As it has in the past, the Russell Sage Foundation came to the rescue by issuing a Presidential Grant for this project.[2] The Weidenbaum Center and its supporters and the Center for the Study of Race, Ethnicity, & Equity were able to top up my t_3 resources with a Research Seed Grant, allowing me to field an oversample of African Americans for the t_3 survey.[3] For an oversample of active college students, a small grant from the Foundation for Individual Rights in Education saved the day.[4]

To round out acknowledging my indebtedness, I also conducted a t_4 survey with the generous support of the Weidenbaum Center and its bene-factors. I am extremely grateful to both Steve Fazzari for his assistance in gaining this support, which went far beyond the call of duty, and to the former director of the center, Steve Smith, who has been a strong supporter of my research agenda over the years.

Regrettably, my efforts to consummate the research design with a major t_5 survey were torpedoed by those who favor greater causal certainty over everything else. I will have more to say throughout this book about the growing and seemingly irreconcilable tension between being relatively more certain about causal processes for small research questions, on the one hand, and taking on large research questions even at the expense of greater causal uncertainty, on the other. The explicit premise of this book is that collecting and assembling empirical evidence in response to research questions of such fundamental magnitude and importance to the welfare of the country are probably worth the sacrifice of a bit of causal certitude. I recognize, how-ever, that I am in a (shrinking if not vanishing) minority on this issue.

Throughout this entire process, the survey firm NORC at the University of Chicago was an invaluable resource. Its AmeriSpeak panel survey pro-vided the respondents for each of the surveys I conducted (including the oversamples). I am grateful to the entire survey team at NORC, especially Dan Costanzo, Jennifer Carter, and Mark Watts.

For research assistance on this project, I am incalculably indebted to my undergraduate assistant, Katie O'Quinn. The book has profited immeasurably from Katie's hard and persistent work. I can only hope that, while doing such a fine job for me, she learned something about the conduct and values of social scientific research. For additional research assistance on the project, I am thankful for the help of Maggie Amjad, Zoe Ang, and Jenna Pedersen. Finally, I am indebted to Donald Patrick Haider-Markel, Lee Slocum, Candis Watts Smith, and Ariel White for comments on various portions of this work.

As always, Michael Nelson has been extremely valuable as one I can bounce my (many half-baked) ideas against. For his patience with me, I am grateful.

In the end, I fully recognize the limitations of a research design that focuses on the views of representative samples of the American people. Coups, insurrections, and revolutions are rarely instigated by representative samples of a population. The success of such actions may ultimately depend on the views of the people, but the drivers of the destruction of democracy are usually unrepresentative elites. Of course, I do not naively assume that the fate of democracy depends on how the majority of people answer questions in an online survey. On the other hand, as I have previously argued regarding anti-Semitism's failure to gain much of a foothold during Russia's political transformation, the ultimate success of elite gambits depends on their ability to attract the support of the people.[5] That being the case, perhaps studies like the one I have produced here are of at least some value.

Finally, I wish this book did not have to be written. But because threats to the health of America's democracy were not readily apparent to all in 2020 and 2021—and perhaps may still not be—intense analysis of rigorous data is essential. In a world of lies and orchestrated attempts to mislead, producing evidence-based analyses and conclusions is the only way to diagnose the health of democratic systems and prevent democracy's destruction—a task of the utmost importance and urgency.

James L. Gibson
Miami, Florida
December 2023

CHAPTER 1

The Consequences of Elections

ON JANUARY 6, 2021, one of the most momentous events in recent American politics took place. The Capitol was stormed by an angry mob seeking to overturn the results of the 2020 presidential election. This assault on the country's democratic system was orchestrated by the sitting president, abetted by his political party and other sycophants, and supported by a vocal minority of the American people. No event in recent U.S. political history is comparable to this effort to subvert American democracy.

The January 6 insurrection was only the most salient and pernicious episode in a series of assaults on America's democratic institutions. Indeed, during Donald Trump's presidency, such attacks were unlike any before in modern American politics. Even a cursory compilation of the influence of Trump's machinations and canards is sobering:

- The attacks arguably originated with the efforts to "delegitimize" Barack Obama's presidency via the "birther" movement.[1]
- U.S. bureaucracy has been undermined through allegations that a "deep state" exists with a will independent of and contrary to that of the president.[2]
- The mass media have been characterized as "the enemy of the people."[3]
- Courts have been politicized, for example, through references to

https://doi.org/10.7758/dvkr4409.8182

"Obama judges" and charges that judges are "incompetent" and "so political."[4]

- Truth in myriad contexts has been under attack through conspiracy theories and disinformation campaigns.[5]

As to the 2020 presidential election itself, even before the balloting began, Trump and the Republicans repeatedly and without evidence predicted that the election would be rigged.[6] After he lost, Trump and the Republicans sought to overturn the results through legal and illegal efforts alike, to no avail and without any meaningful proof of fraud.[7] Trump was impeached for instigating the insurrection, and at his Senate trial, a majority of senators, but not a supermajority, voted to convict him. News about these events has been widely accessible to the American people via social media and 24/7 mass media coverage.[8]

During the election season and its protracted aftermath, pundits often questioned whether the election would fundamentally change American political institutions. The potential effect most widely discussed was the loss of legitimacy. Because the loser refused to accept that he lost the election and made wild and unsubstantiated claims of electoral fraud, pundits hypothesized that many Americans—perhaps as many as 70 million—would lose confidence in electoral processes and the institutions that undergird and sustain them, that Joe Biden's presidency would be delegitimized, and even that the persistence of America's democracy itself would be put at risk. Some of this speculation was no doubt little more than partisan hyperbole. But there is at least some evidence that confidence in the American democratic system was shaken, and that even well-informed elites became more worried than ever that U.S. democracy would not be able to flourish or even survive.[9] And of course, the election did not take place in an institutional vacuum: for instance, the incumbent president, expecting to lose the popular election, sought to pack the U.S. Supreme Court with like-minded justices whom he hoped would award him the election, just as the court had to fellow Republican George W. Bush in 2000.

If some institutional legitimacy was lost in the 2020 election process— and it should not simply be *assumed* that legitimacy was lost—then the election was even more important than it seemed to engaged partisans. Legitimacy is an invaluable resource for institutions, a form of political capital that, while difficult to earn and sustain, can shield an institution when it comes under attack. Indeed, legitimacy is so important that both institutional leaders and scholars have invested enormous resources in recent decades to try to understand its dynamics. Legitimacy theory (addressed more thoroughly in the next section) has become perhaps the single most investigated topic among political scientists who study judicial institutions, and concerns about institutional legitimacy permeate virtually all subfields in political science (and in other disciplines, including law).[10] Political institutions that attempt to govern without legitimacy must have nearly unlimited resources, because they have only three effective means of inducing compliance with their decisions: such an institution can either decide issues in a manner pleasing to all its constituents, which is not possible; pay those who are displeased with policy outputs to comply, using its resources (its purse); or force the displeased to comply, using its means of coercion (its sword). The ability to convince people to accept unwanted policy decisions because they think it is the right thing to do is a form of political capital second to none.

However, apprehensions about a loss of institutional legitimacy are possibly overblown and hyperbolic. Many observers sounded the same sort of alarm on a smaller scale about President Trump's efforts to delegitimize certain federal courts earlier in his term of office.[11] But some empirical research indicates that, whatever his intentions, Trump's impact on the legitimacy of the federal courts was negligible.[12] Moreover, the best evidence demonstrates that the analogous highly contested presidential election of 2000 had little lasting effect on American political institutions, especially the Supreme Court.[13] And perhaps most important of all, institutions are resilient—that is what makes them institutions. Policies change, personnel are replaced, some become delighted while others become disgusted, and, generally speaking, much of institutional life goes on as normal. When power is transferred from an incumbent group to its challengers, many might bemoan that "the sky is falling." But in fact, in modern times at least, the sky's altitude has not been reduced.

Elections have consequences, to be sure, but they rarely have dire, momentous, and immediate consequences. Pundits often overestimate the significance of events, and the 2020 election is no exception. Only rigorous social science inquiry can assess whether institutional damage was done by the run-up to the election, the election itself, and its aftermath. We should not jump to the conclusion that America's democracy was—or was not—

damaged by Trump, the Republicans, and their allies without careful and systematic supportive evidence.

The purpose of this book therefore is to investigate the degree to which the 2020 presidential election and its aftermath did lasting damage to three American national political institutions. My analysis is limited to the U.S. Supreme Court, the presidency, and the U.S. Senate—the institutions that some observers feel were put at risk—as well as on the legitimacy of several hallowed democratic values. The general hypothesis considered in this research is that the election and its aftermath undermined confidence and faith in these American political institutions—and, by extension, perhaps in American democracy as well.

To assess the impact of the 2020 election on American political institutions, I embed the inquiry squarely within legitimacy theory writ large, and in particular in studies of institutional legitimacy. Consequently, this book is not just an analysis of the election of 2020 but also a more general treatise that interrogates a variety of hypotheses about levels of legitimacy and how legitimacy changes. My analysis is heavily weighted toward the Supreme Court, owing in part to the importance of the court as a maker of public policy that lacks the essential fount of democratic legitimacy—accountability to the people—making it widely thought to be more fragile than the presidency and the Senate, and in part to my nearly forty-year-old research agenda on the legitimacy of courts in both the United States and around the world.

At the same time, one of the most important innovations of this book is its extension of legitimacy theory across institutions. Little research exists on the legitimacy of the American presidency,[14] and only limited work on the legitimacy of legislatures has been reported.[15] Scholars have long called for cross-institutional analysis,[16] and some have recently attempted to answer that call.[17] But the research reported here stands as one of the first attempts to measure and assess the legitimacy of three major American political institutions: the Supreme Court, the presidency, and the Senate.

In addressing these legitimacy theory hypotheses, this book relies heavily on survey data measuring Americans' ratings of the institutions that govern them. I turn to several nationally representative surveys I conducted between July 2020 and June 2021. Unfortunately, the research design of this project is a bit untidy, mainly because it is a firehouse study that unfolded as the events themselves unfolded (and as I was able to secure increments of funding).[18] Like those who study the eruption of volcanoes, firehouse researchers try to understand unanticipated events in real time. The actions of Trump and the Republicans to overturn the 2020 presidential election results sent me scurrying to find ways (and means) to get into the field as quickly as possible. In addition to the (preplanned) July 2020 survey, I was able to field a survey in December 2020 and January 2021 (with interviews completed by January 5, 2021), another in February and March 2021, and the last in this series in June 2021. These databases are perhaps unprecedented, but as the crisis unfolded, I responded to events without the luxury of focusing on a single data source planned years in advance. On the other hand, no one can doubt the relevance of these data to the research question at hand.

Another crucial and perhaps unprecedented aspect of this research is its focus on intergroup differences in attitudes toward democratic institutions. In particular, the large oversample of African Americans included in the February and March 2021 survey allowed me to assess the election's consequences for one of the groups most targeted by Republicans seeking to make certain that not all votes counted (or were counted). Moreover, a large proportion of Black respondents were reinterviewed in June 2021, permitting at least some direct assessment of changes over time. When scholars discuss a "democratic political culture" in the United States, they too often seem to (implicitly) assume that different groups subscribe to those cultural values at the same rate. My analysis does not make that assumption, and as the data show, that turns out to have been a wise choice.

To recap, this book makes several contributions to our understanding of the threats to these democratic institutions. First, it expands legitimacy theory beyond its "home court" in judicial studies. Few serious efforts to measure and explain variation in the legitimacy of the presidency have been reported, and only limited research on the legitimacy of Congress has been conducted. Second, this study allows some assessment of how legitimacy changed over time in response to events surrounding the 2020 election, including the midnight appointment of Amy Coney Barrett to the Supreme Court. Third, it directly measures perceptions and assessments of those events rather than assuming that all Americans understood them similarly. Fourth, both inter- and intraracial differences in support for U.S. democracy are investigated with unusually dispositive data. Finally, and perhaps most importantly, my analysis investigates support for these institutions within two discrete time periods: up until January 6 and after the insurrection. This allows me to more precisely pinpoint the election's consequences apart from the consequences of the insurrection. Thus, the question of how the election affected these three institutions will be answered with an unusually variegated set of hypotheses and data.

Central to this analysis is legitimacy theory. Although the theory is well developed and widely understood, a brief overview of what legitimacy is and why it is so important to institutions is perhaps useful.

The Theory of Institutional Legitimacy

The analysis reported in this book concerns itself with the degree to which people have faith in three American democratic institutions—in particular, the degree to which ordinary people (in contrast to elites) are willing to extend legitimacy to some of the political institutions that govern them. Several elements of this approach to understanding how people relate to political institutions must be explained.

Scholars generally agree on the basic contours of legitimacy theory.[19] For instance, most recognize that legitimacy—sometimes referred to as "authority" or "diffuse support"[20]—is a normative concept, having something to do with the (moral and legal) right to make decisions. As Tom Tyler observes:

> Legitimacy is a . . . property of an authority, institution, or social arrangement that leads those connected to it to believe that it is appropriate, proper, and just. Because of legitimacy, people feel that they ought to defer to decisions and rules, following them voluntarily out of obligation rather than out of fear of punishment or anticipation of reward. Being legitimate is important to the success of authorities, institutions, and institutional arrangements since it is difficult to exert influence over others based solely upon the possession and use of power. Being able to gain voluntary acquiescence from most people, most of the time, due to their sense of obligation increases effectiveness during periods of scarcity, crisis, and conflict.[21]

In other words, institutions perceived as legitimate have a widely accepted right to make binding judgments for a political community. Those without legitimacy find that right contested.

In the last few decades, scholarly interest in legitimacy has exploded. Indeed, few institutional theories in contemporary political science are as widely accepted and relied on as legitimacy theory. It has been used to try to understand everything from the role of central banks to corporate social responsibility, legitimacy in international affairs, the legitimacy of the police, and even the legitimacy of algorithms.[22]

Although there are different ways to conceptualize legitimacy, the approach I adopt in this book is typically called "sociological legitimacy"—the beliefs about legitimacy held by the American people.[23] More specifically, as Richard Fallon defines it, "loosely following [Max] Weber . . . sociological legitimacy [is associated] with beliefs that the law and formal legal authorities within a particular regime deserve respect or obedience with a further disposition to obey the law for reasons besides self-interest."[24] This is an empirical concept, not a normative one; it refers to how people actually feel about the institutions that govern them rather than how they ought to feel. As a consequence, those who study this type of legitimacy need not make normative judgments about whether more or less legitimacy is desirable.[25]

Furthermore, scholars of sociological legitimacy typically treat even the question whether institutional legitimacy is necessary for effective democratic governance as an empirical one. Relying on cultural theories of democracy, most scholars believe that the success of democracy itself depends on its legitimacy, on the belief that "democracy is the only game in town." As Larry Diamond famously put it:

> Political competitors must come to regard democracy (and the laws, procedures, and institutions it specifies) as "the only game in town," the only viable framework for governing the society and advancing their own interests. At the mass level, there must be a broad normative and behavioral consensus—*one that cuts across class, ethnic, nationality, and other cleavages*—on the legitimacy of the constitutional system, however poor or unsatisfying its performance may be at any point in time.[26]

Legitimacy (or as David Easton termed it, "diffuse support") is typically distinguished from simple approval (or disapproval) of the actions of an institution (specific support).[27] Diffuse support is often conceptualized as a "reservoir of goodwill" that institutions can draw on to implement disagreeable decisions or in times of crisis.[28] By contrast, specific support is "satisfaction with the performance of a political institution."[29] In other words, diffuse support represents longer-term, global judgments about an institution's authority, whereas specific support represents shorter-term and more fleeting opinions about an institution's particular actions. While diffuse support might be thought of as a form of institutional loyalty, specific support reflects approval or disapproval of recent institutional actions. Thus, a crucial attribute of institutions is the degree to which they enjoy the *loyalty*, not just the approval, of their constituents.

When an institution makes a decision of which all of its constituents approve, discussions of legitimacy are rarely relevant or necessary. Such discussions become particularly apposite, however, when constituents disagree about political judgments. To use a widely cited phrasing, "legitimacy is for losers"; in other words, legitimacy takes on its primary significance in the presence of an "objection precondition."[30] As Lawrence Friedman rightly noted long ago: "We do not need a theory of legitimacy to explain why people obey a person with a gun, or adhere to an order that brings them personal honor or gain; or obey their religions or their moral codes."[31] When an institution's constituents disagree over a decision made by an institution, some may ask whether the institution has the "right" to make the decision.[32] A legitimate institution is one that is recognized as an appropriate decision-making body even when constituents disagree with its outputs; its decisions are respected, enforced, and implemented even in the face of dissent. To be effective, institutions need legitimacy—the leeway to go against public opinion (for instance, to protect unpopular political minorities). It follows from legitimacy's focus on "voluntary acquiescence" that the most important consequence of legitimacy is people's acceptance of and acquiescence to decisions and policies with which they disagree. Consequently, institutional legitimacy is an invaluable and irreplaceable form of political capital. In sum, legitimacy matters greatly to institutions.

Legitimacy theory has been explicated and tested most fully within the context of judicial institutions in the United States, mainly because the federal courts, including the U.S. Supreme Court, lack the essential fount of legitimacy—democratic accountability to the majority.[33] Indeed, in the subfield of judicial politics, perhaps no other research question (with the possible exception of research on the determinants of judicial decision-making) has consumed as many intellectual resources as the study of how both individual courts and the legal system generally acquire, maintain, use, and lose institutional legitimacy. The need for institutional legitimacy is not unique to the U.S. Supreme Court; state courts and courts throughout the world also require legitimacy in order to function as effective institutions.[34]

Concern about institutional legitimacy reaches beyond scholars and democratic theorists. For example, Supreme Court justices have dramatically increased the use of the term "legitimacy" in their opinions, as Dion Farganis notes: "since the Court's 1954 decision in *Brown*, in fact, the justices have made seventy-one such references to the Court's institutional legitimacy, compared with just nine in the 164 years up to that point."[35] Moreover, in the aftermath of the *Dobbs* ruling that overturned the abortion rights declared in *Roe v. Wade*, several justices, including Justice Elena Kagan, have publicly voiced concerns about the court's legitimacy.[36] The mass media have also rediscovered legitimacy theory in recent years, issuing frequent reports on the Supreme Court's ability to attract the loyalty of the American people.[37] Of course, debates about the legitimacy of the presidency/president have long circulated in American politics, as in the challenges to President Barack Obama based on false allegations about his place of birth.[38] "Legitimacy" may not always be rigorously defined in the popular vernacular, but it is clear that the concept has become widely salient and important to many observers of American political institutions.

In short, this book focuses on sociological legitimacy, or what ordinary people think about the authority of the institutions that govern them. Institutional legitimacy means that people extend the right to make binding decisions to an institution (be it a court, a central bank, or whatever), and that right is associated with a presumption in favor of accepting decisions even when they are disagreeable. As a consequence, institutions seek to acquire and maintain legitimacy; its value is recognized by nearly everyone. In addition, many scholars also recognize that legitimacy may be fragile and can be lost. Governance without legitimate institutions is difficult indeed.

The 2020 Presidential Election and Lost Legitimacy?

How institutions acquire legitimacy has been studied widely, but how legitimacy is lost is much less well investigated.[39] Several scholars have examined the impact on judicial legitimacy of disagreement with individual court decisions, but such effects seem to be weak at best.[40] To account for declining support for the Supreme Court among African Americans, Gregory

Caldeira and I have suggested that sustained disappointment with an institution's policy outputs can undermine legitimacy.[41] Events politicizing the judiciary, such as highly contentious and partisan fights over Supreme Court nominations,[42] can also undermine judicial legitimacy by promulgating the view that the court is "just another political institution."[43] Direct elite attacks on institutions have also been examined as possible causes of diminished institutional legitimacy.[44]

That an institution is unfair or has acted unfairly might be a particularly pungent line of criticism of institutions, because people care greatly about fairness in politics.[45] Thus, elite charges that mass media are biased, that elections are rigged, that judges are not impartial, and that processes and procedures are unjust can be particularly persuasive.[46] For such charges to "stick," elites often need to connect them with deeper, more general, and more widely shared values held by ordinary people. "Fair play" is such a value.

What makes the 2020 presidential election different from many contested elections is the sustained attack by elites on the legitimacy of the electoral process and the institutions designed to manage challenges to that process. President Trump, of course, orchestrated the attacks, but he had many willing accomplices, such as Missouri senator Josh Hawley and Texas senator Ted Cruz. Indeed, Republicans in general left few stones unturned in their efforts to undermine the institutions rendering judgments on the election, including state election boards, state courts, the military, federal courts, the U.S. Supreme Court, state legislatures, the president's own cabinet, the Electoral College, Congress (in certifying the election), and unsupportive Republicans (especially RINOs, or "Republicans in Name Only"). Republicans' repeated attacks on the legitimacy of American political institutions may well have resonated with the American people.

And then there was the insurrection.

Whether the assault on the U.S. Capitol on January 6, 2021, produced its intended effects is unclear. Like other attacks on the United States (for example, the Islamist attacks on September 11, 2001), the insurrection may well have raised rather than lowered institutional legitimacy by inducing a "rally round the flag" effect.[47] Events are not always as they seem; indeed, the backlash to events can often be more momentous than the events themselves.[48] When people's values are at risk, they often "double down" on the values under attack, reinvigorating their commitment to them. For instance, a standard finding in public opinion research is that attacks on the country tend to raise rather than lower confidence in American institutions.[49] Given this body of research, it seems quite plausible that the insurrection actually strengthened rather than weakened American political institutions. From this perspective, the January 2021 insurrection possibly marks the beginning of the rebirth of American democracy, not its pending demise.

The alternative to the hypothesis that legitimacy was diminished or lost in the wake of the 2020 election and its aftermath is, of course, the hypothesis that political institutions are resilient and therefore were little affected by the election or the insurrection. That is, their "reservoir of goodwill," as suggested by conventional legitimacy theory, guarded them from attacks on their authority. From this perspective, the efforts of Trump and the Republicans to undermine institutional legitimacy likely failed.

Still, people exposed to elite challenges to institutional legitimacy could reasonably be more likely to be influenced by such challenges and therefore to withdraw legitimacy from the institutions. That is the central hypothesis of this research. Specifically, I expect both awareness of and judgments about the key events in the 2020 presidential election and the insurrection to be associated with lower levels of institutional support for the Supreme Court, the Senate, and the presidency.[50] I also consider the connection of these events to generalized support for America's democratic institutions.

The attacks of Trump and the Republicans on American political institutions could have undermined the popular legitimacy of those institutions. Elections have consequences, as both Democrats (Obama) and Republicans (Trump) have reminded us.[51] Few elections in the recent history of American politics were more consequential than the presidential balloting of 2020. Indeed, the 2020 election could well be remembered as a watershed event for the evolution of American democracy. Not only did the sitting president fail to concede that he lost the vote, but more than in any recent election the loser sought to overturn the outcome through a variety of legal, illegal, and political gambits, including efforts that threaten the very essence of American democracy.[52] Elections certainly have consequences; as of the close of 2021, many people feared that President Trump's perhaps unintended legacy would be widespread and growing distrust in and dissatisfaction with American democratic institutions coupled with a grave threat to the legitimacy of the Biden presidency—and conceivably worse.

The overriding research question this book attempts to answer is whether the 2020 election and its aftermath reduced, perhaps irretrievably, the legitimacy of America's political institutions and possibly of democracy itself. In testing this hypothesis, I take a somewhat distinctive approach to assessing the impact of events on the public's opinions.

Events and Perceptions Thereof

Following a considerable body of extant research, the overall objective of this project is to assess whether so-called exogenous events—the 2020 presidential election—affected attitudes toward political institutions. Since such events unfold over time, as do people's reactions to them, a panel survey in which the same people are repeatedly interviewed is the obvious preferred research design.

However, despite their important benefits for causal attributions, panel surveys often make it difficult to discern precisely what the independent variable is. For example, scholars who study the impact of Supreme Court decisions on attitudes toward the judiciary typically assume that all respondents are aware of important court decisions.[53] Obviously, that is a fallacious assumption, even for landmark court rulings.[54] More generally, as scholars of public opinion have long recognized, it is unwise to assume that political facts are accurately and uniformly understood.[55] Truth, as we have learned, is often contested in American politics.

The difficulty with approaches that focus on citizen perceptions and evaluations of events is that citizens must be asked what their perceptions and evaluations actually are. This requires the researcher to identify the relevant events in advance, which is easy to do when the researcher is addressing Supreme Court decisions, but more difficult in a study focused on the impact of events (including Supreme Court confirmations) on public opinion. Nevertheless, because events such as those associated with the 2020 presidential election are obviously not self-evident truths, my research includes empirical measures of how people perceived and understood the election.

The events surrounding the insurrection and the 2020 presidential election more generally had many legitimacy-threatening elements, the most important of which may have been Trump's efforts to delegitimize the election outcome. Here two activities stand out. First, both before and after the election, President Trump repeatedly called the balloting "rigged." Second, especially after the Electoral College vote confirmed Biden as the president-elect, Trump engaged in a variety of efforts to overturn the results of the balloting.[56]

Then the insurrection and the second impeachment process took place in January and February 2021. On January 6, pro-Trump rioters stormed the Capitol building, largely in an effort to block the completion of the 2020 presidential election. President Trump was charged with inciting the riot and was impeached by the House of Representatives. A majority of senators voted to convict ex-president Trump, but that vote fell short of the required supermajority. At that point, Trump retired to Florida, though he did not retire from politics.

As to threats to judicial legitimacy, Barrett's confirmation to the Supreme Court just weeks before Trump lost the election, especially in the context of the failed Merrick Garland nomination in 2016 and the likely litigation over the election outcome, could not help but politicize the nominee and perhaps the court itself.

In this book, I therefore focus on measuring awareness and evaluations of five potentially delegitimizing sets of events: (1) allegations that the election was rigged or somehow manipulated so that it did not represent the actual votes of the American people; (2) President Trump's efforts to overturn and reverse the election outcome; (3) the insurrection of January 6, 2021, and the ransacking of the Capitol building; (4) the impeachment of President Trump and the failure to sanction him at the Senate trial; and (5) the nomination and confirmation of Barrett to the Supreme Court in the run-up to the election.

My surveys asked questions about both levels of awareness and assessments of each set of events, since, as discussed earlier, I do not assume, as many researchers do, that political events are perceived by everyone and, once perceived, are understood and evaluated in the same way. Most specifically, I hypothesize that the legitimacy of American democratic institutions is most likely to be rejected by those who believe that the 2020 presidential election was rigged or somehow manipulated so that it did not represent the actual votes of the American people; those who endorse President Trump's efforts to overturn and reverse the outcome of the election;

those who regard the insurrection of January 6, 2021, as not harmful to American democracy; those who opposed the impeachment of Trump and approved of the Senate's failure to sanction him; and those who see nothing inappropriate about the nomination and confirmation of Barrett to the Supreme Court during the last weeks of the presidential election.

This project's research design has the advantage of allowing me to distinguish the effects of the election events themselves from the insurrection events and the subsequent Trump impeachment. The first portion of the book addresses the consequences of the election, based on a survey that was completed on January 5, 2021. (For details, see the appendix.) The book's second portion focuses on the aftermath of the insurrection and impeachment, based mainly on a survey conducted in February and March 2021. That analysis, of course, incorporates the effects of the election itself but also seeks to determine whether the insurrection uprising had any lasting consequences for the legitimacy of American democratic institutions.

Interracial Differences in Institutional Legitimacy

Not all Americans were affected by the election events in the same fashion. Indeed, as I argue in greater detail later in this book, African Americans were uniquely part of the subtext of nearly all the election events, and their reactions to the insurrection events could reasonably be expected to differ from those of White people. First, at least in a somewhat different but temporally related context, Black people in America have been found to be more willing than White people to tolerate rioting as a means of expressing a group's grievances. For instance, a Monmouth poll fielded in the summer of 2020 reported that African Americans were somewhat more likely than White people to judge that summer's widespread rioting as "fully justified" (27 percent versus 15 percent), while White people were considerably more likely than Black people (45 percent versus 21 percent) to say that rioting was "not at all justified."[57]

Second, Black people in general are more likely than White people to have had run-ins with the police that they judge to have been unfair.[58] That said, African Americans are not necessarily more critical of the police in general.[59] Third, as Michael Nelson and I have shown, Black people are less strongly committed to democratic institutions and processes and therefore may be less likely to see the insurrection events as representing an existential threat to America's democracy.[60] On the other hand, Black people as a group were far less likely to have voted for Trump in the 2020 presidential election.[61] Moreover, the efforts of Trump and the Republicans to overturn the election often sought the disenfranchisement of Black voters.[62] Relatedly, many insurrectionists were sympathetic to White nationalists, a fact well illustrated by the flying of the Confederate flag during the siege on the Capitol.[63] Thus, my analysis recognizes that a mixture of forces may uniquely affect Black Americans, mainly alienating them from America's democratic institutions.

Not much research has addressed whether and why racial minorities extend less legitimacy to political institutions than does the racial majority. For instance, Nelson and I have reported that Black people are considerably less willing than White people to ascribe legitimacy to the Supreme Court.[64] We conclude that one important reason why African Americans extend less diffuse support to the Supreme Court is that they are less committed to basic democratic values, institutions, and processes than White people.

In sum, this book investigates interracial differences in the willingness to extend legitimacy to three political institutions, the Supreme Court, the Senate, and the Biden presidency, using a representative sample of Americans that includes a substantial oversample of African Americans. Second, because research on public opinion shows that so-called objective events are not necessarily perceived and evaluated the same by different people and groups, I examine interracial differences in awareness and assessments of the insurrection events. Finally, I draw conclusions about the connections between the insurrection events and the legitimacy of these institutions.

Although confidence in my causal inferences admittedly varies with the type of analysis possible given the structure of the survey data, my cross-sectional analysis at least is able to control for more fundamental (and presumably obdurate) democratic values, and in some instances I also make use of panel data. In the end, I show that important interracial differences exist in reactions to the insurrection events, and that these differences help advance a theory of why Black and White Americans differ in their support for America's democratic institutions and processes.

As noted earlier, Black Americans were no doubt subjected to countervailing forces in the aftermath of the presidential election. Few Black people voted for Trump, Trump is often associated with White nationalists, and many people believe that Trump is a racist. On the other hand, Black people are less offput by political violence and less strongly committed to American political institutions in the first place, and they have vastly more experience than White people with unfair treatment by legal authorities. In light of how few studies have addressed interracial differences in support for democratic institutions and processes, framing specific hypotheses is difficult. Some exploratory analysis is therefore required.

Summary of the Chapters

By the time of this writing in the fall of 2022, the attempted coup of Trump and the Republicans seemed to have failed, gone underground, or been transferred to some state governments. President Biden seemed to be secure in his presidency. That the coup failed does not necessarily mean that no damage was done to America's democratic institutions, however, or to democracy itself. Many observers, pundits and scholars alike, have pointed to potentially momentous consequences of the Trump-led coup attempt. Indeed, the belief that the legitimacy of American political institutions has been unaffected by the Trump machinations seems to many to be little more than wishful thinking.[65]

At the same time, however, institutional theories suggest that legitimacy is obdurate, or at least resistant to short-term change. Besides Easton's characterization of legitimacy as a "reservoir of goodwill,"[66] it is also likened to interpersonal loyalty.[67] Loyalty in a relationship usually protects against a single indiscretion, but repeated indiscretions may result in its termination. When legitimacy is accorded, people also tend to suspend instrumental calculations (cost-benefit analyses) and may continue to support an institution, at least for a while, even when they are displeased with its performance. Consequently, premature conclusions about whether America's political institutions have been damaged by Trump and the Republicans should not be made without rigorous empirical evidence. The specific purpose of this book is to provide such evidence.

In chapter 2, which focuses on the measurement of institutional legitimacy, I present the empirical indicators of the legitimacy of the Supreme Court, the Senate, and the presidency/president that I analyze throughout this book. Measuring legitimacy validly and reliably is a task of utmost importance. I ground the measurement of Supreme Court legitimacy in the voluminous literature on that subject, but for the Senate and the presidency I develop new measures and present the necessary empirical evidence validating them. I also create and explicate original measures of support for American democratic institutions in general, as well as measures of several key democratic values (such as support for the rule of law).

As noted earlier, an important argument of this book is that so-called exogenous events are not truly exogenous, because they must be perceived and, more importantly, assessed if they are to influence people. In chapter 3, I present evidence that the events of the 2020 presidential election and its aftermath were widely perceived by the American people, but that they had vastly different understandings of those events—very few "truths" were "self-evident." This chapter sets up the book's tests of its central hypotheses by developing the indicators of awareness and assessments that become the crucial independent variables in the various analyses I undertake.

Chapter 4 begins to test the central hypothesis of this book: that awareness and assessments of the election events and their aftermath poisoned attitudes toward democratic institutions and processes. The analysis is based on a survey that was completed on a noteworthy date: January 5, 2021. The timing of this survey allows me to distinguish between the consequences of the election and the consequences of the insurrection, which took place on January 6, 2021.

Obviously, the insurrection and its aftermath are of vast potential importance. Chapter 5 focuses on the consequences of the riots at the Capitol building for support for democratic institutions and processes. A new survey, fielded in February and March 2021, provides the data. I investigate not only the election events but also awareness and assessments of the riots and the Trump impeachment. Although I cannot specify the exact consequences of the insurrection alone—after all, it was intimately tied up with the election controversy—this research design does allow me to draw conclusions about the consequences of the election specifically (chapter 4) and the consequences of the election, the insurrection, and the impeachment (chapter 5).

Chapter 6 changes course by focusing on whether different racial groups extend the same level of support to America's democratic institutions, values, and processes. I present some limited evidence on four categories of race, but most of the chapter focuses on differences between Black and White Americans.

Chapter 7 continues my spotlight on African Americans by testing a variety of hypotheses about intra-Black variability in change in support for democratic institutions. Importantly, while the chapter still considers the role of the election and the insurrection in attitude change, its most important contribution is its inclusion of measures of experiences with unfair treatment by legal authorities and measures of in-group identifications and attachments (including a sense of linked fate). Because the additional measures are drawn from the t_4 survey (June 2021), I focus exclusively on Black Americans.

After briefly summarizing my major findings, chapter 8 turns to its main objective: to anticipate—and attempt to rebut—the obvious criticisms of the analyses presented in chapters 1 through 7. The most urgent question I address here concerns the temporal limits of my findings. My conclusions from an analysis of survey data ranging from July 2020 to June 2021 pertain to what might be considered the opening round of what has become a sustained attack on the legitimacy of America's democracy and its democratic institutions. I readily acknowledge that my data do not speak to round two of this assault. Thus, my generally sanguine conclusions about the initial assault on democracy by Trump and the Republicans may not be generalizable to the future. Given my findings, democrats—both Democratic and Republican democrats—should perhaps worry most about the future, rather than the past.

CHAPTER 2

Cross-institutional Approaches to Institutional Legitimacy: Conceptualization and Measurement

HOW DO WE know whether ordinary people are committed to the maintenance of democratic institutions, processes, and values in America?[1] It turns out that, despite investing a great deal of energy in measuring support for democracy, scholars have come to little consensus on how to operationalize democratic attitudes or support thereof. Indeed, in some senses, the different approaches to thinking about support for democratic institutions, processes, and values are pursued in essentially separate silos and often even do not acknowledge the existence of alternative conceptualizations. This diversity of approaches therefore requires that considerable attention be given to conceptualizing and measuring support for democracy and its institutions. That is the central purpose of this chapter.

Conceptualizing Support for Democracy

My approach to support for democracy begins with a fairly simple definition of the concept of democracy—or more specifically, the liberal variant of that concept. Simply put, liberal democracy is a system of majority rule with institutionalized opportunities for the minority to become a majority.[2] At its core, it means little more than "majority rule with minority rights." Such rights are defined primarily in terms of the ability of all groups and ideas to compete for political power.

https://doi.org/10.7758/dvkr4409.9941

Support for majority rule is not the same as support for minority rights. Indeed, as I and others have argued, ordinary people more widely embrace support for majority rule, in part because most people think of themselves as belonging to the majority.[3] The minority rights half of the democratic equation is the hard part; it typically means extending the rights of contestation—free speech, assembly, access to mass media, and so on—to those with whom we disagree, perhaps even to those holding unconscionable views. The term "illiberal democracy" describes political regimes that have some degree of majority rule but limit or constrain rights of contestation for political minorities.[4]

Because the concept of democracy encompasses at least two distinct parts, asking people whether they are satisfied with "democracy" elicits inherently ambiguous answers.[5] People who say that they support democracy may believe that decisions ought to be made by majority rule rather than by oligarchs, monarchs, tyrants, or elites. Or they may believe that all political points of view, even distasteful ones, should be allowed to compete for power under unbiased rules (such as equal access to the mass media). Some respondents possibly have no clear idea of what "democracy" means; some even may confuse it with an economic system, such as a market economy.[6]

Consequently, to allow respondents themselves to define "democracy" is unwise. The more valid approach is for scholars to specify what democratic institutions, processes, and values are and then to provide concrete and specific measures of attitudes toward these components of democracy—often (if not typically) without even using the word "democracy" in the survey questions.

My colleagues and I have gone some distance toward breaking "democracy" down into its various institutions and processes, then measuring attitudes toward these individual components.[7] We have addressed attitudes toward democratic institutions (for example, the mass media), democratic values and principles (such as political tolerance), and processes (such as attitudes toward the rule of law). Another crucial characteristic of democratic politics is the willingness to compete *peacefully* for power.[8] Some scholars have pointed to a recent rupture in the consensual rejection of political violence, especially among Republicans.[9] Therefore, the broadest definition of commitment to democratic institutions, processes, and values should include the unwillingness to endorse political violence.

In sum, this research employs multiple measures of support for democratic institutions, processes, and values: (1) willingness to extend legitimacy to major national political institutions; (2) willingness to stand by and support American democratic institutions in general; and (3) general democratic values.[10] I begin with a recap of the most well-trodden and central concept—institutional legitimacy.

The Legitimacy of Institutions as an Indicator of Support for Democracy

As noted in chapter 1, legitimacy is a precious form of political capital. Institutions can assume that people will accept policy decisions with which they agree, but they cannot rely solely on manipulating costs and benefits to get its constituents to accept decisions with which they disagree. Indeed, because legitimacy engenders voluntary compliance, no institutional resource is more valuable or more coveted.

Despite decades of research, progress on measuring the sociological legitimacy of institutions has been uneven. Over time, generally accepted measures of the legitimacy of courts have developed, whereas advances in the measurement of legislative legitimacy have been limited, and those of presidential legitimacy are practically nonexistent. And even regarding the courts, a recently developed revisionist school urges some modifications to the conventional indicators of judicial legitimacy.[11] Thus, although most scholars acknowledge the importance of institutional legitimacy, consensus on how it should be measured, especially across institutions, has not yet emerged.

Consequently, this chapter devotes considerable effort to measuring legitimacy within various institutional contexts. I first explicate judicial legitimacy, the focus of so much scholarly attention, then move on to the chapter's most important contribution: addressing the meaning and measurement of legislative and presidential legitimacy, which have received so little previous research attention. The indicators I develop are well grounded in the theory of institutional legitimacy, but many have not been used in any prior research.

Before we turn to the data, it should be remembered that legitimacy is much more than mere satisfaction with an institution's performance. Indeed, legitimacy requires constituents to stand by an institution even when they are dissatisfied with its performance. Legitimacy, in Easton's famous phrase, is a "reservoir of goodwill," which means that performance lapses do little, at least in the short run, to subtract from an institution's legitimacy.[12] Winners are naturally always pleased to win and therefore extend support to institutions that make what they consider favorable policy decisions, but losers do not as easily or readily offer such support. Institutional legitimacy is thus a means by which losers can be induced to accept their loss.[13]

Recalling Easton's terms for two different attitudes toward institutions, I equate what he called "diffuse support" with legitimacy (and with other terms as well).[14] "Specific support," by contrast, refers to performance satisfaction.[15] That concept is well represented by presidential popularity (which is largely retrospective), performance evaluations, and confidence that the institution will make reasonable public policy in the future (which is largely prospective). Driven by evaluations of the outputs of institutions, specific support is typically more volatile than diffuse support.[16] At the same time, diffuse support is far more valuable to institutions than specific support.

Measuring Institutional Legitimacy

A primary focus of this research is attitudes toward three of the four major American national political institutions: the presidency, the Supreme Court, and the Senate.[17] I choose to ask questions about the Senate—and not the House of Representatives—owing to its roles in the confirmation of Supreme Court justice nominees and as the "jury" in the impeachment process.

For at least some political institutions, the measurement of institutional legitimacy is quite well developed. Research on attitudes toward the Supreme Court, for instance, has made considerable advances in creating valid, reliable, and widely used measures of its institutional legitimacy.[18] Such measurements may have become so well established in part because legitimacy is such an important form of political capital for the court.[19]

The legitimacy of other institutions has been much discussed, but little attempt has been made to rigorously develop the concept, and precious little hypothesis testing has been conducted. For example, both scholars and pundits often reference "presidential legitimacy" yet rarely if ever give rigorous empirical content.[20]

Some thinking about legitimacy theory has been applied to Congress, though it is not particularly well developed. While John Hibbing and Elizabeth Theiss-Morse have made important advances in understanding public attitudes about Congress as an institution, most scholars tend to focus on performance evaluations (on which Congress does quite poorly) or on evaluations of respondents' own representatives rather than on more fundamental commitments to the legislative institution.[21] Thus, the court indicators employed in this research are well grounded in the literature on judicial legitimacy, but I have found it necessary to create some new measures of the popular legitimacy of the presidency/president and the Senate.[22]

The Legitimacy of the Supreme Court

In the surveys I conducted, six widely used items were employed to measure institutional support for the Supreme Court (see figure 2.1). For most indicators, more respondents gave legitimacy-affirming responses than not legitimacy-affirming ones. For some statements, such as the "do away with the Court altogether" item, the differences are substantial, but for others, such as the "U.S. Supreme Court ought to be made less independent" indicator, the differences are considerably smaller. On one of the propositions, "the U.S. Supreme Court gets too mixed up in politics," the percentage of respondents that gave an anti-legitimacy response was larger than the percentage that gave a pro-legitimacy response. Although conclusions from these data are clouded by the sizable percentages of respondents who neither agreed nor disagreed with the statement, support for the court, while certainly not overwhelming, seems moderately high.[23] Still, on judicial independence—an attribute of courts that some scholars consider essential to an effective judiciary—the percentage of Americans who rejected the view that the court should be less independent is significantly, but not greatly, larger than the percentage who agreed that the court's independence should be reduced. Certainly, not much unequivocal support for an independent judiciary exists in these data.

The analysis in this book relies on a legitimacy index derived from these six items.[24] The index of judicial legitimacy is the average response to the six indicators.[25] Just less than 21 percent of the respondents (20.6 percent) gave no responses supportive of the court, while 14.8 percent gave supportive replies to all six propositions. As I have noted, the answers to at least

Figure 2.1 The Sociological Legitimacy of the U.S. Supreme Court

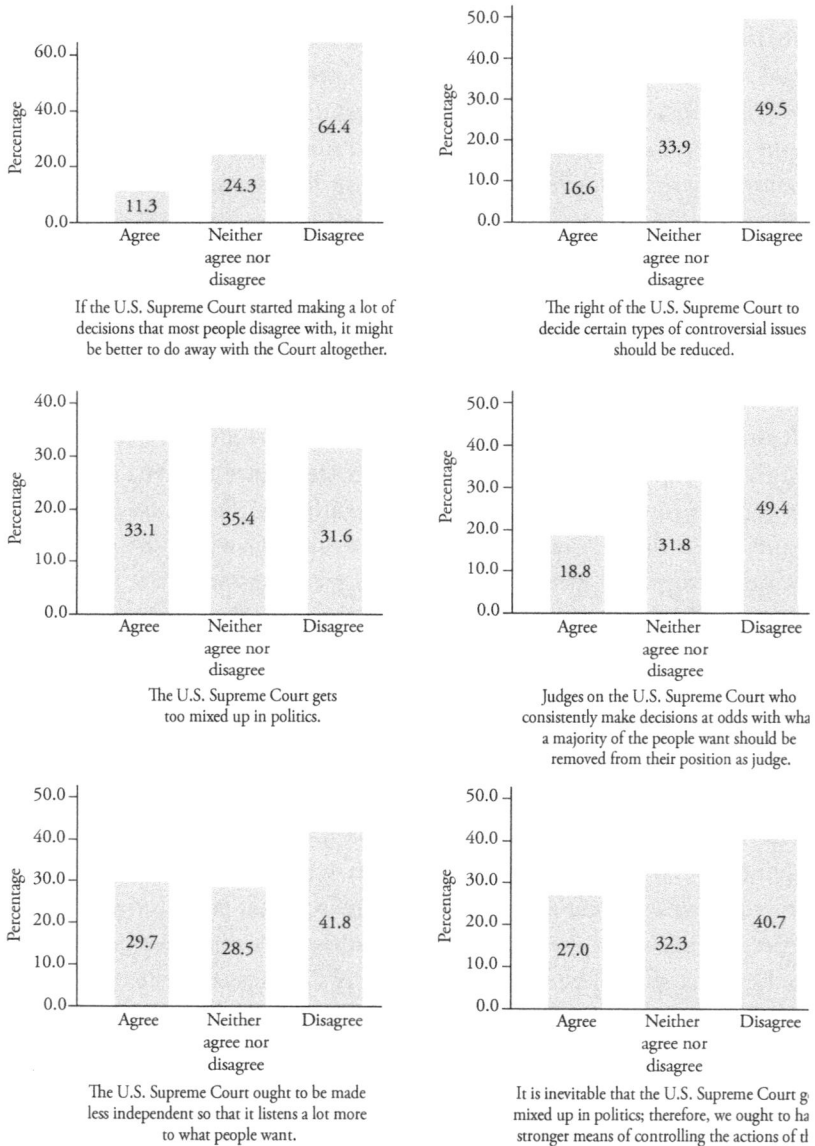

If the U.S. Supreme Court started making a lot of decisions that most people disagree with, it might be better to do away with the Court altogether.

The right of the U.S. Supreme Court to decide certain types of controversial issues should be reduced.

The U.S. Supreme Court gets too mixed up in politics.

Judges on the U.S. Supreme Court who consistently make decisions at odds with what a majority of the people want should be removed from their position as judge.

The U.S. Supreme Court ought to be made less independent so that it listens a lot more to what people want.

It is inevitable that the U.S. Supreme Court g mixed up in politics; therefore, we ought to ha stronger means of controlling the actions of t

Source: The 2021 Insurrection and Impeachment Survey (t₃), February and March 2021.
Notes: Weighted $N \approx 2{,}010$. Respondents were asked to assess these statements using a five-point Likert response set. The percentages reported in this figure collapse "disagree" and "disagree strongly" replies into "legitimacy-affirming" responses and "agree" and "agree strongly" replies into "not legitimacy-affirming" responses.

two items indicate that a nontrivial proportion of Americans approve of reining in the independence of the Supreme Court.

The Legitimacy of the Presidency/President

Pundits often discuss efforts to "delegitimize" presidents, such as the "birther" scheme to delegitimize President Obama or the 2020 attempt of Trump and the Republicans to delegitimize the incoming Biden presidency.[26] Without legitimacy, presidents are less persuasive and efficacious; the opposition aims to take away legitimacy from the presidency/president to diminish the power—attenuate the political capital—of the office/incumbent and thus limit what the president can do through unwelcome policy initiatives.

As I noted earlier, legitimacy is a normative concept having to do with the right to govern and citizens' consequent obligation to fulfill their side of the social contract by complying with government. In a democratic theory nutshell, if a leader achieves power through a fair process and makes decisions through fair procedures, then citizens feel obliged to accept and comply with the leader's policies.

The four indicators I developed to measure the Biden presidency's legitimacy (see figure 2.2) reflect whether Biden's method of attaining the office of president is seen by people as undermining the legitimacy of the office, and in particular whether Americans recognize a perceived normative obligation to cooperate with the president and obey laws passed by his administration. The first item stands as a summary rejection of the Biden presidency, and especially Biden's claim to be the president of all Americans.

The data in figure 2.2 indicate that Biden's presidency has a substantial store of legitimacy. For example, on the first item, only about 12 percent of the respondents asserted that Biden "will never be my president." Nearly 57 percent of all respondents (data not shown) gave four pro-legitimacy responses to these indicators; only 12 percent gave no legitimacy-affirming responses. By these measures, the Biden presidency seems to have the support of a substantial proportion of Americans—at least as of February and March 2021—suggesting that efforts to delegitimize the Biden presidency met with little success.

The measurement hypothesis that the responses to these items reflect an

Figure 2.2 The Sociological Legitimacy of the Biden Presidency

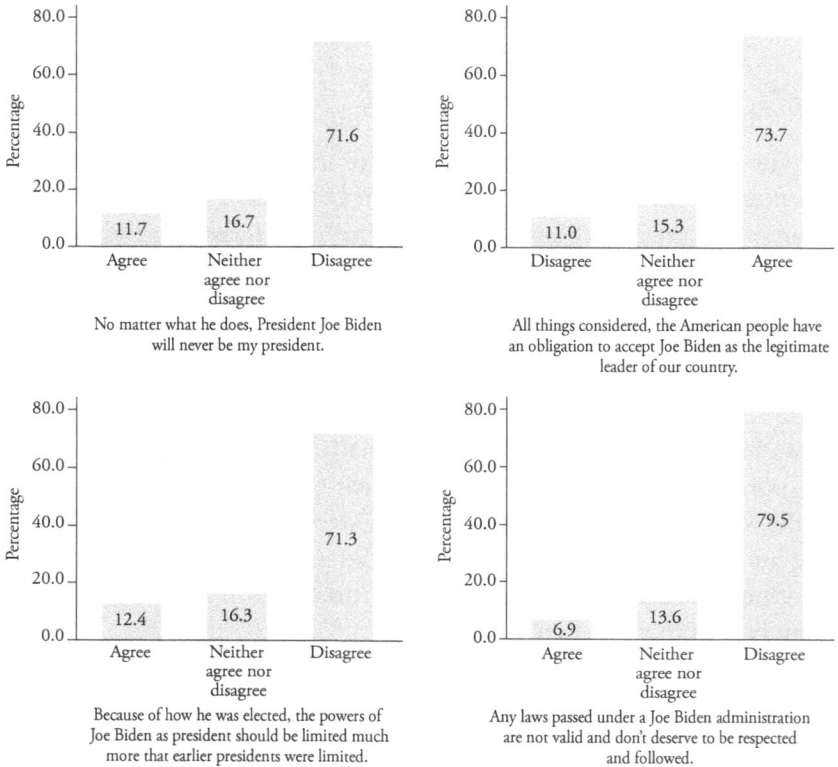

No matter what he does, President Joe Biden will never be my president.

Agree: 11.7
Neither agree nor disagree: 16.7
Disagree: 71.6

All things considered, the American people have an obligation to accept Joe Biden as the legitimate leader of our country.

Disagree: 11.0
Neither agree nor disagree: 15.3
Agree: 73.7

Because of how he was elected, the powers of Joe Biden as president should be limited much more that earlier presidents were limited.

Agree: 12.4
Neither agree nor disagree: 16.3
Disagree: 71.3

Any laws passed under a Joe Biden administration are not valid and don't deserve to be respected and followed.

Agree: 6.9
Neither agree nor disagree: 13.6
Disagree: 79.5

Source: The 2021 Insurrection and Impeachment Survey (t_3), February and March 2021.
Notes: Weighted $N \approx 2,010$. Respondents were asked to assess these statements using a five-point Likert response set. Except for the "have an obligation" item," the percentages reported in this figure collapse "disagree" and "disagree strongly" replies into "legitimacy-affirming" responses and "agree" and "agree strongly" replies into "not legitimacy-affirming" responses. For the "have an obligation" item, "disagree" and "disagree strongly" replies are "not legitimacy-affirming."

underlying latent legitimacy construct is strongly supported by psychometric analysis.[27] I created an index of presidential legitimacy from the responses to the four items. For further evidence on the validity of this measure, see the appendix.

To entirely separate attitudes toward the legitimacy of the presidency and support for the incumbent holding the office would no doubt be impossible. Across a variety of tests, however, my analysis shows that presidential legitimacy reflects more than mere partisanship (or even ideology), as it should. These measures are far from perfect, but they nevertheless seem adequate for this analysis, in the sense that they are reliable and valid indicators and derive from the same conceptualization of legitimacy used throughout this book.

The Legitimacy of the Senate

Researchers have made few attempts to measure attitudes toward the Senate as an institution.[28] In one partial exception, Gregory Caldeira, Lester Kenyatta Spence, and I compared the legitimacy of Congress with the popular legitimacy of the Supreme Court and discovered, perhaps surprisingly, that the court had more legitimacy than Congress, though the legitimacy gap between the two institutions was not large.[29]

My approach to measuring the Senate's legitimacy draws on measures of Supreme Court and presidential legitimacy. The February and March 2021 survey used four indicators of institutional support for the Senate (see figure 2.3). The fourth item represents a nod to G. R. Boynton and Gerhard Loewenberg's question in the 1950s about proposals to change the size of the German Bundestag.[30] To increase the size of the Senate to match the House's 435 members would fundamentally alter the nature of the Senate.

The responses to these items reveal considerable variability in how Americans feel about the legitimacy of the Senate. At one extreme, only a small minority would support doing away with the Senate, although about 26 percent of all respondents were uncertain of their views on this proposal. A majority would oppose eliminating the Senate. Similar responses were given to the proposal that the Senate be changed to be more similar to the House of Representatives, although here a smaller majority rejected the idea. At the other extreme, almost 34 percent of respondents would support replacing every currently serving senator, though roughly 36 percent of all respondents were uncertain as to how they felt about this idea. Only about 38 percent rejected the notion that the Senate would "never represent me and people like me." Even though the considerable proportions of people unwilling or unable to express an opinion on Senate legitimacy cloud the findings to some degree, the fact that a majority of respondents extended legitimacy to the Senate on only two of the four items suggests that the Senate's legitimacy is less than omnipresent.

Figure 2.3 The Sociological Legitimacy of the U.S. Senate

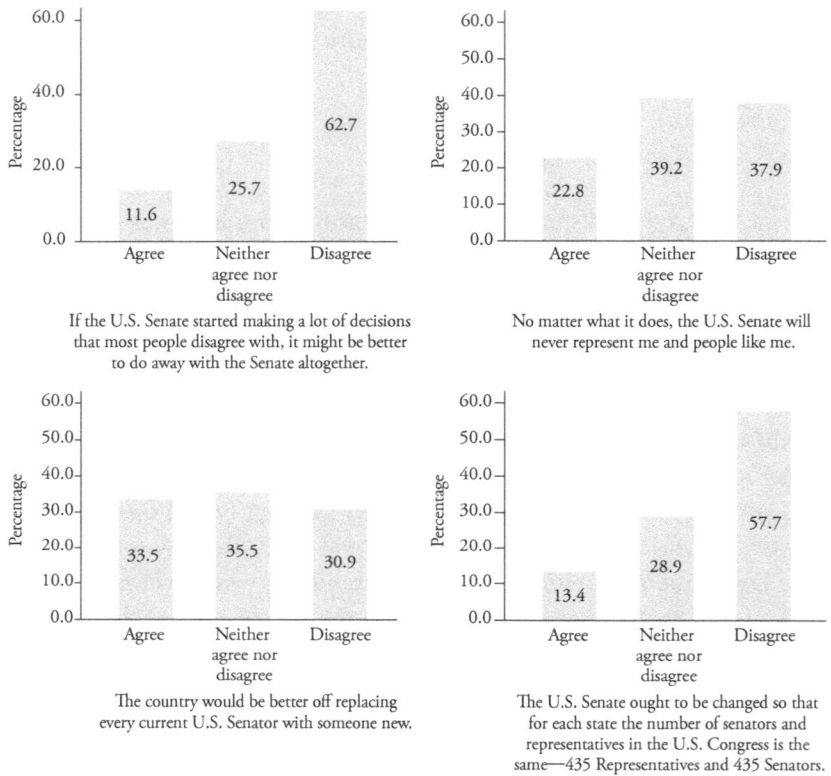

If the U.S. Senate started making a lot of decisions that most people disagree with, it might be better to do away with the Senate altogether.

No matter what it does, the U.S. Senate will never represent me and people like me.

The country would be better off replacing every current U.S. Senator with someone new.

The U.S. Senate ought to be changed so that for each state the number of senators and representatives in the U.S. Congress is the same—435 Representatives and 435 Senators.

Source: The 2021 Insurrection and Impeachment Survey (t₃), February and and March 2021.
Notes: Weighted *N* ≈ 2,010. Respondents were asked to assess these statements using a five-point Likert response set. The percentages reported in this figure collapse "disagree" and "disagree strongly" replies into "legitimacy-affirming" responses and "agree" and "agree strongly" replies into "not legitimacy-affirming" responses.

When compared to the legitimacy of the Supreme Court, these findings echo those Caldeira, Spence, and I reached in 2005: the court has slightly more legitimacy than the Senate, but not a great deal more.[31] While 64 percent of respondents rejected doing away with the court, 63 percent rejected doing away with the Senate. Compared with the president, however, the Senate's legitimacy pales. While 72 percent of respondents rejected the notion that Biden would never be their president, only 38 percent disagreed with the statemen that the Senate would never represent them or people like them. The evidence suggests that, of the three institutions considered here, the Senate enjoys the least amount of institutional legitimacy.

As measures of Senate legitimacy, these items have reasonably strong psychometric properties.[32] For further evidence on the validity of this measure, see the appendix.

Are Institutional Attitudes Distinguishable?

To a significant degree, respondents held distinguishable attitudes toward these three institutions. Although support for the Supreme Court and support for the Senate are strongly correlated ($r = 0.63$, so only less than one-half of the variance is shared), neither is strongly related to support for the Biden presidency ($r = 0.18$ and 0.31, respectively). Each of these indices should therefore be analyzed individually.

Conceptualizing and Measuring General Support for U.S. Democratic Institutions

A different approach to measuring attitudes toward democratic institutions is concerned with the degree to which people have faith in America's democratic institutions writ large. According to cultural theories of democracy, the views of ordinary people are important. Consequently, I gave the national survey respondents three statements pertaining to their overall assessments of the state of American democratic institutions. Figure 2.4 reports their responses (with the five-point responses collapsed for illustrative purposes).

These data suggest a somewhat mixed level of support for U.S. political institutions. On the one hand, substantial majorities rejected the view that the existing institutional setup should be scrapped and is not worth saving. At the same time, only about 31 percent of respondents said that they had not lost faith in these institutions. These responses suggest that, for a large majority of Americans, U.S. political institutions are on "probation," in the sense that people are displeased with the institutions but have not yet given up on them.

I hypothesize that the three items posed to respondents are valid and reliable indicators of a latent construct: allegiance to American democratic

Figure 2.4 Support for American Democratic Institutions

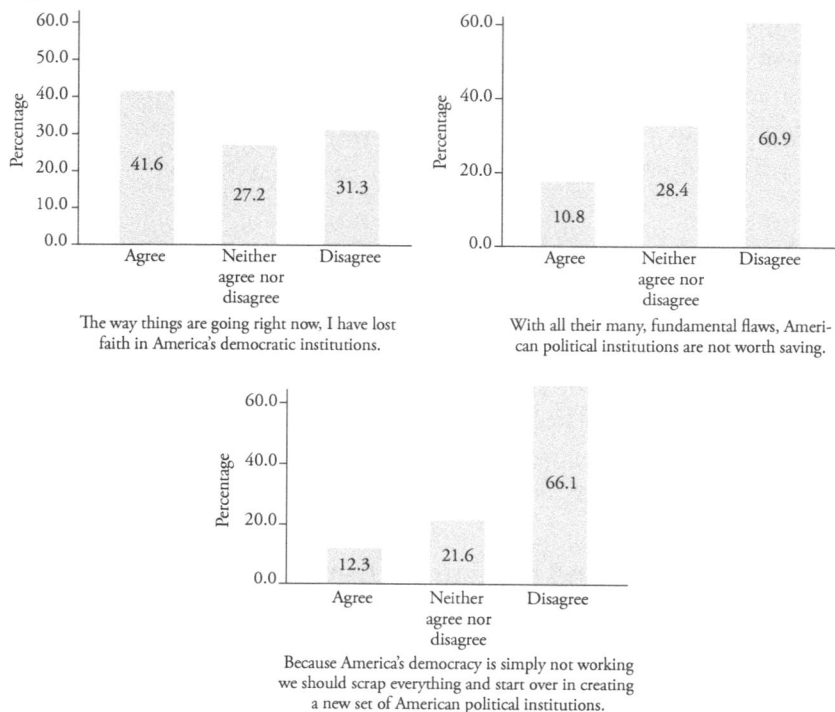

The way things are going right now, I have lost faith in America's democratic institutions.

With all their many, fundamental flaws, American political institutions are not worth saving.

Because America's democracy is simply not working we should scrap everything and start over in creating a new set of American political institutions.

Source: The 2021 Insurrection and Impeachment Survey (t₃), February and March 2021.
Notes: Weighted *N* ≈ 2,010. Respondents were asked to assess these statements using a five-point Likert response set. The percentages reported in this figure collapse "disagree" and "disagree strongly" replies into "pro-democracy" responses and "agree" and "agree strongly" replies into "not pro-democracy" responses.

institutions. Psychometric analysis supports that hypothesis.[33] With validity and reliability established, I created an index of democratic support as the mean of the responses to the three items. Only 26 percent of respondents gave three pro-democracy answers to these items. Strikingly, 27 percent of the sample gave no pro-democracy answers.[34] For further evidence of the validity of the measure, see the appendix.

Democratic Values

Extant research conventionally conceptualizes support for democratic values and processes as separate from attitudes toward democratic institutions.[35]

Following that research, the various analyses reported in this book include measures of these values.

Support for the Rule of Law

Support for the rule of law is conceptualized as ranging from universalism to particularism. Some people are deeply committed to law, believing that law ought to be strictly enforced even when the consequences are not necessarily positive, whereas others believe that law ought to be obeyed only to the extent that the outcome is desirable. In this sense, support for the rule of law is a procedural commitment.

Earlier research has widely used the following items to measure rule-of-law attitudes.[36] The percentage of respondents who espoused the rule-of-law position by disagreeing are listed in parentheses:

It is not necessary to obey a law you consider unjust. (Disagree: 72 percent)

Sometimes it might be better to ignore the law and solve problems immediately rather than wait for a legal solution. (Disagree: 60 percent)

The government should have some ability to bend the law in order to solve pressing social and political problems. (Disagree: 55 percent)

It is not necessary to obey the laws of a government I did not vote for. (Disagree: 85 percent)

When it comes right down to it, law is not all that important; what's important is that our government solve society's problems and make us all better off. (Disagree: 69 percent)

As has been found in earlier research, Americans, to a remarkable degree, are strongly committed to the rule of law.[37]

Valuation of Individual Political Liberty

The following items, which have been often used in earlier research, measure the degree to which respondents favored social order when it conflicts with the liberty of political minorities.[38] The percentage of respondents who espoused the pro-order position by agreeing are listed in parentheses:

Society should not have to put up with those who have political
   ideas that are extremely different from the majority. (Agree: 14
   percent)
It is better to live in an orderly society than to allow people so much
   freedom that they can become disruptive. (Agree: 27 percent)
Free speech is just not worth it if it means that we have to put up
   with the danger to society of extremist political views. (Agree:
   14 percent)

Prioritizing individual liberty over social order was quite commonplace
among respondents.[39]

Support for Civil Liberties

As a measure of the willingness to extend civil liberties to all groups and
ideas, the survey asked four questions about whether particular groups
should be allowed to hold public demonstrations. The question stem read:

> Next, let's suppose that [THE GROUP] wanted to hold public rallies and
> demonstrations in your community to advance their cause, but that the au-
> thorities decided to prohibit it. How would you react to such a ban by the
> authorities of a public demonstration by [THE GROUP]? Would you
> strongly support the ban, support the ban, oppose the ban, or strongly op-
> pose the ban?

The groups about which I asked (and the percentage willing to tolerate
their demonstrations) were radical Muslims (57 percent), a group of people
who are against all churches and religion (70 percent), White nationalists
(47 percent), and Christian fundamentalists (76 percent).[40]

Open-Mindedness

Tolerance researchers has long found open-mindedness—the opposite of
dogmatism, the primary indicator of psychological insecurity—to be a powerful predictor of political tolerance.[41] The items I employ, with the percentage taking the dogmatic position by agreeing, are as follows:

> To compromise with our political opponents is dangerous because it
>   usually leads to the betrayal of our own side. (Agree: 19 percent)

There are two kinds of people in this world: those who are for the truth
and those who are against it. (Agree: 44 percent)
A group which tolerates too many differences of opinion among its
own members cannot exist for long. (Agree: 24 percent)

Open-mindedness is measured with a simple summated index of the
responses to these items.[42]

Interracial Differences in Institutional Support

I defer full consideration of the influence of race on institutional support
to chapter 6, but here I test the simple hypothesis that support for these
institutions varies by race. Figure 2.5 reports the interracial difference-of-
means tests (as indicated by respondents' self-classifications of their race)
for each of the three indices of institutional support.

The biggest cross-race difference in support (as indexed by the eta statistic) is for the legitimacy of the Senate, followed by the Supreme Court and
the presidency. White Americans support the Senate and the Supreme
Court to a considerably greater extent than other Americans. For both institutions, the differences among the other three minority racial groups are
not great; Hispanic people extended slightly less legitimacy to the Senate
than did Black people and those of other races, and those of other races
granted slightly more legitimacy to the Supreme Court.[43]

Presidential legitimacy reveals a distinctive pattern. Black Americans are
considerably more likely to extend legitimacy to the Biden presidency, and
Hispanic people are considerably less likely to grant legitimacy to the Biden
presidency. White people, on average, are in between. Still, all these differences are within the context of relatively high legitimacy for the presidency
(and less substantial intergroup differences). The conclusion that emerges
from this analysis is that race seems to matter for institutional legitimacy:
minorities generally support American political institutions less than White
people do, although not to a great extent. The exception is the attitude of
African Americans toward the Biden presidency.

Thus, analyses of support for democratic institutions in America must
not ignore the omnipresent influence of interracial differences. Of course,
these groups differ on many attributes other than their race, so firm conclusions about the role of race in structuring these attitudes must await the
multivariate analysis reported later in this book.

Figure 2.5 Interracial Differences in Institutional Support

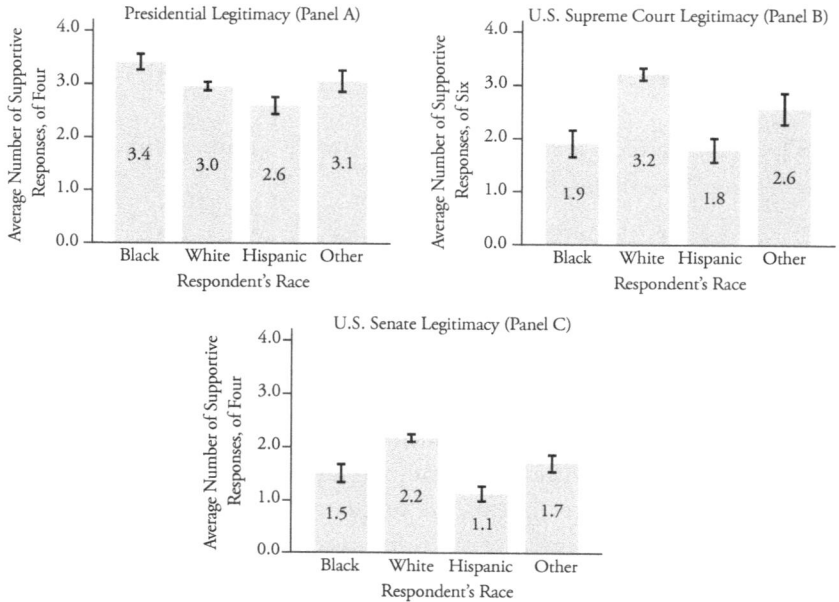

Source: The 2021 Insurrection and Impeachment Survey (t₃), February and March 2021.
Notes:
Panel A: N = 2,023; difference of means: *p* < .001; eta = 0.15. Confidence intervals of 95 percent are shown around the means. The measure of institutional support ranges from 0 to 4.
Panel B: N = 2,027; difference of means: *p* < .001; eta = 0.29. Confidence intervals of 95 percent are shown around the means. The measure of institutional support ranges from 0 to 6.
Panel C: N = 2,026; difference of means: *p* < .001; eta = 0.31. Confidence intervals of 95 percent are shown around the means. The measure of institutional support ranges from 0 to 4.

Summary and Concluding Thoughts

This chapter primarily intended to introduce measures of institutional legitimacy for the presidency, the Supreme Court, and the Senate. Although research on judicial legitimacy is well-trodden turf, few attempts have been made to address the legitimacy of the other two institutions. The measures of the legitimacy of the presidency and the Senate that I have developed are perhaps not perfect—in part because, compared with their judicial counterpart, they are not as well grounded in long-established thinking about and empirical analyses of institutional legitimacy—but they have desirable empirical properties when it comes to validity and reliability.

By these indicators, Americans grant legitimacy to the Supreme Court and the Senate in about equal measure and at levels that suggest moderate degrees of support. The Biden presidency is granted considerably more legitimacy. Making these cross-institutional comparisons is not without risk, however, because we do not yet understand a great deal about the structure of legitimacy attitudes within different institutional contexts.

The results reported in this chapter pertain to Americans' attitudes toward the presidency, the Senate, and the Supreme Court after the presidential election of 2020 and the insurrection, impeachment, and related events of early 2021, and they therefore reflect any influence these events may have had on support for these institutions. Ideally, we would be able to assess change from before to after the election (and even beyond). Given the available data, such change in institutional support can be assessed only for the Supreme Court (as reported in chapter 4).

And of course, there is much more to the story of why some Americans support the legitimacy of these institutions and others do not, and especially how the events of the 2020 election are associated with Americans' legitimacy attitudes. To conduct that analysis, understanding more fully how Americans perceived and evaluated that election is essential. That is the purpose of the next chapter.

CHAPTER 3

Awareness and Assessments of the 2020 Presidential Election Events

> Misinformation is not like a plumbing problem you fix. It is a social condition, like crime, that you must constantly monitor and adjust to.
>
> —Tom Rosenstiel, director of the American Press Institute and senior fellow at the Brookings Institution, quoted on the Pew Research Center website

> In the arms race between those who want to falsify information and those who want to produce accurate information, the former will always have an advantage.
>
> —David Conrad, chief technology officer, Pew Research Center, quoted on the Pew Research Center website

SINCE MY OVERRIDING objective in this project is to interrogate the linkage between events and institutional attitudes, I need to give some attention to how people understand and assess what happened in the 2020 presidential election. Unfortunately, however, if anything is universally true about contemporary politics in the United States (and throughout the world), it is that truths are not inherently self-evident. Not only are some truths inconvenient, but they are also very difficult to measure (How much is the globe warming?), and the truth of causation is even more complex and difficult to establish (What are the causes of global climate change?). In comparison to issues such as climate change, the truth of who won an election in which millions and millions of ballots were cast might seem simple. In many elections, however, it seems not to be for the losers.

Unfortunately, scholars often assume that truth—or at least the truth of events—is self-evident, and consequently that all people perceive and evaluate events in the same way. This assumption may sometimes be valid—for

https://doi.org/10.7758/dvkr4409.3440

instance, few Americans, I suspect, would disagree with the proposition that a presidential election took place in the United States in November 2020.

At the same time, the burden of most (but not all) scholarly research is that Americans generally are amazingly clueless about political affairs.[1] And even when they do tune in, these scholars note, they often get the message wrong.[2] Prominent psychological models account for the fact that, for a considerable proportion of Americans, attitude change cannot take place in response to external events because they are oblivious to the occurrence of these events. Thus, for many, if not most, Americans, few truths are self-evident.

It is statistically handy not to have to worry about variability in awareness and evaluations of events when considering the impact of allegedly exogenous factors such as changes in laws, court decisions, and elections. Scholars are motivated to treat events as exogenous, because great methodological advantages accrue if the causes of changes can be assumed to be independent of the outcome variables of interest.[3] However, these scholars' studies often make no allowances for (a) people who are oblivious to the events and (b) differences in how those who are aware of events perceive and evaluate them. Since events must be perceived and evaluated in order to have effects on individuals, seemingly exogenous occurrences are not actually exogenous.[4]

In this book, my primary objective is to consider the hypothesis that events shape legitimacy attitudes and, more specifically, that the allegations about the 2020 election influenced the willingness of Americans to extend legitimacy to their national political institutions. In pursuit of this hypothesis, I cannot assume that individuals do not vary in their awareness of events or especially in their assessments of those events. Consequently, this chapter has several objectives. First, I report measures of both awareness and evaluations of the events of the 2020 presidential election and its aftermath. Second, and more important, I consider whether individual variability in reactions to these events is systematic, that is, whether, as part of a motivated reasoning hypothesis, substantive attitudes prior to the events predict awareness and assessments of them.

My most important conclusion from these analyses is that Americans' perceptions and assessments of this election were strongly influenced by pre-existing attitudes—especially by ideological and partisan self-identifications, but by other values as well—and therefore that these judgments cannot be considered exogenous in any meaningful sense. The possibility thus arises that the 2020 election results did not really change anyone's views of America's democratic institutions.

Previous Research on the Influence of Events on Public Opinion

Many social scientists are beginning to recognize the truth of the contention that few truths are actually self-evident.[5] For instance, race and ethnic politics researchers have paid considerable attention to variability in how people perceive and evaluate seemingly exogenous events. For some time now, scholars have known that Black and White Americans perceive and evaluate racially charged events in entirely different ways.[6] In perhaps the most theoretically sophisticated of the various studies that demonstrate this, Hakeem Jefferson, Fabian Neuner, and Josh Pasek report a recent analysis of these differences.[7]

These authors document a tremendous chasm in how Black and White Americans view and judge the events associated with the shooting of Michael Brown in Ferguson, Missouri, in 2014.[8] They report interracial differences in both perceptions of facts (for example, whether Brown had a weapon) and normative judgments (for example, whether Darren Wilson, the police officer who shot Brown, should be charged).[9] On normative items, interracial differences are unsurprisingly gigantic. They are markedly smaller on empirical items, but still substantial. Clearly, the truths surrounding the shooting of Brown by Wilson are anything but self-evident.[10]

In a similar vein, Periloux Peay and Tyler Camarillo establish that White people are likely to see a potential for violence in demonstrations in which more of the protesters are Black.[11] Preexisting stereotypes about Black people, fueled by sensationalist media reports, shape conclusions about the likelihood of violence. Devorah Manekin and Tamar Mitts report similar findings, concluding that "violence is not a simple, objective category but rather is often subjectively shaped through biased human perceptions."[12]

In their investigation of willingness to believe false political information, Timothy Ryan and Amanda Aziz note that several studies concluding that conservatives are more likely to endorse fake news than liberals fail to account for the fact that, on the supply side, more right-leaning and fake or misinformative news are available.[13] To test whether Republicans really have a greater proclivity to believe fake news, they used entirely fictional rumors created for the purpose of the experiment in which the aggrieved party was interchangeable. The participants were shown two rumors: one that favored their party and one that favored the opposing party. Ryan and Aziz find that Democrats and Republicans endorsed the false rumors about their political opponents to nearly the exact same degree.

Nicolas Berlinski and his colleagues find that elite attacks on the legitimacy of election outcomes have effects, although largely among copartisans.[14] Importantly, they also discover that these attacks have no impact on support for democracy itself. One implication of their findings is that belief in the integrity of elections is *not* an important predictor of support for democracy. The authors speculate that the failure of elite claims to influence the mass public may be related to poor source credibility.[15]

Jefferson, Neuner, and Pasek identify two processes by which "bias" in perceptions may be generated.[16] One process relies on social identity theory and claims that perceptual bias is associated with the psychological need to protect the value and integrity of the group with which the person identifies through reasoning motivated by identity protection. They report only mixed support for the hypotheses associated with social identity theory processes.[17]

The second mechanism does not rely on in-group attachments. Instead, the theory posits that people have experiences with (in this case) legal authorities and that those experiences shape their expectations about how those authorities *should* behave, and ultimately perceptions of how they *do* behave, through biased information processing. For example, there is more to the story than

> Blacks and whites reflexively defending their racial groups in a manner consistent with a pure identity-protective motivating reasoning account. Instead, the persistent racial divide observed in responses to officer-involved shootings appears rooted in the markedly different beliefs and expectations Blacks and whites hold about the behavior of Black Americans and the fairness of the criminal justice system.[18]

These beliefs and expectations, I might add, are rooted in both personal and vicarious experiences with legal authorities. Focusing on beliefs and expectations about the behavior of Black Americans and the fairness of the criminal justice system, Jefferson and his colleagues claim that their data support a reasonably simple process:

experiences → beliefs → future expectations → judgments

This and other studies generate the fairly uncomplicated conclusion that the facts of events are rarely, if ever, self-evident. To claim that events are exogenous, at least in any analysis attempting to discover the psychological consequences of those events, would therefore be unwise. To assume here that the "facts" of the 2020 presidential election, its aftermath, the insurrection, and the ensuing impeachment are objective and exogenous in any meaningful sense would be particularly unwise.

Measuring Perceptions and Evaluations of the Election, Insurrection, and Impeachment Events

The attacks on American political institutions during the Trump years were unprecedented in modern American politics. In an era of fake news and misinformation, however, to assume that all people perceive and evaluate events like these in the same way would be a mistake. Instead, subjective perceptions must be measured and incorporated into analyses.

The challenge with an approach that focuses on citizen perceptions and evaluations of events is that citizens must be asked what their perceptions and evaluations actually are. To do so, the researcher must identify in advance the relevant events—an easy task for a study focused on court decisions, but more difficult for one concerned with the impact of unfolding events (including Supreme Court confirmation hearings) on public opinion. Nevertheless, because events such as the 2020 presidential election are obviously not self-evident truths, this research includes empirical measures of how the respondents perceived and understood the election.

I ask two types of questions about the major political events relating to the 2020 election and its aftermath: one relating to the degree to which the respondent was aware of the events, and another to how the respondent evaluated those events. This approach allows me to test at the micro level the hypothesis that events shape institutional legitimacy ; events as "constants" are transformed into events as "variables." At the same time, of course, these perceptions and evaluations also become endogenous variables to some degree, through processes such as selective perception and exposure and motivated reasoning. I would also note that, owing mainly to motivated reasoning, misinformation is quite resistant to change, even with concerted efforts to bring about such change.[19]

The events surrounding the 2020 presidential election included many legitimacy-threatening elements, the most important of which may have been Trump's efforts to delegitimize the election's outcome. These efforts included calling the balloting "rigged" and fraudulent, both before and after the election, and making several attempts (some possibly illegal) to overturn the balloting results, especially after the Electoral College vote confirmed that Biden was the president-elect.[20] And as noted earlier, Barrett's confirmation to the Supreme Court just weeks before Trump lost the election and the likelihood that the election results would be litigated before the court could not help but politicize the nominee and perhaps the court itself.[21]

In this research, I initially focused on perceptions and evaluations of three events: (1) Barrett's nomination and confirmation to the Supreme Court in the run-up to the presidential election; (2) allegations that the 2020 presidential election was rigged or somehow manipulated so that it did not represent the actual votes of the American people; and (3) President Trump's efforts to have the outcome of the 2020 presidential election overturned and reversed. To be clear, I contend that it is factually and objectively correct that (1) Barrett was nominated and confirmed, (2) allegations of election rigging were made, and (3) Trump tried to overturn the election's outcome. I measured both levels of awareness and judgments of each event. Table 3.1 reports the responses to these questions in the December 2020 and January 2021 survey (t_2).

Perhaps unsurprisingly, awareness of these happenings was extremely commonplace, with very large majorities of respondents claiming to be "very" or "somewhat" aware of them. Indeed, probably few events in American politics have attracted such widespread attention from the mass public. Nevertheless, some variability in claimed awareness does exist, and that variability will be incorporated into the analyses that follow.[22]

Much greater variability exists in the assessments of these events. For instance, a bare majority of the respondents judged the Barrett nomination and confirmation to have been appropriate within the context of democratic politics, while less than a majority regarded Trump's efforts to over-

Table 3.1 Perceptions and Assessments of the Major Events of the 2020 U.S. Presidential Election

	Awareness of Events				Assessments of Events			
	Very or Somewhat Aware	Mean	Standard Deviation	N	Entirely or Somewhat Appropriate or Certain	Mean	Standard Deviation	N
Appropriateness of Barrett nomination	81%	0.76	0.30	1,017	53%	0.53	0.39	1,004
Appropriateness of Trump's efforts to overturn election	94%	0.88	0.22	1,016	40%	0.40	0.42	1,012
Certainty that the election was rigged	92%	0.88	0.23	1,016	39%	0.39	0.39	1,016

Source: The 2020 Pre-insurrection Survey (t_2), December 2020 and January 2021.
Notes: The response set for the first two assessment items asks the degree to which the activity was "appropriate for a democracy like ours." The item on whether the election was rigged uses a response set measuring the degree of certainty about the assessment. For that statement, the percentage shown is the percentage of respondents who were "very" or "fairly" certain that the election was rigged. All six measures are scored to vary between 0 and 1. See the appendix for the text of these questions.

turn the election results as appropriate to at least some degree. A larger majority concluded that the election was not rigged. In general, only a minority of the American people judged the election to have been rigged and concluded that Trump's efforts to subvert the election were appropriate. These data document an unsurprising conclusion: reality and perceptions and assessments of reality often diverge among Americans.[23]

Predictors of Event Evaluations

As conceptualized, assessments of events cannot be assumed to be exogenous variables. I therefore begin this analysis by investigating the predictors of evaluations of the Barrett affair at t_2, using attributes of the respondents at t_1. Because the t_1 survey was not designed to focus on election events (instead it was the 2020 entry in my Freedom and Tolerance Surveys), my most complete analysis investigates approval of the Barrett nomination and confirmation at t_2 (December 2020 and January 2021) using Supreme Court attitudes and other predictors measured at t_1 (July 2020). Cross-time analyses such as these earn some greater degree of (though, of course, far from perfect) confidence in causal inferences.

I first consider whether institutional attitudes at t_1 are associated with attitudes toward the Barrett nomination and confirmation at t_2. Recall that the dependent variable is not measured as support for Barrett becoming a Supreme Court justice; instead, the question reads as follows:

> Regarding the Barrett nomination, some say the president and the U.S. Senate should have waited until after the presidential election to fill the vacant seat on the Supreme Court, while others say that the president and the U.S. Senate had every right to fill the seat before the election. Would you say that the nomination and confirmation process for Amy Coney Barrett was entirely appropriate for a democracy like ours, somewhat appropriate for a democracy like ours, not very appropriate for a democracy like ours, [or] entirely inappropriate for a democracy like ours?

A majority (54.4 percent) judged the nomination appropriate, while 45.6 percent thought it at least not very appropriate.[24]

Two obvious hypotheses require testing: because Barrett was nominated by a Republican president and is a conservative, I hypothesize that both Republicans and conservatives are more likely to think her nomination appropriate. Figure 3.1 reports the bivariate relationships, using party and ideological identifications from the t_1 survey. For expository purposes only, I report the percentages of respondents judging the nomination to be at least somewhat appropriate.

Both partisan and ideological self-identifications are strongly related to judgments of the Barrett nomination and confirmation. Republicans of every stripe strongly approved of the nomination and confirmation, while Democrats were somewhat more mixed in their views. Democrats in general were less opposed to the nomination and confirmation than Republicans were supportive of it. For example, support among strong Democrats was somewhat of the inverse of support among moderate Republicans, as well as those leaning toward the Republican Party. Independents (about 15 percent of the sample) were in between and were fairly evenly divided.

Ideological identifications reveal a similar pattern: conservatives approved of the nomination much more than liberals disapproved of it, with moderates (33 percent of the sample) in the middle. Together these two

Figure 3.1 Partisan and Ideological Self-Identifications and Attitudes toward the Barrett Nomination

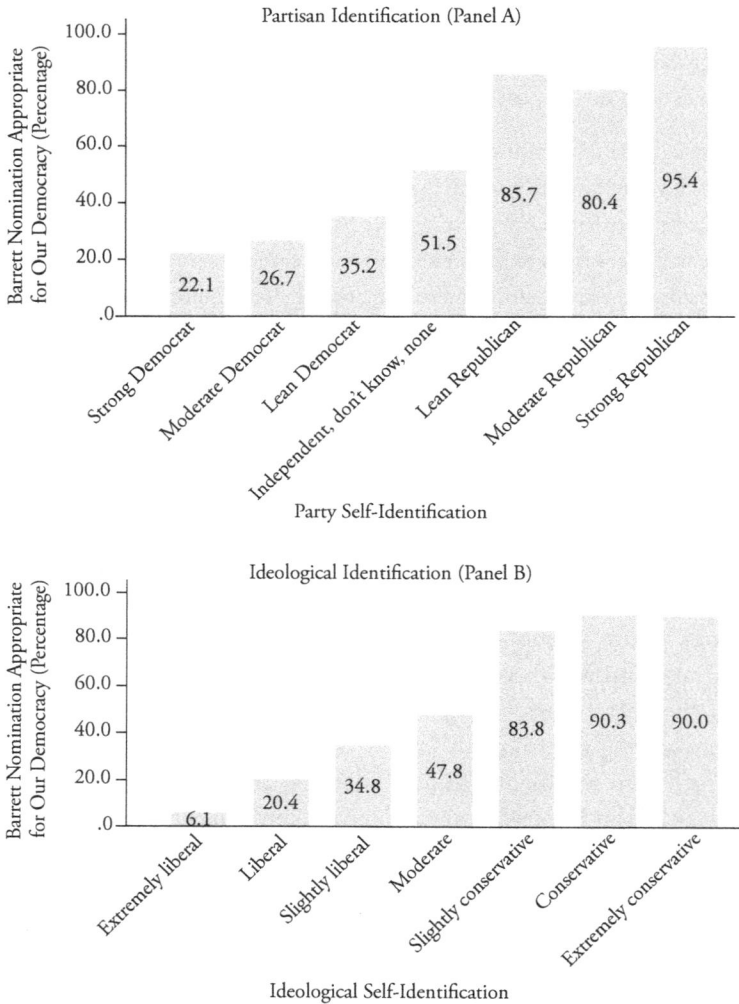

Partisan Identification (Panel A)

Ideological Identification (Panel B)

Source: The 2020 Freedom and Tolerance Survey (t₁), July 2020, and the 2020 Pre-insurrection Survey (t₂), December 2020 and January 2021.

Notes:

Panel A: N = 656; *p* ≤ .001; r = 0.60.

Panel B: N = 680; *p* ≤ .001; r = 0.61.

The measures of partisan and ideological self-identifications were taken from the t₁ survey while the evaluations of the Barrett nomination were taken from the t₂ survey.

variables can account for about 43 percent of the variance in approval of the nomination and confirmation, with ideology playing a slightly stronger role than partisanship.[25] Assessments of the appropriateness of the Barrett nomination and confirmation are closely connected to respondents' ideological and partisan self-identifications.

The data in figure 3.2 reveal an entirely different relationship. The figure shows the percentages of respondents who approved of the nomination and confirmation according to their degree of willingness to extend legitimacy to the Supreme Court. The data reveal some relationship—those more supportive of the court at t_1 were more likely to approve (at t_2) of the Barrett nomination—but the relationship is obviously far from strong (and even includes some slight deviations from monotonicity). Preexisting attitudes toward the court have some, though not much, impact on attitudes toward the Barrett nomination and confirmation.[26] This finding may, of course, be peculiar to the relatively even split of public opinion on the nomination and confirmation and the relative lack of controversy over Barrett herself (in contrast to the president and political party that nominated her).

As an aside, support for the Supreme Court's institutional legitimacy (at t_1) is entirely unrelated to both partisanship and ideology (also at t_1). Because this relationship is sometimes not fully appreciated, figure 3.3 reports

Figure 3.2 Diffuse Support for the U.S. Supreme Court and Attitudes toward the Barrett Nomination

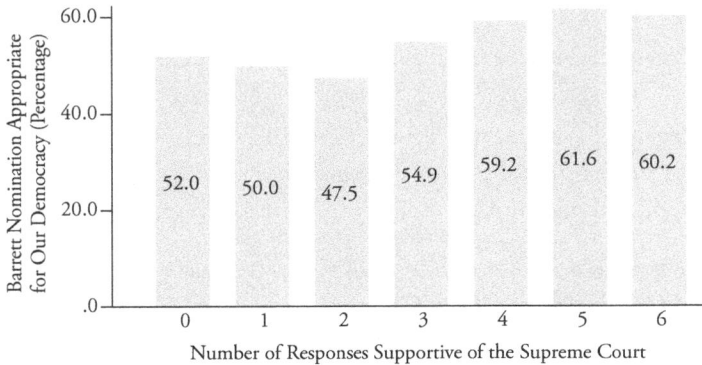

Source: The 2020 Freedom and Tolerance Survey (t_1), July 2020, and the 2020 Pre-insurrection Survey (t_2), December 2020 and January 2021.
Notes: N = 680; p = .013; r = 0.14.

Figure 3.3 Partisan and Ideological Self-Identifications and Diffuse Support for the U.S. Supreme Court

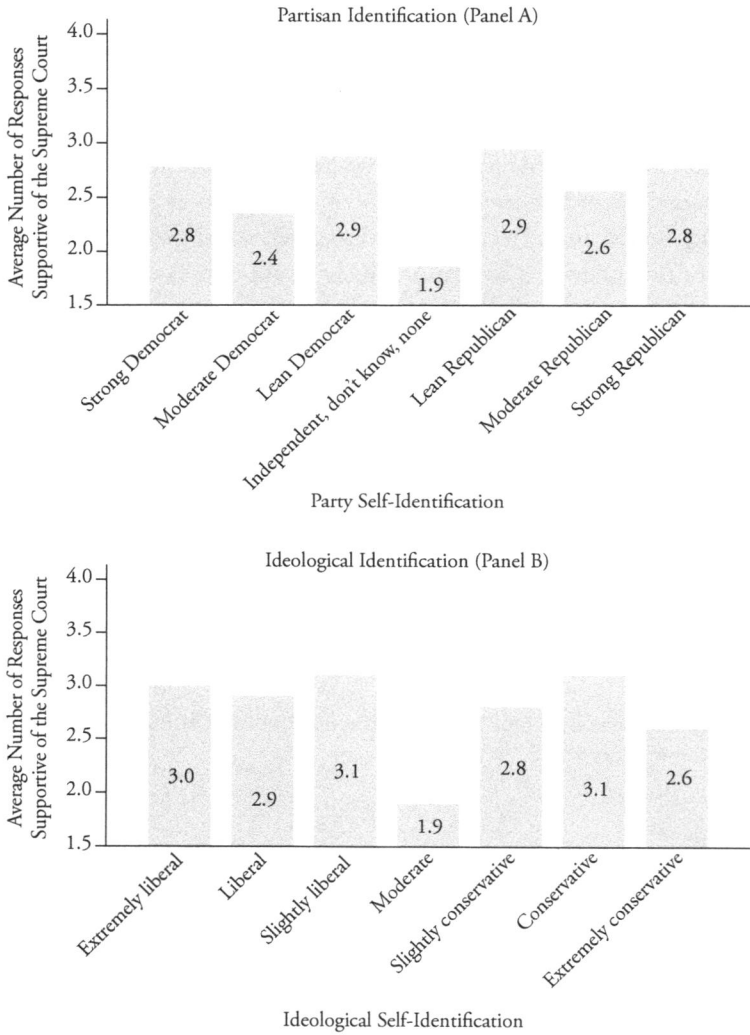

Partisan Identification (Panel A)

Ideological Identification (Panel B)

Source: The 2020 Freedom and Tolerance Survey (t_1), July 2020, and the 2020 Pre-insurrection Survey (t_2), December 2020 and January 2021.
Notes:
Panel A: $N = 664$; $p = .126$; r = 0.03.
Panel B: $N = 686$; $p = .003$; r = –0.03.
The measures of partisan and ideological self-identifications were taken from the t_1 survey while the evaluations of the Barrett nomination were taken from the t_2 survey.

the data using the number of legitimacy items endorsed by the respondent as the measure of Supreme Court support (again, for expository purposes). As the figure shows, strong Republicans and strong Democrats register the same institutional support average. Independents are the least supportive, no doubt because those without a party attachment tend to be relatively uninformed and disengaged from politics. The same can be said of moderates (as shown in the second part of the figure). In general, individuals' ideology provides practically no traction in predicting their support for the court. Indeed, neither partisanship nor ideology has any relevance for institutional support.

Bivariate relationships can be revealing as estimates of total effects. However, several of the independent variables are themselves intercorrelated, making multivariate analysis essential. Figure 3.4 reports the results of regressing attitudes toward the Barrett nomination and confirmation on several sets of independent variables, all measured at t_1: ideological and partisanship self-identifications; institutional attitudes, including diffuse and specific support; political knowledge; support for democratic institutions and processes; open-mindedness; and a variety of demographic control variables. In anticipation of analyses of the other two event assessments later in this chapter, I also report separate equations for three dependent variables (all measured at t_2).

The results reported in figure 3.4 conclusively demonstrate that judgments of the events of the Barrett nomination and confirmation are not exogenous variables (see panel A). Many of the findings in the table are noteworthy. First, a quite sizable proportion of the variation in Barrett nomination and confirmation assessments can be accounted for by the equation. That these assessments are so well predicted should give caution to researchers who would evaluate the effects of seemingly exogenous events on public opinion.

Second, and not surprisingly, the strongest predictors of these assessments, by far, are partisan and ideological identifications, with Republicans and conservatives being considerably more supportive of the nomination and confirmation. Only two additional variables contribute much to predicting approval of the nomination: the level of institutional support for the Supreme Court from well before Justice Ruth Bader Ginsberg's death and support for the rule of law (both measured, of course, at t_1). Replicating the bivariate results, respondents more supportive of the court were more

Figure 3.4 Predictors of Assessment of Events at the December 2020 and January 2021 Survey, Using Predictors at the 2020 Freedom and Tolerance Survey

Dependent Variable: Barrett Nomination (Panel A)

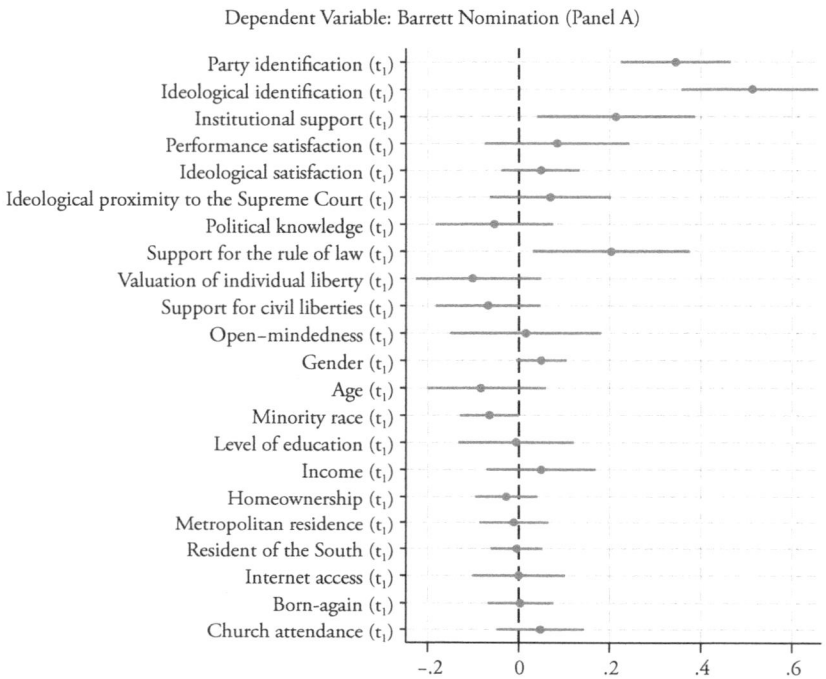

Source: The 2020 Freedom and Tolerance Survey (t_1), July 2020, and the 2020 Pre-insurrection Survey (t_2), December 2020 and January 2021.

Notes:

Panel A: Equation:

$R^2 = 0.49$***

$N = 634$

Significance of unstandardized OLS regression coefficients:

* $p \le .05$

    Gender (t_1)

    Minority race (t_1)

** $p \le .01$

    Institutional support (t_1)

    Support for the rule of law (t_1)

*** $p \le .001$

    Party identification (t_1)

    Ideological identification (t_1)

Figure 3.4 (*continued*)

Dependent Variable: Efforts to Overturn the 2020 Election (Panel B)

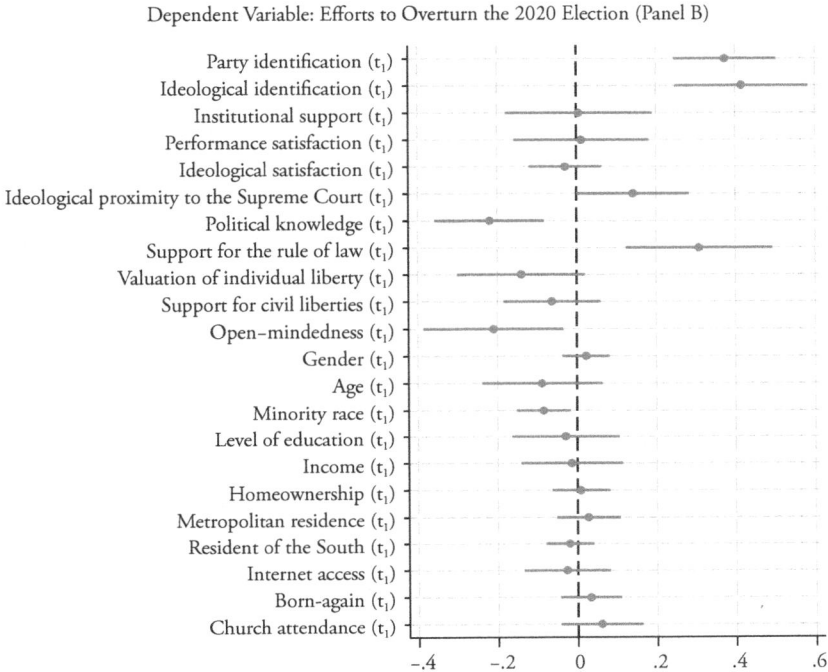

Source: The 2020 Freedom and Tolerance Survey (t_1), July 2020, and the 2020 Pre-insurrection Survey (t_2), December 2020 and January 2021.

Notes:

Panel B: Equation:

R² = 0.48***

N = 634

Significance of unstandardized OLS regression coefficients:

* *p* ≤ .05

Ideological proximity to the Supreme Court (t_1)

Valuation of individual liberty (t_1)

** *p* ≤ .01

Open-mindedness (t_1)

Minority race (t_1)

*** *p* ≤ .001

Party identification (t_1)

Ideological identification (t_1)

Political knowledge (t_1)

(*continued*)

Figure 3.4 *(continued)*

Dependent Variable: 2020 Election Was Rigged (Panel C)

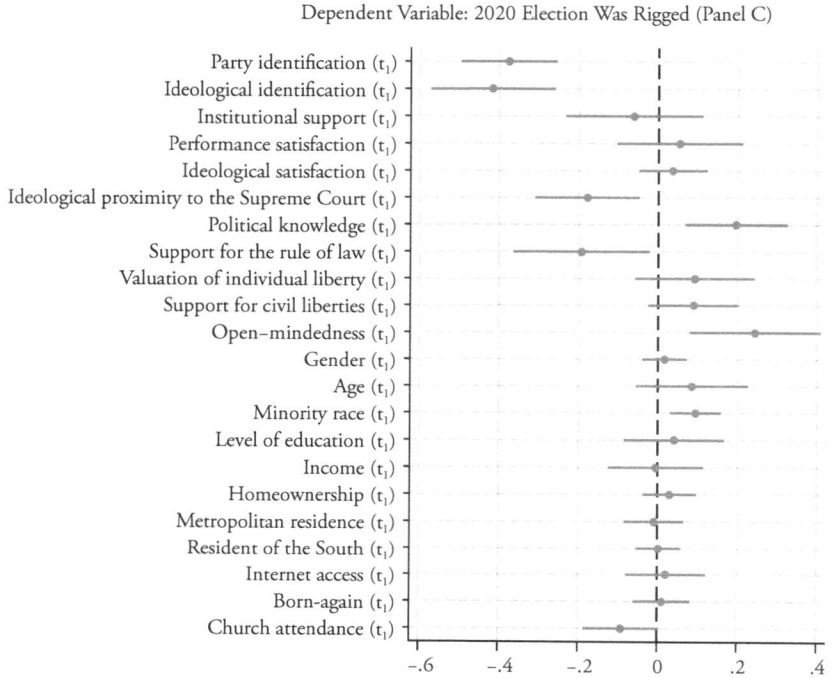

Source: The 2020 Freedom and Tolerance Survey (t_1), July 2020, and the 2020 Pre-insurrection Survey (t_2), December 2020 and January 2021.

Notes:

Panel C: Equation:

   $R^2 = 0.50$***

   $N = 634$

Significance of unstandardized OLS regression coefficients:

* $p \leq .05$

   Church attendance (t_1)

** $p \leq .01$

   Ideological proximity to the Supreme Court (t_1)

*** $p \leq .001$

   Party identification (t_1)

   Ideological identification (t_1)

   Political knowledge (t_1)

   Support for the rule of law (t_1)

   Open-mindedness (t_1)

   Minority race (t_1)

For the full regression table from which these results are derived, see table A.3. All variables are scored to range from 0 to 1. For their distributions, see table A.4. Shown are the unstandardized regression coefficients and their confidence intervals. For details on the measurement of the predictors, see the appendix.

likely to judge Barrett's nomination and confirmation as appropriate, ceteris paribus. Notably, those more supportive of the rule of law were also more likely to approve of the Barrett nomination and confirmation (which, of course, was perfectly legal irrespective of its political context and machinations). Quite small and marginally significant relationships are also observed between Barrett support and the respondent's gender and racial minority status.

In sum, the most important finding from the analysis in this table is that about half of the variance in assessments of the Barrett nomination and confirmation can be explained by respondents' preexisting attributes.

Figure 3.4 also reports the results of regressing assessments of Trump's efforts to overturn the election (panel B) and claims that the election was rigged (panel C). These two perceptions, not unexpectedly, are strongly intercorrelated ($r = -0.88$). For both assessments, party and ideological self-identifications are strong predictors of views. As with assessments of the Barrett nomination, attitudes toward the rule of law are quite consequential, with stronger supporters of the rule of law being less likely to approve of Trump's efforts to overturn the election and to reject the conclusion that the election was rigged. Levels of political knowledge, as well as open-mindedness, are also connected to these judgments.[27] Generally, the equations are strong predictors of perceptions at t_2, using only variables measured at t_1. I conclude that assessments of these election events were most likely motivated.[28]

Indeed, the most general story of this analysis is one of partisan and ideologically motivated reasoning. Republicans and conservatives saw and judged the election events differently from Democrats and liberals. Other preexisting attitudes, especially support for universal applications of the rule of law, also seemed to shape these assessments.

Discussion and Concluding Comments

This chapter introduced some of the main independent variables for the analyses that follow: the perceptions and assessments of the events of the 2020 presidential election. The data reveal a very high level of attentiveness to these happenings—perhaps unusually high. In addition, the t_2 survey reveals that Americans are divided in their assessments of each of these issues, with the divisions on all three generally in the range of one-half versus one-half.

How people viewed the 2020 election depended mightily on their attitudes and values well before the election. Unsurprisingly, partisanship played an important role in structuring these assessments; that ideology is at least as important as partisanship may be more surprising.

Perhaps the greatest twist revealed by this analysis is the strong connection of rule-of-law attitudes to all three assessments, suggesting that each may have been to some degree principled, and not purely concocted according to the respondents' self-interested partisan and ideological attachments. Rule-of-law attitudes have been shown—and increasingly are being shown—to be wide-ranging predictors of all sorts of political attitudes. I will have more to say about this in later chapters; here I would simply note that the coefficients attached to rule-of-law attitudes in all three equations are impressive indeed.

As is often the case in the multivariate context, demographic attributes hold little predictive power. Gender effects, for example, are entirely trivial. Perhaps a bit more surprising is the muted role of level of education (although its effect may be absorbed by my indicators of political knowledge). A possible exception to this general finding is the respondent's race, about which I will have much more to say in chapter 6.

In sum, the simplest and perhaps most important conclusion of this chapter is that individual assessments of the events associated with the 2020 presidential election were very much a function of preexisting and, I submit, relatively stable attitudes, identities, and values. Indeed, perhaps none of the truths of the 2020 presidential election should be held to be self-evident. The psychological and political impacts of seemingly exogenous events are far from exogenous; instead, they are dependent on the attitudinal makeup of the people assessing the events.

CHAPTER 4

The Election's Consequences: Did Trump's Canards Undermine the Legitimacy of U.S. Political Institutions?

> All of us here today do not want to see our election victory stolen by emboldened radical-left Democrats, which is what they're doing. And stolen by the fake news media. That's what they've done and what they're doing. We will never give up, we will never concede. It doesn't happen. You don't concede when there's theft involved.
>
> —President Donald Trump, speech, January 6, 2021

THE ANALYSIS in the preceding chapter established that Americans viewed the events associated with the 2020 election and its aftermath in varying and idiosyncratic ways associated with their preexisting attitudes and values. The task at hand in this chapter is to explore the consequences of those perceptions and evaluations. In particular, the overriding research question asked here is whether perceptions and evaluations of the election events undermined support for American democracy, and specifically the legitimacy of the Supreme Court, the Senate, and the presidency.

To briefly recap, scholars recognize that legitimacy (also referred to as "diffuse support" and "authority") is a normative concept concerned with the (moral and legal) right to make widely accepted decisions for a political community; institutions without legitimacy find their authority contested. We know little about how institutional legitimacy is undermined and diminished, although anything that politicizes the Supreme Court does seem to detract from its legitimacy. I hypothesize that people exposed to elite attacks on the legitimacy of institutions are more likely to be influenced by such challenges and therefore to withdraw legitimacy from the institutions than those who are not exposed. Specifically, I expect both awareness of and

https://doi.org/10.7758/dvkr4409.4182

judgments about the key events in the 2020 presidential election to be associated with lower levels of institutional support for both the presidency and the Senate and with a decline in support for the Supreme Court. These are the electoral consequences on which the analysis in this chapter focuses.

The alternative hypothesis, of course, is that these institutions are resilient and therefore were little affected by the election and its aftermath. That is, their reservoir of goodwill, as suggested by conventional legitimacy theory, largely immunized them from the legitimacy-threatening attacks of Trump and the Republicans.

Data and Analytical Strategy

As a reminder, my analysis in this chapter primarily relies on a nationally representative survey conducted by NORC's AmeriSpeak in July 2020 (t_1) and a pre-insurrection follow-up survey also conducted by NORC in December 2020 and January 2021 (t_2). The follow-up survey consists of two segments: first, the reinterviewing of 689 respondents from the July 2020 survey, and second, the interviewing of a fresh sample of 337 AmeriSpeak panelists. All interviews were completed before the January 6, 2021, insurrection. (For technical details about the surveys, see the appendix)

On a wide variety of tests, I find no significant difference between the new respondents and those who completed both surveys, and therefore I collapse them into a single database for the cross-sectional analysis.[1] Some analyses focus on change in institutional support from before (July 2020) to after the election (December 2020). The appendix also reports the results of an analysis indicating that attrition bias is unlikely to have any significant consequences for my conclusions.

A Brief Note on Causality

Some earlier projects have attempted to identify the impact of decisions and events on the legitimacy of courts. Most are correlational studies, although experimental studies have also become popular.[2] Increasingly, scholars are turning to panel surveys positioned before and after events or decisions, because such surveys enable us to estimate the causal effects of decisions at the micro-level by treating the decisions *as exogenous events* that interact with preexisting attitudes. Indeed, these decisions are similar to the experimental treatments in various studies (e.g., Bartels and Johnston 2013), but with greater external validity as these are real decisions occurring in real time.[3]

In this chapter, change in Supreme Court legitimacy is measured in the panel survey, with the initial interview in July 2020 and the subsequent interview in December 2020. Causal inferences about attitudes toward the presidency/president and the Senate must be drawn much more cautiously, because measures of these were included only in the December 2020 survey.[4]

Change in Support for the Supreme Court

I begin this investigation by focusing on attitudes toward the Supreme Court, because data on attitudes toward that institution are available for the same individuals from both before and after the election (a true panel survey). As I have noted, one way in which researchers can increase confidence in their causal inferences is by using panel data. Although panel surveys are still not the norm in studies of institutional legitimacy—they are often costly, and many have their own serious problems (such as attrition) that make them less than a panacea—scholars have gravitated toward panel research designs owing specifically to their strong ability to support causal inferences. As Nelson and I concluded in our review of the Supreme Court legitimacy literature: "The most pressing need for those seeking to understand judicial legitimacy is data capable of supporting dynamic analysis. . . . Attitudes toward legal institutions are not set in stone, even if they do not change easily; future research should seek to understand how and why these attitudes evolve."[5]

At t_1, institutional support for the Supreme Court was measured by the same six items (which also have very strong psychometric properties).[6] Table 4.1 reports summary data on support for the court at both t_1 (July 2020) and t_2 (December 2020). In the aggregate, support for the court increased slightly between the two surveys. The change is certainly not large; the mean of the distribution of individual-level change scores is 0.03. In-

Table 4.1 Change in Diffuse Support for the U.S. Supreme Court between the Freedom and Tolerance Survey and the Pre-Insurrection Survey

	Index of Support			Number of Supportive Responses		
	Mean	Standard Deviation	N	Mean	Standard Deviation	N
July 2020 Survey (t₁)	0.58	0.21	688	2.60	2.08	688
December 2020 and January 2021 Survey (t₂)	0.61	0.20	688	2.92	2.16	688
Change	0.03	0.15	688	0.32	1.57	688

Source: The 2020 Freedom and Tolerance Survey (t₁), July 2020, and the 2020 Pre-insurrection Survey (t₂), December 2020 and January 2021.

Notes: This table reports the responses of those t₁ respondents who were also interviewed at t₂. The "index of support" is the average response to the six items measuring diffuse support for the Supreme Court and is scored to range from 0 to 1, with higher scores indicating more support. The "number of supportive responses" is the number of items, out of six, on which the respondent expressed diffuse support for the court (that is, irrespective of intensity and with "uncertain" respondents in the denominator). "Change" is change at the individual level between responses at t₂ and t₁. Positive change scores represent increases in institutional support.

creases in institutional support are more common than decreases: the t_2 score of 50 percent of the respondents was higher than their t_1 score; diffuse support declined for only 34 percent of the respondents, and only 15 percent registered the same score at t_2 as at t_1 (data not shown). Some observers might expect that a controversial confirmation battle would politicize the court, resulting in a decline in institutional support.[7] In this instance, that seems not to have been the case.

Figure 4.1 reports the results of estimating the following equation:

$$y_i = \alpha_i + \lambda Legit_{it_1} + \beta_k X_k + \varepsilon_i,$$

where y_i is perceptions of legitimacy at t_2, $\lambda Legit_{it_1}$ is the effect of perceived legitimacy measured at t_1, β_k is the effects of the $N \times K$ matrix of covariates X_k, and ε_i is the error term. Figure 4.1 reports the analysis of the predictors of Supreme Court legitimacy at t_2. Several aspects of the analysis are important to note.

First, and critically important, the equation controls for levels of diffuse support at t_1. Second, most of the control variables, including democratic values and partisan and ideological identifications, were measured at t_1, not t_2.[8] Third, knowledge and assessments of events, of course, were measured

Figure 4.1 Cross-panel Predictors of Institutional Support for the U.S. Supreme Court

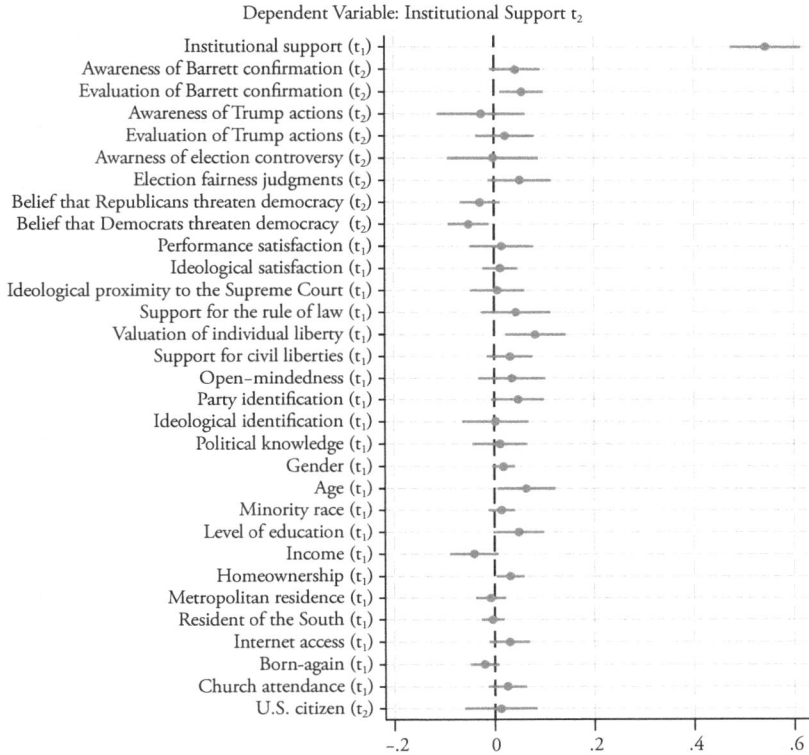

Dependent Variable: Institutional Support t_2

Source: The 2020 Freedom and Tolerance Survey (t_1), July 2020, and the 2020 Pre-insurrection Survey (t_2), December 2020 and January 2021.

Notes: Equation:

$R^2 = 0.60$***

$N = 622$

Significance of unstandardized OLS regression coefficients:

* $p \le .05$

Evaluation of Barrett confirmation (t_2)

Belief that Democrats threaten democracy (t_2)

Age (t_1)

** $p \le .01$

Valuation of individual liberty (t_1)

*** $p \le .001$

Institutional support (t_1)

For the full regression table from which these results are derived, see table A.5. All variables are scored to range from 0 to 1. For their distributions, see table A.6. Shown are the unstandardized regression coefficients and their confidence intervals.

at t_2. This equation allows for inferences about causality that, while certainly not perfect, are superior to those reported from cross-sectional analyses. Finally, given their important role in the literature on Supreme Court legitimacy, I also control for t_1 measures of specific support (performance satisfaction), satisfaction with the court's policy outputs (ideological satisfaction), and ideological proximity (the ideological distance between the individual and the court; see the appendix).[9]

Unsurprisingly, institutional support at t_1 strongly predicts institutional support at t_2. With such a potent control variable (and including essential controls for support for democratic institutions and processes), the other variables in the equation no doubt struggle to register an independent impact on institutional support in December 2020.

To what degree do perceptions and assessments of the events between the two surveys affect attitudes toward the Supreme Court? The awareness variables have practically no independent impact on institutional support, but evaluations of the Barrett affair do. Those respondents who viewed the confirmation as inappropriate significantly—but not greatly—reduced their support for the court from before the nomination and confirmation to after it. On the other hand, neither perceptions nor evaluations of the election and Trump's efforts to overturn it affected institutional support for the Supreme Court.

As I documented in chapter 3, the respondents were almost evenly divided on their judgments of the appropriateness of the Barrett nomination and confirmation, with a slight edge going to those who considered her placement on the Supreme Court appropriate. The simplest and most direct way to understand the relationship between these assessments and changes in court support is to examine the bivariate relationship between assessments of the Barrett nomination and confirmation and changes in supportive responses to the institutional legitimacy items. Figure 4.2 reports this relationship.

I first note that the bivariate relationship between assessments of the Barrett nomination and confirmation and change in Supreme Court support is neither statistically nor substantively significant. Among respondents who judged the Barrett nomination most harshly, support for the court barely changed (mean = 0.01). Those who judged the nomination most favorably did increase their support for the court the most, but only slightly and not significantly so.

Figure 4.2 Assessments of the Barrett Nomination and Change in Institutional Support for the U.S. Supreme Court

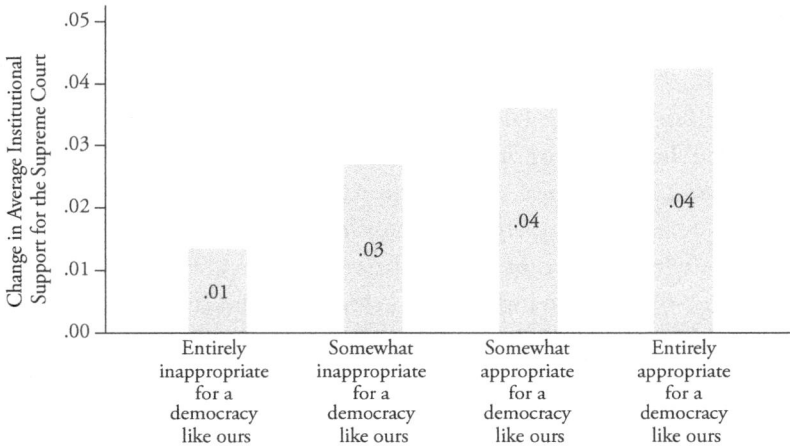

The nomination and confirmation process for Amy Coney Barrett was . . .

Source: The 2020 Freedom and Tolerance Survey (t_1), July 2020, and the 2020 Pre-insurrection Survey (t_2), December 2020 and January 2021.
Notes: $N = 680$; $p = .295$; $r = 0.07$. Change in the number of supportive responses varies from –0.46 to 0.67, with a mean of 0.03 and a standard deviation of 0.15.

Returning to the multivariate findings reported in figure 4.1, the regression coefficient for evaluations of the Barrett nomination and confirmation is 0.06. Because all variables are scored to range from 0 to 1, the effect of these assessments from the lowest to highest evaluation scores is 0.06 on a dependent variable that ranges from 0 to 1 and that has a mean of 0.61. This coefficient may be distinguishable from 0, but it is also fairly small. This is an important finding because respondents who judged the Barrett nomination and confirmation as appropriate increased their support, while those who found the nomination and confirmation inappropriate did not reduce their institutional support compared to July 2020.

The primary purpose of this chapter is to assess the effects of the election controversy on the legitimacy of American political institutions. That said, several ideological, partisan, and performance variables fail entirely to predict change in Supreme Court support. Republicans did not become more supportive than Democrats did; the same is true of conservatives and liberals. The equation in figure 4.1 controls for performance satisfaction, satisfaction with the court's ideological outputs, and ideological proximity to the court. None of these variables is a significant predictor of institutional support.

The Barrett nomination and confirmation were intensely controversial and partisan events, as documented at least in part by the Senate vote of fifty-two Republicans in favor of confirmation and forty-seven Democrats, plus Republican senator Susan Collins, voting against confirmation. We could expect, therefore, to see that the events surrounding the nomination affected Democrats and Republicans differently.

Thus, under the hypothesis that partisanship provided a filter (motivated reasoning) for understanding the events, I interact the partisan self-identification measure with each of the three evaluation variables and added the three interaction terms to the equation reported in figure 4.1. None of the interaction terms even approaches statistical significance. As far as Supreme Court legitimacy is concerned, Democrats and Republicans seem to have reacted to the events of the 2020 election in similar ways. The results from interacting ideological self-identifications with the evaluation variables are largely the same.[10]

I have been careful to emphasize that these conclusions pertain only to the legitimacy of the Supreme Court, because measures of the legitimacy of the presidency and the Senate are not available in the t_1 survey. Considerable debate exists in the academic literature over whether the court's legitimacy is obdurate. Some scholars argue that unpopular decisions undermine the Supreme Court's legitimacy,[11] and others argue that controversial nominations—such as the Brett Kavanaugh nomination—damage the court's legitimacy.[12] My findings run counter to those conclusions, perhaps in part because the Barrett nomination, while quite salient to the American people (see table 3.1), was not "alive" long enough to become as intensely politicized as, for instance, the Kavanaugh nomination. Moreover, no charges of untoward behavior were leveled against Barrett, as they were against Kavanaugh. Thus, unsurprisingly, only a minority of Americans judged the Barrett nomination and confirmation to be inappropriate.

Finally, despite Trump's tirades against the Supreme Court, the election itself also unsurprisingly had few consequences for the court's legitimacy. The Court largely avoided ruling on Republican claims of voting irregularities, and when it did, its opinions were limited, legally focused, and far from inflammatory (see the appendix). From this analysis, the Supreme Court appears to have come out of the various events associated with the 2020 presidential election largely unscathed.

Summary

This analysis of change in support for the Supreme Court yields several important conclusions. First, the election brouhaha seems to have had few consequences for the court's institutional legitimacy. Second, the Barrett nomination and confirmation do appear to have had some consequences, but largely to *boost* support in the aggregate as a result of an increase in support for the Court among those favoring the nomination and little change in support among those opposing the nomination. Third, partisanship and ideology played only a limited role in this process; they shaped assessments of the Barrett nomination and confirmation but otherwise had little impact on court support. Finally, support for the court at t_1 seems not only to have structured assessments of the nomination and confirmation but also to have had a significant influence on support at t_2.

Cross-Sectional Analysis: Cross-institutional Legitimacy

I continue this investigation with an analysis of the 2020–2021 cross-sectional data.[13] My basic hypothesis is that perceptions and evaluations of events are associated with the perceived legitimacy of the presidency/president, the Supreme Court, and the Senate. Although cross-sectional analysis allows only for confident conclusions about covariation (what goes with what), I include a significant number of theoretically derived control variables, thereby mitigating omitted variable bias to at least some degree. For example, it is well established that support for the Supreme Court is connected to an individual's general support for democratic institutions and processes, as well as levels of exposure to the court (that is, "to know them is to love them").[14] Because earlier investigations of the legitimacy of the presidency and the Senate are few and far between, not much theory exists on the predictors of support for these institutions. Nevertheless, I include controls for democratic values[15] and for political knowledge,[16] as well as for a host of additional attitudinal and demographic factors, including an individual's ideological and partisan self-identifications. Still, even with this panoply of controls, I acknowledge that only the weakest of causal inferences can be drawn (except, of course, inferences about fixed demographic variables).

To reiterate, support for the presidency, the Supreme Court, and the Senate are hypothesized to be associated with: (1) awareness and perceptions of events associated with the 2020 election; (2) judgments about the fairness of the election; (3) evaluations of the actions of the two political parties during the election controversy; (4) general support for democratic institutions and processes; (5) open-mindedness; (6) ideological and partisan self-identifications; (7) political knowledge; and (8) various demographic control variables. (See the appendix for details on the measurement of these concepts.)

Figure 4.3 reports the ordinary least squares (OLS) results for the three dependent variables. The equation I estimate is:

$$Y_i = \beta_0 + \beta_k X_k + \varepsilon_i,$$

where Y_i is the reported perception of legitimacy measured for each institution at t_2, β_0 is the intercept, $\beta_k X_k$ is an $N \times K$ matrix of t_2 covariates and their associated effects, and ε_i is the residual error.

The results reported in this figure support a variety of conclusions. First, the legitimacy attitudes toward each of the institutions are quite well predicted by the equations, especially attitudes toward the legitimacy of the presidency ($R^2 = 0.69$). Second, the coefficients confirm the long-standing finding that legitimacy attitudes are connected to more general support for democratic institutions and processes.[17] Indeed, across the three equations, support for the rule of law is one of the strongest and most consistent predictors (b ≈ 0.16). Relatedly, open-mindedness, one of the three primary antecedents of support for civil liberties (a democratic value), is also a strong and consistent predictor of legitimacy attitudes (the regression coefficients range from 0.19 to 0.30).[18]

Generally, the measures of awareness of the election events are not particularly useful predictors of legitimacy attitudes, no doubt owing in part to the very high salience of these events (as documented in table 3.1). Awareness of the Barrett nomination and confirmation varies more (standard de-

Figure 4.3 Predictors of Support for Institutional Legitimacy before the January 6, 2021, Insurrection

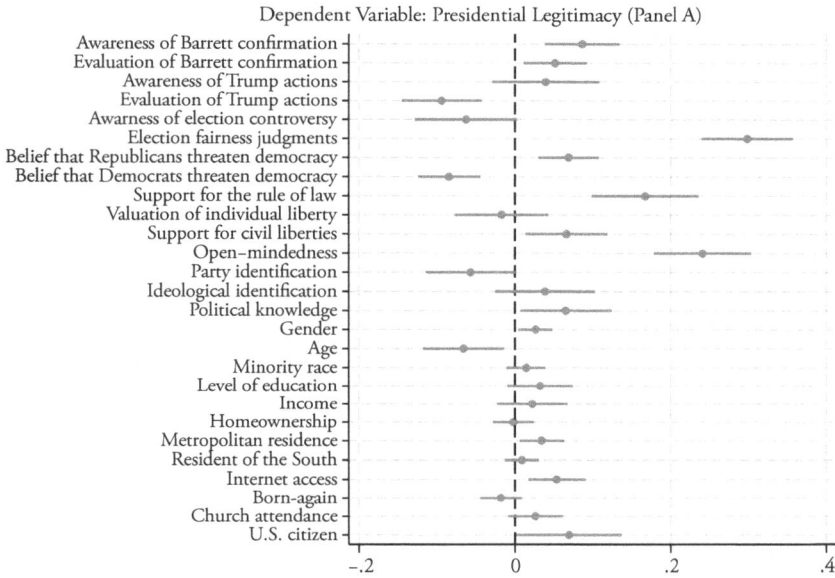

Dependent Variable: Presidential Legitimacy (Panel A)

Source: The 2020 Freedom and Tolerance Survey (t₁), July 2020, and the 2020 Pre-insurrection Survey (t₂), December 2020 and January 2021.
Notes:
Panel A: Equation:
  $R^2 = 0.69$***
  $N = 958$
Significance of unstandardized OLS regression coefficients:
* $p \leq .05$
    Evaluation of Barrett confirmation
    Support for civil liberties
    Political knowledge
    Gender
    Age
    Metropolitan residence
    U.S. citizen
** $p \leq .01$
    Evaluation of Trump's actions
    Internet access
*** $p \leq .001$
    Awareness of Barrett confirmation
    Election fairness judgments
    Belief that Republicans threaten democracy
    Support for the rule of law
    Open-mindedness

(continued)

Figure 4.3 (*continued*)

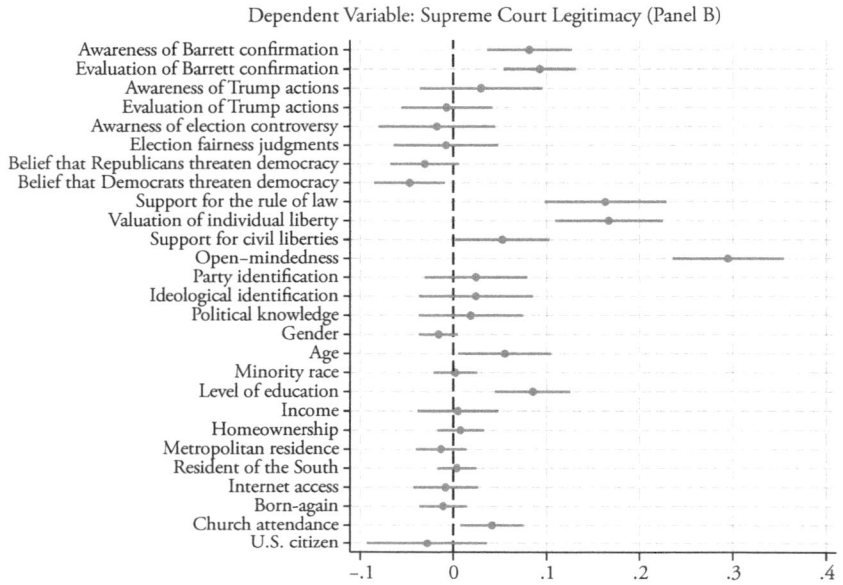

Dependent Variable: Supreme Court Legitimacy (Panel B)

Source: The 2020 Freedom and Tolerance Survey (t₁), July 2020, and the 2020 Pre-insurrection Survey (t₂), December 2020 and January 2021.

Notes:

Panel B: Equation:

$R^2 = 0.44$***

$N = 958$

Significance of unstandardized OLS regression coefficients:

* $p \leq .05$

    Belief that Democrats threaten democracy

    Support for civil liberties

    Age

    Church attendance

** $p \leq .01$

    [None]

*** $p \leq .001$

    Awareness of Barrett confirmation

    Evaluation of Barrett confirmation

    Support for the rule of law

    Valuation of individual liberty

    Open-mindedness

    Level of education

Figure 4.3 (*continued*)

Dependent Variable: Senate Legitimacy (Panel C)

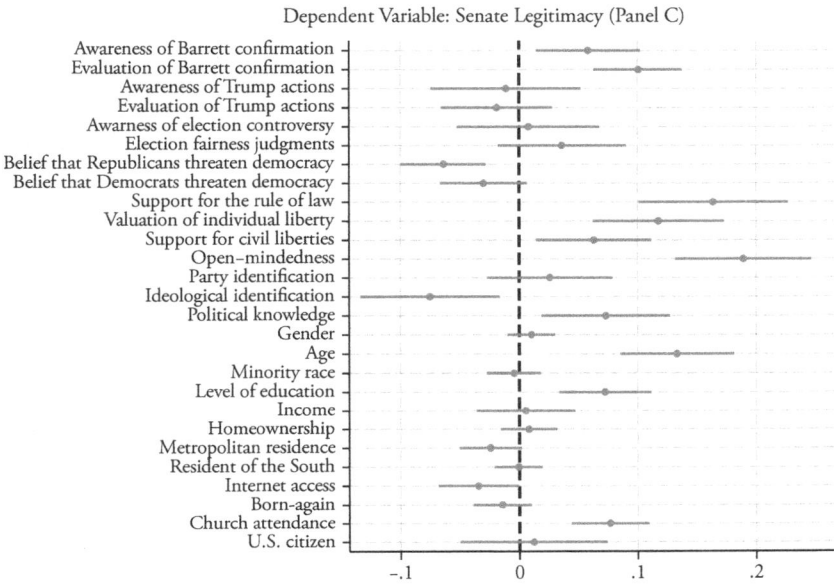

Source: The 2020 Freedom and Tolerance Survey (t₁), July 2020, and the 2020 Pre-insurrection Survey (t₂), December 2020 and January 2021.

Notes:

Panel C: Equation:

    $R^2 = 0.44^{***}$

    $N = 958$

Significance of unstandardized OLS regression coefficients:

* $p \le .05$

    Internet access

** $p \le .01$

    Awareness of Barrett confirmation

    Support for civil liberties

    Ideological identification

    Political knowledge

*** $p \le .001$

    Evaluation of Barrett confirmation

    Belief that Republicans threaten democracy

    Support for the rule of law

    Valuation of individual liberty

    Open-mindedness

    Age

    Level of education

    Church attendance

For the full regression table from which these results are derived, see table A.7. All variables are scored to range from 0 to 1. For their distributions, see table A.8. Shown are the unstandardized regression coefficients and their confidence intervals.

viation = 0.30), and that variability is associated with slightly higher levels of support for two of the three institutions (at p < .001), a finding consistent with the conventional "to know them is to love them" hypothesis (the coefficients range from 0.06 to 0.09). At the same time, however, general political knowledge has little connection to legitimacy attitudes, while level of education is marginally related to Senate legitimacy (b = 0.07) and Supreme Court support (b = 0.09), as is often the case.

I next turn to the most important findings of this chapter: evaluations of the various events are connected to the willingness to grant legitimacy to these institutions. One of the strongest relationships found in figure 4.3 is between presidential legitimacy and the belief that the 2020 presidential election was rigged: respondents who believed that the election was rigged were very much less likely to extend legitimacy to the Biden presidency (b = 0.30).[19] However, that beliefs about the election have decidedly not spilled over to affect the legitimacy of the Supreme Court or the Senate is particularly noteworthy. Indeed, none of the four election variables (knowledge and evaluations) has any connection whatsoever to attitudes toward the legitimacy of the Supreme Court or the Senate. These institutions seem to have escaped from the 2020 presidential election imbroglio largely unscathed.

On the other hand, both Supreme Court and Senate legitimacy are significantly associated with perceptions of the Barrett nomination and confirmation. Although the causal connections among these variables are cloudy and the panel analysis results suggest that attitudes toward the Supreme Court are more complicated, respondents who judged the Barrett nomination and confirmation to have been more inappropriate were substantially less likely to extend legitimacy to either the Senate or the Supreme Court. Neither of these relationships is particularly strong (b ≈ 0.10, and recall that all variables are scored to range from 0 to 1), but each suggests that the Barrett affair may have undermined these two institutions to a minor degree.[20]

Judgments of the threat to democracy posed by either Democrats or Republicans are both related to the willingness to grant legitimacy to the Biden presidency, although with opposite signs (as expected). Respondents who viewed the Democrats as less of a threat to America's democracy and the Republicans as more of a threat were more likely to acknowledge Biden's legitimacy (b = –0.08 and 0.07, respectively). That both variables are influential, especially in the context of an equation that includes the specific events variables, is noteworthy. The effects of Trump's actions seem to have spilled over to empower fears about the two major political parties. However, these variables have considerably weaker or more inconsistent connections to the legitimacy of the Supreme Court and the Senate.

Some literature on polarization suggests that attitudes toward the Supreme Court's legitimacy have not become polarized.[21] However, considerable debate exists on this issue.[22] On this score, figure 4.3 reports no independent effect of either partisan or ideological identification on support for the Supreme Court. Nor are the multivariate coefficients mainly a function of the other variables in the equation. The bivariate relationship between Supreme Court legitimacy and partisan self-identification is only 0.07; for ideological self-identification, it is 0.05. Nor are attitudes toward the other two institutions connected to partisanship or ideology. From these data, Democrats and Republicans do not differ much in their attitudes toward these institutions.[23]

As is typically the case, the demographic predictors of legitimacy attitudes, such as class-related differences, are generally of little consequence. A few exceptions exist. For example, older Americans seem to extend somewhat more legitimacy to the Senate (all else equal).

Perhaps the most important conclusions of this portion of my analysis pertain to the variables that are *not* connected to institutional legitimacy: the legitimacy of the Supreme Court and the Senate do not seem to have been undermined by the presidential election of 2020—even if the election, perhaps fairly naturally, had at least some connections to perceptions of the legitimacy of the Biden presidency. Attitudes toward the presidency seem to be more politicized than attitudes toward the other two institutions.

Discussion and Concluding Comments

The analysis reported in this chapter draws a simple theoretical conclusion: institutions are often more resilient than many people think. The strongest single bit of evidence in support of this inference is that between July to December 2020 diffuse support for the Supreme Court actually grew slightly, despite a contentious dispute over the Barrett nomination and confirmation, a highly divisive presidential election, and the intrigues of a bombastic president. Support grew not just in the aggregate but also at the individual level, with only about one-third of respondents withdrawing even a small amount of support from the court. This finding is in part a function of the fact that most Americans did not perceive the Barrett nomination and confirmation as untoward. Nevertheless, the Barrett affair seemingly did less damage to the Supreme Court than was done, for instance, by the Samuel Alito nomination.[24] Put most conservatively, no evidence suggests that the net effect of the Barrett nomination and confirmation, the election, and its aftermath on the Supreme Court's legitimacy was detrimental.

These findings are reminiscent of two sets of earlier findings on the Supreme Court's legitimacy. First, Michael Nelson and I also discovered that Trump's attacks on judges and the judiciary were ineffective, in part because most Americans did not view Trump as a credible source.[25] Second, the findings here differ little from the conclusions of many scholars on the effect of the 2000 presidential election on the legitimacy of the Supreme Court. Researchers agree that if that election, including the ruling in *Bush v. Gore*, had any impact on the institution, it was to *increase* its legitimacy with the American people. Of course, 2000 was different from 2020 from the viewpoint of the Supreme Court. In 2000, the court decided the election; in 2020, it refused to do so. Still, no evidence in either case suggests that the court's legitimacy suffered from being asked by the election participants to rule on the outcome of the balloting.

A related finding of institutional resilience is that, as of the very beginning of 2021, Biden and his presidency had overwhelming support from Americans, despite President Trump's concerted effort to undermine Biden's victory. This is perhaps not a startling finding—by the start of the new year, most Americans had come to reject Trump's claims of a rigged and fraudulent election.[26] The percentage of all Americans who disavowed the statement that Biden would "never be my president" was far greater than the percentage of Americans who voted for Biden for president, in spite of the vituperative attacks on the presidential election over an extended period of seventy-seven days.[27] The wild punches thrown by Trump and the Republicans did not seem to land with weighty force on the Biden presidency— even if, as the data have shown, presidential legitimacy is a bit more volatile and responsive to external events than the legitimacy of the Supreme Court and the Senate.

Most of the conclusions that pertain to the Supreme Court also pertain to the Senate (recall that the legitimacy indices for these two institutions are fairly strongly correlated). Whether this finding is surprising is unclear; the sociological legitimacy of the Senate as an institution has not been investigated before to any great extent. Much more research on the legitimacy of legislatures is necessary, especially because Congress profits from electoral legitimacy while the Supreme Court does not, and it seems intuitively obvious that people's normative expectations of the two institutions would differ. Moreover, recall that the fieldwork for the surveys on which this chapter relies was completed prior to Congress's involvement in certifying the outcome of the 2020 presidential election (and the concomitant attack on the Capitol).

Practically none of my results are simple extrapolations of people's partisanship. Indeed, a striking thread that runs through these analyses is the weak and limited effects of partisan attachments. Undoubtedly, some people will find these results difficult to fathom. But the legitimacy of these institutions seems not to have fallen prey to the hyperpartisan context of the 2020 election.

As my analysis has shown, the lack of volatility in institutional legitimacy is at least in part a function of legitimacy's close connection to support for democratic institutions and processes and of the relatively obdurate nature of democratic values. We have long known that the legitimacy of the Supreme Court is rooted in the democratic values of citizens, but this research has shown that those values are reasonably closely connected to the willingness to extend legitimacy to the Biden presidency and to the Senate as well.[28] An attack on the legitimacy of these institutions is indeed ultimately an attack on basic commitments to democratic values. To date, little direct evidence suggests that the health of those democratic values has been compromised, in part because citizens develop such values early in life, making them fairly resistant to change.

In addition to producing these important (and perhaps startling) substantive conclusions, this research makes several theoretical and methodological contributions. First, and most obviously, in taking advantage of an existing survey to create a panel research design bookended around an important public controversy, this project is exemplary of the so-called firehouse studies that are mobilized in response to events.[29]

Second, the analysis extends legitimacy theory from the courts to the presidency/president and the Senate, producing some new (though perhaps not perfect) empirical measures of public attitudes toward these institutions. Legitimacy theory indubitably will profit from being expanded and tested within a cross-institutional context.

Third, by actually measuring individual-level awareness and assessments of seemingly exogenous events, this research shows the folly of assuming that all citizens pay similar attention to politics and understand seemingly objective political events in the same way. Perhaps this contribution seems to be obvious; nevertheless, as is increasingly clear, even court decisions are understood and evaluated differently by different people. Partisanship may play a role in how individuals filter their understandings of events, but mass perceptions not only often deviate from those of elites but also vary in seemingly random ways. Political events are not self-evident truths.

Of course, this analysis has some important limitations, the most telling of which are temporal. First, the survey wrapped up on the day before the Capitol insurrection. I have argued that my research design allows an assessment of the election events unconfounded by the violent attack in Washington, D.C. Fortunately, the next chapter is able to address the post-insurrection support for these democratic institutions.

A second limitation is perhaps more serious—this study can conclude nothing definitive about the long-term consequences of the 2020 election. Grounding legitimacy in democratic values suggests that legitimacy has some staying power, but just as political tolerance seems to have changed in recent times among college students in the United States, democratic values themselves are not guaranteed to be entirely unresponsive to external forces.[30]

Finally, for some subgroups of Americans, these processes may differ. Survey samples these days cannot guarantee that the disaffected or the lumpenproletariat participate in proportion to their population numbers. Nor, it should be remembered, did it take anything more than a tiny sliver of the American population to rain down chaos on the country's political system by its attack on the Capitol. Consequently, chapter 6 presents some extensive subgroup analysis.

A number of other limitations to the analyses reported in this chapter require extra consideration in future research. Undoubtedly, the measurement of the legitimacy of institutions other than the Supreme Court requires additional thought and empirical investigation; mine is only an initial stab at the problem. Efforts to measure the legitimacy of institutions must tap loyalty toward the institution rather than simple approval of the incumbents and their actions. For the Supreme Court, with its relatively low-salience incumbents, this is not a particularly difficult task. For other institutions—especially the presidency—the obstacles remain formidable.

Finally, I would be remiss not to point out that legitimacy theory, even within its home field of the Supreme Court, is very much in flux these days: a variety of important revisionist challenges are being made to the conventional wisdom. My findings in this chapter largely comport with the button-down understandings of legitimacy (for example, partisanship has little connection to legitimacy). The revisionists, it seems, face two vital unanswered questions. First, even if there is a very short-term negative reaction to an unwanted ruling or event, does it persist? Or is legitimacy instead subject to some sort of "values-based regeneration" or other processes of forgetting the bad news, thereby allowing the good views to resurface?[31] Second, how does legitimacy transfer from individuals to institutions? In the case of the Supreme Court, do one or two bad apples spoil the whole bunch? At the most general level, how are attitudes toward institutions connected to attitudes toward the incumbents in those institutions—and of course, how does this vary across institutions?

Consequently, this chapter is far from being the last word on many unanswered legitimacy questions. The events I study do underscore, however, the importance of legitimacy for democracy. Without legitimacy for its political institutions, democracy itself is threatened in America. That institutional legitimacy has not yet been lost does not mean that it cannot be lost.

As mentioned, this survey was wrapped up on January 5, 2021, one day before the Trump-inspired attack on the Capitol and on America's democracy. Fortunately, a new survey, addressing these same issues of support for democratic institutions, was fielded shortly after the close of the second Trump impeachment trial. Determining whether the findings of this chapter characterize the post-insurrection period is the objective of chapter 5.

The Riots' Consequences: Did the Attack on the U.S. Capitol Undermine the Legitimacy of U.S. Political Institutions?

If Dr. Eastman and President Trump's plan had worked, it would have permanently ended the peaceful transition of power, undermining American democracy and the Constitution. If the country does not commit to investigating and pursuing accountability for those responsible, the Court fears January 6th will repeat itself.

— Judge David Carter, quoted in *Eastman v. Thompson*, 2022

A stake was driven through the heart of American democracy on January 6, 2021, and our democracy today is on a knife's edge.

— Judge J. Michael Luttig, statement before the U.S. House of Representatives January 6 Committee hearing, June 16, 2022

THE PRECEDING CHAPTER reported analyses of the effects of the 2020 presidential election and its aftermath on the public's attitudes toward America's democratic institutions. The election, however, was only one of several momentous events taking place during the transition away from Trump rule. Perhaps more consequential for the health of America's democracy was the insurrection of January 6, 2021, and the subsequent impeachment and trial of President Donald Trump. These events made painfully evident that the challenges to the election outcome were being mounted not only in courts and legislatures but also in the streets and by surreptitious elite-driven efforts to implement a coup against democracy in America. The failure of that attempt—perhaps only by a Mike Pence shoestring—does not necessarily mean that the effort was of no consequence.

https://doi.org/10.7758/dvkr4409.8259

In this chapter, I examine public support for democracy after the close of the impeachment trial, based on a nationally representative survey fielded in February and March 2021.[1] In some respects, the analysis in this chapter parallels that reported in chapter 4. For example, my primary purpose here is to evaluate the hypothesis that awareness and assessments of the insurrection and impeachment events are associated with the willingness or unwillingness to extend legitimacy to the Supreme Court, the Senate, and the presidency. In a fashion analogous to the analysis in chapter 3, this requires that I begin by documenting how people perceived and judged these events. And as in chapter 4, I address the role of democratic values, under the hypothesis that values such as support for the rule of law influence legitimacy attitudes more than perceptions of the insurrection and impeachment events do.

In other respects, this chapter breaks new ground. First, the March 2021 survey—the Insurrection and Impeachment Survey (the t_3 survey)—did not include a panel component, as the December 2020 (the t_2 survey) survey did. Second, in addition to the measures of the legitimacy of the Supreme Court, the Senate, and the presidency/president, the t_3 survey included a new summary measure of support for America's democratic institutions in general. Finally, and perhaps most important, the inclusion of a large oversample of African Americans in the March 2021 survey made possible an analysis of heterogeneity in support for democratic institutions, processes, and values. The Black oversample is particularly important because it became the first interview in a two-wave panel, with the second interview conducted in June 2021. The results of this panel survey—which includes additional indicators of experiences with legal authorities and in-group attachments—are reported in chapters 6 and 7.

As a one-shot cross-sectional survey, the March 2021 data are, of course, limited in their ability to support strong causal inferences, and thus much of the analysis presented in this chapter should be understood as descriptive. However, by comparing the results of the March 2021 survey with the December 2020 and July 2020 surveys, slightly stronger evidence of aggregate-level change can be adduced. I therefore begin this chapter by presenting data on the change in attitudes toward various political institutions over the nine-month period between the first and last surveys.

Changes in Institutional Support, July 2020 to March 2021

The Legitimacy of the Supreme Court

I first focus on attitudes toward the Supreme Court, the institution for which the survey data are most complete. Figure 5.1 reports a comparison of aggregate-level support for the Supreme Court from about July 2020 to March 2021. The indicators of diffuse support for the court discussed in chapter 2 are also used here, with the same question wording used in each of the three NORC surveys.

The surveys reveal that the average number of items on which respondents expressed support for the court increased from July 2020 to March 2021; thus, the null hypothesis of no change over time can be rejected. Moreover, for each of the six indicators of institutional attitudes, the largest percentages of respondents expressing support for the court are found in the last survey, conducted in February and March 2021 (data not shown). To be sure, the differences are often small and are not always of much substantive significance. Still, these data support minimalist and maximalist conclusions: At the minimum, no evidence indicates that the election-related events between July 2020 and March 2021 took a toll on the legitimacy of America's highest court. At the maximum, the events may have even enhanced the court's legitimacy.

This is not the first study to conclude that when the Supreme Court gets involved in a highly salient political or legal dispute, its support actually increases. The "poster child" for such findings is the court's intervention in the 2000 presidential election, the capstone of which was its ruling in *Bush v. Gore*.[2] That research gave rise to one of the most venerable findings in research on attitudes toward the court: to know it is to love it.[3] Such a characterization of public opinion may seem trite, but it is grounded in theory and research on the effects of symbols on people's attitudes toward institutions.[4] Greater awareness results in increased support because it is associated with more exposure to the legitimizing symbols of judicial authority.

To reiterate, repeated cross-sectional surveys such as those presented in this book are certainly limited in their ability to describe and explain change.[5] At the same time, however, these data seem to be incompatible with the view that either the election or the insurrection (or both) seriously

Figure 5.1 Change in Institutional Support Attitudes from 2020 to 2021

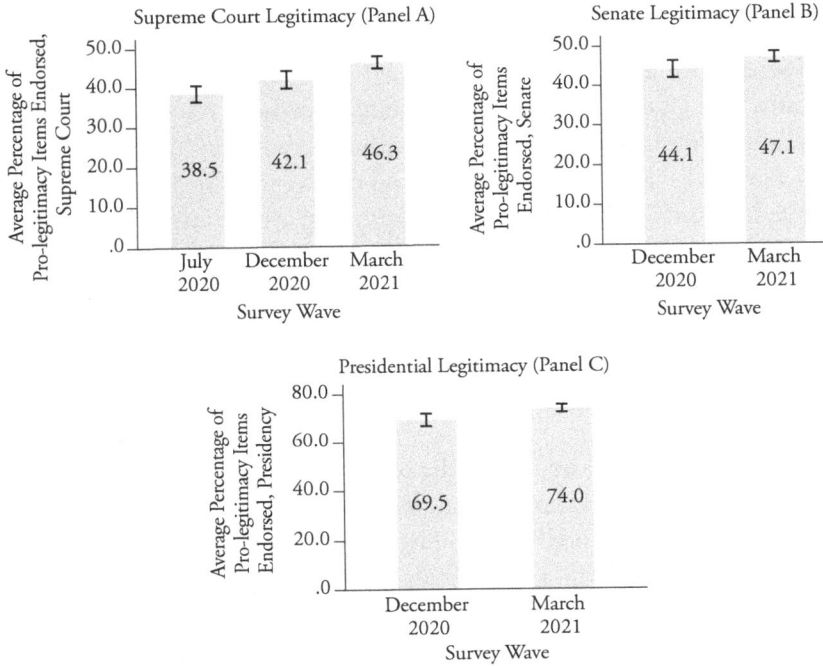

Supreme Court Legitimacy (Panel A)

38.5   42.1   46.3

July 2020   December 2020   March 2021

Survey Wave

Senate Legitimacy (Panel B)

44.1   47.1

December 2020   March 2021

Survey Wave

Presidential Legitimacy (Panel C)

69.5   74.0

December 2020   March 2021

Survey Wave

Source: The 2020 Freedom and Tolerance Survey (t₁), July 2020; The 2020 Pre-insurrection Survey (t₂), December 2020 and January 2021; and The 2021 Insurrection and Impeachment Survey (t₃), February and March 2021.

Notes: Supreme Court: $p < .001$, $r = 0.09$, $N \approx 1,003$. Senate: $p = .021$, $r = 0.04$, $N \approx 1,026$. Presidency: $p = .002$, $r = 0.06$, $N \approx 2,007$. These figures report the average percentage of pro-legitimacy statements endorsed by the respondent. For the Supreme Court, this is the average of six statements; for the Senate and the presidency, it is the average of four statements.

undermined support for the Supreme Court. Indeed, perhaps the opposite conclusion is the most warranted.

The Legitimacy of the Senate

I can conduct a similar sort of analysis of the legitimacy of the Senate, though in the absence of pre-election data—the December 2020 survey was the first to ask questions about support for the Senate—the analysis can undertake a comparison of these results at only two points in time. Figure 5.1 also reports the survey answers pre- and post-insurrection.

Although perhaps not as strong as the results regarding the Supreme Court, these data provide little or no evidence of a decline in the aggregate legitimacy of the Senate from December 2020 to March 2021. As the index of Senate attitudes indicates, support for the institution increased significantly, though certainly not strongly. Since the mean response on each of the four items is, at best, nominally larger at t_3 than at t_2 (data not shown), I acknowledge that the hypothesis of no change is difficult to reject. Still, on at least one item ("reform the Senate"), supportive responses increased by almost ten percentage points from the t_2 to the t_3 survey. Again, the minimalist conclusion is that the legitimacy of the Senate did not decline in the aftermath of the insurrection and impeachment.

The Legitimacy of the Presidency/President

With respect to attitudes toward the presidency/president, two caveats are necessary. First, as with Senate attitudes, the December 2020 survey was the first to ask questions about these items, so only two time points are available for consideration. Second, one of the items asked at t_2 was not asked at t_3 because my empirical analysis deemed it too redundant with the other items; consequently, the t_3 survey posed a new proposition to the respondents. Figure 5.1 reports these results as well.

The index of presidential legitimacy confirms the slight increase in support, although once more the differences between t_2 and t_3 are small (even if statistically significant). These data thus support the conclusions that the legitimacy of the Biden presidency is relatively high and that no evidence points to a decline in that legitimacy between the December 2020 and January 2021 (pre-insurrection) survey and the February and March 2021 (post-impeachment) survey. Moreover, on each of the individual items on which a t_2 to t_3 comparison is possible, support for the Biden presidency was more widespread at t_3. None of these differences is particularly large, but the results are consistent across both items.

Summary

An analysis such as this one obviously has limited probative value for many reasons, including the oft-noted observation that aggregate-level stasis is compatible with considerable micro-level change. Nevertheless, the simple hypothesis that the insurrection and the subsequent impeachment and ac-quittal of Trump are associated with an overall decline in the legitimacy of American political institutions does not receive support from these data. The legitimacy that the Supreme Court, the Senate, and the presidency en-joyed was no lower after the insurrection and impeachment than it was before those events.

As I have noted, a serious limitation of this sort of analysis is that the analyst never knows what the independent variables are. I have focused my attention on the impact of the insurrection and impeachment, but of course many events took place between January 5 and March of 2021. Some events may have enhanced institutional legitimacy (for example, the presi-dential inauguration), while others may have undermined legitimacy. Some Americans (although admittedly very few) may have been oblivious to the insurrection and the impeachment, and undoubtedly, people's evaluations of those events varied considerably. Moreover, the insurrection in particular may have had the backlash effect of motivating at least some people to ex-tend more support to the country's political institutions.[6] Therefore, addi-tional analysis is certainly warranted.

Measuring Perceptions and Evaluations of Events

The insurrection and the impeachment process took place in January and February 2021. On January 6, pro-Trump rioters stormed the Capitol build-ing, largely in an effort to block the completion of the 2020 presidential election. President Trump was charged with inciting the riot and was im-peached by the House of Representatives. A majority of senators voted to convict Trump, but the tally fell short of the supermajority required.

In the t_3 survey, I measured perceptions and evaluations of five sets of events: (1) the nomination and confirmation of Amy Coney Barrett to the Supreme Court; (2) allegations that the 2020 presidential election was rigged; (3) President Trump's efforts to overturn the outcome of the 2020 presidential election; (4) the insurrection of January 6, 2021; and (5) the impeachment of President Trump. I asked questions about both levels of awareness and assessments of each event. Table 5.1 reports the responses to these questions. For comparison, note that chapter 3 examined perceptions of election-related events in the December 2020 survey, which, of course, was conducted before the insurrection.

Table 5.1 Perceptions and Assessments of the Major Events of the 2020 U.S. Presidential Election and Its Aftermath

	Awareness of Events				Assessments of Events			
	Very or Somewhat Aware	Mean	Standard Deviation	N	Entirely or Somewhat Appropriate or Certain	Mean	Standard Deviation	N
Appropriateness of Barrett nomination	82%	0.76	0.31	2,017	54%	0.55	0.38	2,000
Certainty that the election was rigged	92%	0.87	0.24	2,010	34%	0.34	0.37	2,001
Appropriateness of Trump's efforts to overturn election	94%	0.89	0.22	2,020	36%	0.35	0.40	2,000
Belief that the Capitol insurrection was not harmful	96%	0.92	0.19	2,017	21%	0.24	0.32	2,004
Belief that the Trump impeachment and trial were not harmful	95%	0.90	0.20	2,014	54%	0.53	0.39	2,001
Approval of no conviction of Trump in the impeachment and trial	—	—	—	—	42%	0.43	0.43	2,005

Source: The 2021 Insurrection and Impeachment Survey (t_3), February and March 2021.

Notes: The response set for the first and third assessments asks the degree to which the activity is "appropriate for a democracy like ours." The item on whether the election was rigged uses a response set measuring the degree of certainty of the assessment. For that statement, the percentage shown is the percentage of respondents who were "very" or "fairly" certain that the election was rigged. For the insurrection and the impeachment trial, the response set was calibrated in terms of the degree of "harm to American democracy." The final item in the table reports those who "strongly" or "somewhat" approved of Trump not being convicted. All measures are scored to vary between 0 and 1. See the appendix for the text of these questions.

Unsurprisingly, awareness of these events was extremely widespread, with large majorities of respondents claiming to be "very" or "somewhat" conversant with the developments. The Barrett nomination and confirmation is something of an exception, although recall that a considerable amount of time had elapsed between the confirmation and the March 2021 interview. Nevertheless, some variability in claimed awareness emerged, which the following analysis takes into account.

Variability in assessments of these events was much greater. For instance, a bare majority of the respondents judged the Barrett nomination and confirmation to be appropriate within the context of democratic politics, while considerably less than a majority regarded Trump's efforts to overturn the election results as, to at least some degree, appropriate. A similar minority concluded that the election was rigged. Only one in five Americans believed that the insurrection was not harmful to American democracy, while a slight majority asserted that the impeachment process was not harmful. Less than a majority approved of the outcome in the Senate. These data confirm an unsurprising conclusion: reality and perceptions and assessments of reality often diverge among Americans. Moreover, only a relatively small percentage of Americans supported the pro-Trump positions on the election and the insurrection.

Hypotheses and Analyses

Figure 5.2 reports the data necessary to test the general hypothesis that awareness and assessments of the election, insurrection, and impeachment events shaped attitudes toward the legitimacy of the Supreme Court, the Senate, and the presidency, as well as sundry other hypotheses first introduced in chapter 4.[7]

The coefficients in this figure demonstrate that a substantial amount of the variance in the three dependent variables can be explained by each of the equations: more than two-thirds of the variance for presidential legitimacy (69 percent), nearly one-half for the Supreme Court (49 percent), and 41 percent for the Senate.[8] In light of voluminous extant research capable of explaining only a very small amount of the variance in the dependent variable of concern, these percentages are impressive.[9]

The high levels of explained variance also go some way toward minimizing concern over omitted variable bias. As with all research, these equations undoubtedly could suffer from some such bias. However, other variables not already included in the equations would be unlikely to contribute much independently to an explanation of the variance in the dependent variables. This conclusion seems especially apposite in light of the reasonably well-developed theory of the etiology of the Supreme Court's institutional legitimacy.[10]

Many of the coefficients in figure 5.2 are either indistinguishable from zero or trivial in magnitude. Some of these coefficients are of unusual importance for this analysis because they suggest the conclusion of no causal effect. (More specifically, they indicate no association, causal or otherwise.)[11] Moreover, with some of these variables—for example, homeownership—

Figure 5.2 Predictors of Support for Institutional Legitimacy after the January 6, 2021, Insurrection

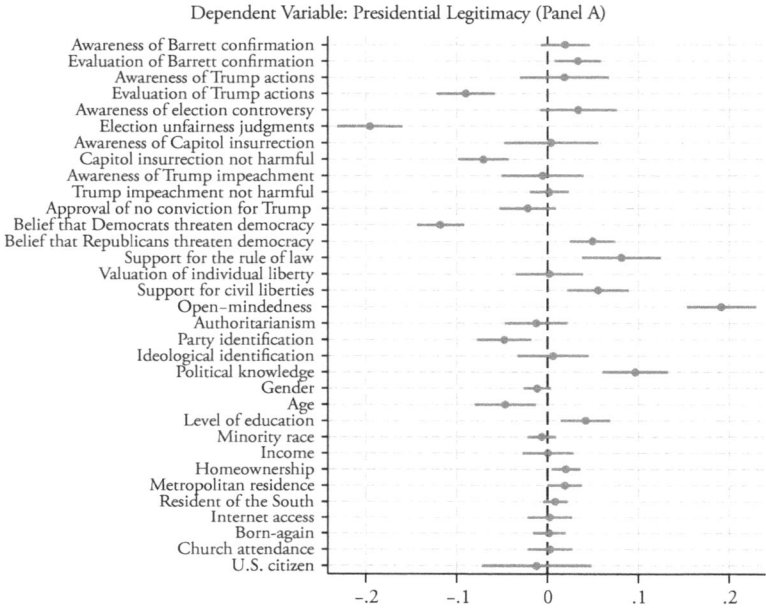

Dependent Variable: Presidential Legitimacy (Panel A)

Source: The 2021 Insurrection and Impeachment Survey (t₃), February and March 2021.

Notes:

Panel A: Equation:

$R^2 = 0.69^{***}$

$N = 1,864$

Significance of unstandardized OLS regression coefficients:

* $p \leq .05$

Homeownership

Metropolitan residence

** $p \leq .01$

Evaluation of Barrett confirmation

Party identification

Age

Level of education

*** $p \leq .001$

Evaluation of Trump actions

Election unfairness judgments

Capitol insurrection not harmful

Belief that Democrats threaten democracy

Belief that Republicans threaten democracy

Support for the rule of law

Support for civil liberties

Open-mindedness

Political knowledge

Figure 5.2 (*continued*)

Dependent Variable: Supreme Court Legitimacy (Panel B)

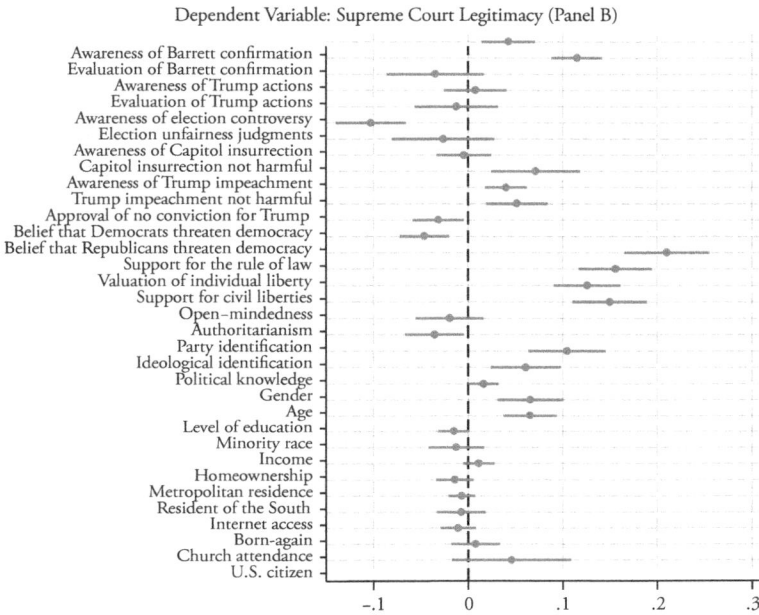

Source: The 2021 Insurrection and Impeachment Survey (t₃), February and March 2021.
Notes:
Panel B: Equation:

R² = 0.49***

N = 1,864

Significance of unstandardized OLS regression coefficients:

* *p* ≤ .05

  Belief that Democrats threaten democracy
  Party identification
  Gender

** *p* ≤ .01

  Awareness of Barrett confirmation
  Awareness of Trump impeachment
  Approval of no conviction for Trump

*** *p* ≤ .001

  Evaluation of Barrett confirmation
  Election unfairness judgments
  Trump impeachment not harmful
  Belief that Republicans threaten democracy
  Support for the rule of law
  Support for individual liberty
  Support for civil liberties
  Open-mindedness
  Ideological identification
  Political knowledge
  Age
  Level of education

(*continued*)

Figure 5.2 (*continued*)

Dependent Variable: Senate Legitimacy (Panel C)

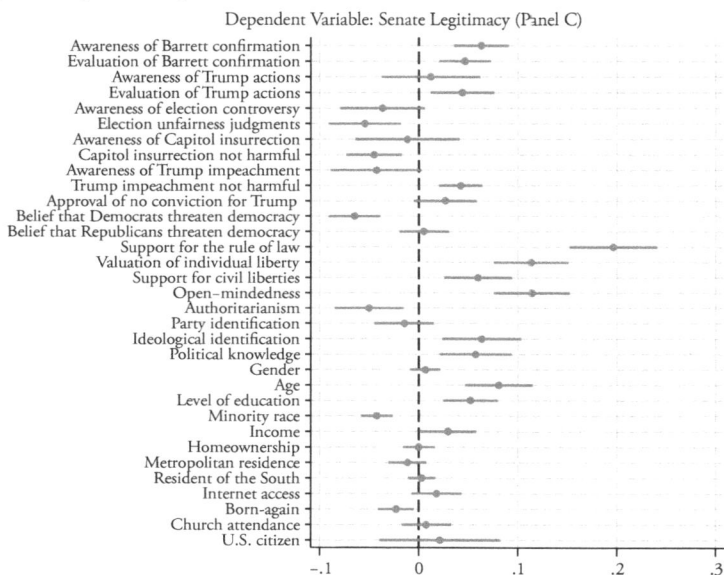

Source: The 2021 Insurrection and Impeachment Survey (t₃), February and March 2021.
Notes:
Panel C: Equation:
  $R^2 = 0.41$***
  $N = 1,864$
Significance of unstandardized OLS regression coefficients:
* $p \leq .05$
  Income
  Born-again
** $p \leq .01$
  Evaluation of Trump actions
  Election unfairness judgments
  Capitol insurrection harmful
  Authoritarianism
  Ideological identification
  Political knowledge
*** $p \leq .001$
  Awareness of Barrett confirmation
  Evaluation of Barrett confirmation
  Trump impeachment not harmful
  Belief that Democrats threaten democracy
  Support for the rule of law
  Support for individual liberty
  Support for civil liberties
  Open-mindedness
  Age
  Minority race
  Level of education
All variables are scored to range from 0 to 1. For their distributions, see table A.11. For the full regression table from which these results are derived, see table A.9. Shown are the unstandardized regression coefficients and their confidence intervals. For details on the measurement of the predictors, see the appendix.

the hypothesis that legitimacy attitudes cause the independent variable is simply not tenable.

Although the demographic variables are not of much substantive interest, this causal logic is of considerable importance when it comes to the events-related variables, many if not most of which appear to be disconnected from legitimacy attitudes. If I were to find a significant connection, some might wonder whether the dependent variable caused the independent variable (although in some instances that logic would certainly be tortured). Consider the variable measuring evaluations of Trump's actions to overturn the election, which is weakly connected to presidential legitimacy ($p < .001$), but not at all to Supreme Court legitimacy ($p > .05$) and not much to Senate legitimacy ($p < .01$)—findings that seem quite logical. I believe I am entitled to conclude from these findings that whether people approved or disapproved of what Trump attempted had practically no causal consequences for either Supreme Court or Senate legitimacy because the variables are not empirically interconnected in any meaningful way. (Recall that all variables are scored to range from 0 to 1.)

Regarding presidential legitimacy, however, the analysis reveals a significant relationship. Here the question of causality becomes more clouded. Did those respondents who extended more legitimacy to the Biden presidency adjust their views of Trump's actions to align them with their presidential support, or did those who approved of what Trump attempted withdraw support from the Biden presidency? Undoubtedly, Trump's efforts predated Biden's inauguration, although I do not put much stock in that as a basis for causal ordering. In most senses, a superior logic supports the latter conclusion: some of the respondents who approved of Trump's efforts to "right" the perceived election "wrongs" decided not to extend legitimacy to the Biden presidency. But the opposite causal structure cannot be ruled out entirely by cross-sectional analysis of the type reported here. At a minimum, the two variables covary (but only slightly).

With these general findings and considerations in mind, I now turn to the specifics of each of the institutional equations.

The Legitimacy of the Presidency

Variation in presidential legitimacy is best accounted for by the equation in figure 5.2. Four variables stand out as substantial predictors of presidential legitimacy: judgments about whether the election was unfair, open-mindedness, estimates of how much Democrats threaten American democracy, and political knowledge. Each of these connections functions as expected: for instance, more open-minded people are more likely to extend legitimacy to the presidency, in part, I suspect, because they are less likely to view the world in stark and threatening black-and-white terms.[12] More knowledgeable Americans extend greater support for presidential legitimacy perhaps because they have a more complete understanding of the role of the presidency in the American political system. Almost by definition, people who see the 2020 election as more unfair are less likely to extend legitimacy to the Biden presidency.

At the same time, however, most of the events variables have little connection with presidential legitimacy, especially the limited variability in awareness of the events. The data reveal a slight tendency among respondents who viewed the insurrection as not harmful to withhold legitimacy from the Biden presidency, although the relationship is quite small. (Recall that all variables are scored to range from 0 to 1, so that a coefficient of –0.07 borders on being trivial, whatever its level of statistical significance.)

Two other very small relationships are noteworthy: neither party identification nor ideological identification is substantially connected with presidential legitimacy in the multivariate equation, with one caveat. Some of the effect of partisanship is likely to be captured in this equation by the estimates of how much Democrats threaten American democracy.[13] the effect of partisanship, therefore, may not be related to how strongly individuals are attached to their own party but rather to how strongly they reject the opposition party. Still, the effect of the Democrat threat variable is not particularly strong, even if my general conclusion is that, of the three measures of institutional legitimacy, presidential legitimacy is no doubt the most closely connected to partisan conflict and attitudes. This connection is perhaps best signaled by beliefs that the election outcome was unfair—beliefs grounded to some degree in partisanship.

The Legitimacy of the Supreme Court

The equation predicting the legitimacy scores for the Supreme Court reveals considerably different relationships. The overall equation is less predictive than that for the legitimacy of the presidency, probably because the partisan variables play a much smaller role in structuring attitudes toward the court.

Instead, the big predictor of Supreme Court legitimacy is belief in democratic values, with support for the rule of law dwarfing the coefficients for the other variables. People with a stronger abstract commitment to the rule of law are much more likely to extend legitimacy to the court, a finding that fits well with the voluminous research (here and elsewhere) showing that rule-of-law attitudes are a bedrock of support for democratic institutions and processes. Furthermore, the most interesting finding from the court equation in figure 5.2 is that the main substantively significant predictors of legitimacy are the values variables. Even in a fairly strong and broad equation, support for the rule of law, the valuation of individual liberty, open-mindedness, and support for civil liberties are moderately strong predictors of legitimacy (although authoritarianism is clearly not). Institutional support for the Supreme Court seems to be rooted in more fundamental democratic values and personality attributes.

The equation also shows that two of the events variables are significant predictors of Supreme Court legitimacy. People who judged the Barrett nomination and confirmation as appropriate were more likely to support the court (although stating the relationship in the opposition direction— that those who opposed the Barrett nomination and confirmation were less likely to support the court—is perhaps more interesting). Similarly, those who rated the presidential election as unfair were less likely to support the court. These two relationships cannot be ignored when assessing how events affect Supreme Court attitudes. That said, evaluations of Trump's actions to overturn the election, assessments of whether the Capitol insurrection was harmful, and impeachment attitudes are not at all connected to a willingness to extend legitimacy to the court. Overall, the events of 2020 and 2021 do not seem to have had many consequences for the legitimacy of the Supreme Court.

Finally, I note that, even in the multivariate equation, people who identified as more conservative were more likely to extend legitimacy to the Supreme Court, even if Republicans were no more or less likely to support the court. I also observe that the demographic attributes are generally not useful predictors of court support.

The Legitimacy of the Senate

Finally, the results from the analysis of willingness to extend legitimacy to the Senate are generally similar to those for willingness to extend legitimacy to the Supreme Court. For example, Senate legitimacy seems to be grounded in more general democratic values, although perhaps slightly less strongly than with Supreme Court legitimacy. Partisan and ideological identifications are not useful predictors of attitudes toward the Senate. The measures of awareness and assessments of the various events are entirely disconnected from support for the Senate. Generally, the demographic variables do little to distinguish between people extending more legitimacy to the Senate and those extending less legitimacy.

Perceptions That the Election Was Rigged: Reprise

In light of these multivariate results, it is worth examining the bivariate relationships between willingness to grant legitimacy to the three institutions and perceptions that the election was rigged. Figure 5.3 reports that the effect of believing that the election was rigged varies from moderately strong (with respect to the presidency) to weak (the Senate) to trivial (the Supreme Court), It is worth examining these relationships in greater detail. Figure 5.3 reports the bivariate relationships under the reasonable assumption that an antecedent to a respondent's willingness to extend legitimacy to these institutions is their assessment of the election.

Three quite different relationships are depicted in figure 5.3. For the presidency, the relationship is quite strong: those who believed that the election was rigged were much less likely to extend legitimacy to the Biden presidency. Indeed, rarely do we see a relationship of this magnitude.

Clearly, perceived election illegitimacy has little effect on institutional attitudes toward the Supreme Court. Indeed, the relationship is not even monotonic. Tellingly, respondents who were very certain that the election was rigged extended the same degree of legitimacy to the Supreme Court as those who were fairly certain that it was not rigged. Whatever the causal structure, election perceptions and Supreme Court attitudes are not closely connected.

The relationship is slightly stronger with respect to willingness to extend legitimacy to the Senate. Again, however, the mean legitimacy score for respondents who were fairly certain the election was rigged is actually higher than the mean for those who were fairly certain that the election was not rigged. And as the analysis has shown, this bivariate relationship becomes even more attenuated in the multivariate context. How people feel about

Figure 5.3 Assessments of Whether the 2020 Presidential Election Was Rigged and Institutional Legitimacy

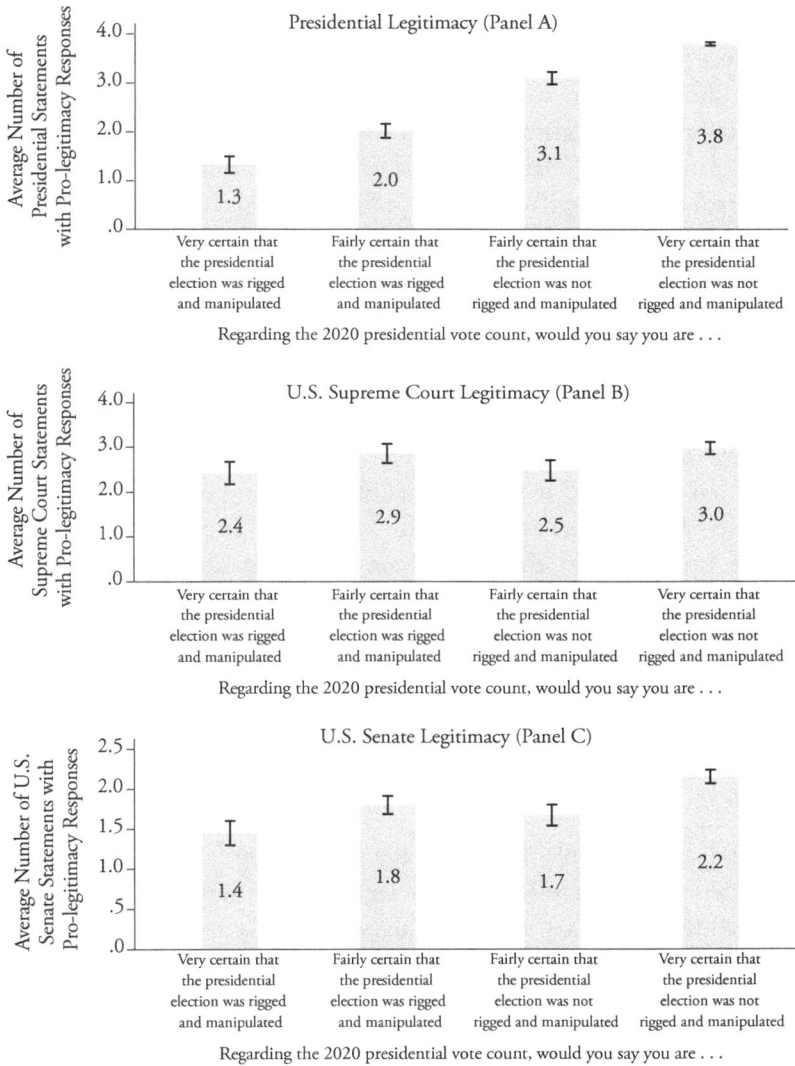

Presidential Legitimacy (Panel A)

Average Number of Presidential Statements with Pro-legitimacy Responses

| Very certain that the presidential election was rigged and manipulated | Fairly certain that the presidential election was rigged and manipulated | Fairly certain that the presidential election was not rigged and manipulated | Very certain that the presidential election was not rigged and manipulated |
| 1.3 | 2.0 | 3.1 | 3.8 |

Regarding the 2020 presidential vote count, would you say you are . . .

U.S. Supreme Court Legitimacy (Panel B)

Average Number of Supreme Court Statements with Pro-legitimacy Responses

| Very certain that the presidential election was rigged and manipulated | Fairly certain that the presidential election was rigged and manipulated | Fairly certain that the presidential election was not rigged and manipulated | Very certain that the presidential election was not rigged and manipulated |
| 2.4 | 2.9 | 2.5 | 3.0 |

Regarding the 2020 presidential vote count, would you say you are . . .

U.S. Senate Legitimacy (Panel C)

Average Number of U.S. Senate Statements with Pro-legitimacy Responses

| Very certain that the presidential election was rigged and manipulated | Fairly certain that the presidential election was rigged and manipulated | Fairly certain that the presidential election was not rigged and manipulated | Very certain that the presidential election was not rigged and manipulated |
| 1.4 | 1.8 | 1.7 | 2.2 |

Regarding the 2020 presidential vote count, would you say you are . . .

Source: The 2021 Insurrection and Impeachment Survey (t₃), February and March 2021.
Notes:
Panel A: $p < .001$; r = 0.75; N = 1,996.
Panel B: $p < .001$; r = 0.06; N = 1,983.
Panel C: $p < .001$; r = 0.18; N = 2,000.

the Senate is (at best) only modestly connected to their perceptions of the election.

Of course, by the time of the t_3 interview, other events had taken place, including the insurrection and the second Trump impeachment trial. Figure 5.2 shows that the second impeachment seemed to have practically no connection to the legitimacy of any of the three institutions, but further consideration of the relationships may be illuminating.

The survey measured attitudes toward the insurrection by asking respondents whether the insurrection was harmful to American democracy. Figure 5.4 reports the bivariate relationships between responses to this question and each of the three institutional support measures.

The story here is much the same as that regarding perceptions of whether the election was rigged, with the exception that for none of the institutions are assessments of much predictive value in the multivariate equation. In the bivariate case, attitudes toward the presidency are at least somewhat connected to assessments of the rioting in a monotonic relationship of moderate strength. In the case of the Supreme Court and the Senate, however, the relationships are practically nonexistent, whatever the nature of the posited causality. Those who hold different assessments of the January 6, 2021, insurrection do not hold different attitudes toward the Supreme Court and the Senate, even if their views of the Biden presidency do covary.

Summary

The findings from this portion of my analysis are fairly straightforward. Consistent with the pre-insurrection legitimacy findings in chapter 4, views of the Biden presidency are indeed shaped to some degree by the events of the election, the insurrection, and the second impeachment. Either I did a relatively poor job of measuring the institutional legitimacy of the presidency or many Americans do not distinguish their views of the institution from their views of the incumbent. In some sense, attitudes toward the presidency can stand as a benchmark against which to compare attitudes toward the Supreme Court and the Senate.

The insurrection and impeachment seem to have had little impact on the legitimacy of the Supreme Court or the Senate, although the court appears to have a slightly stronger connection to some of the happenings

Figure 5.4 Assessments of the Insurrection of January 6, 2021, and Institutional Legitimacy

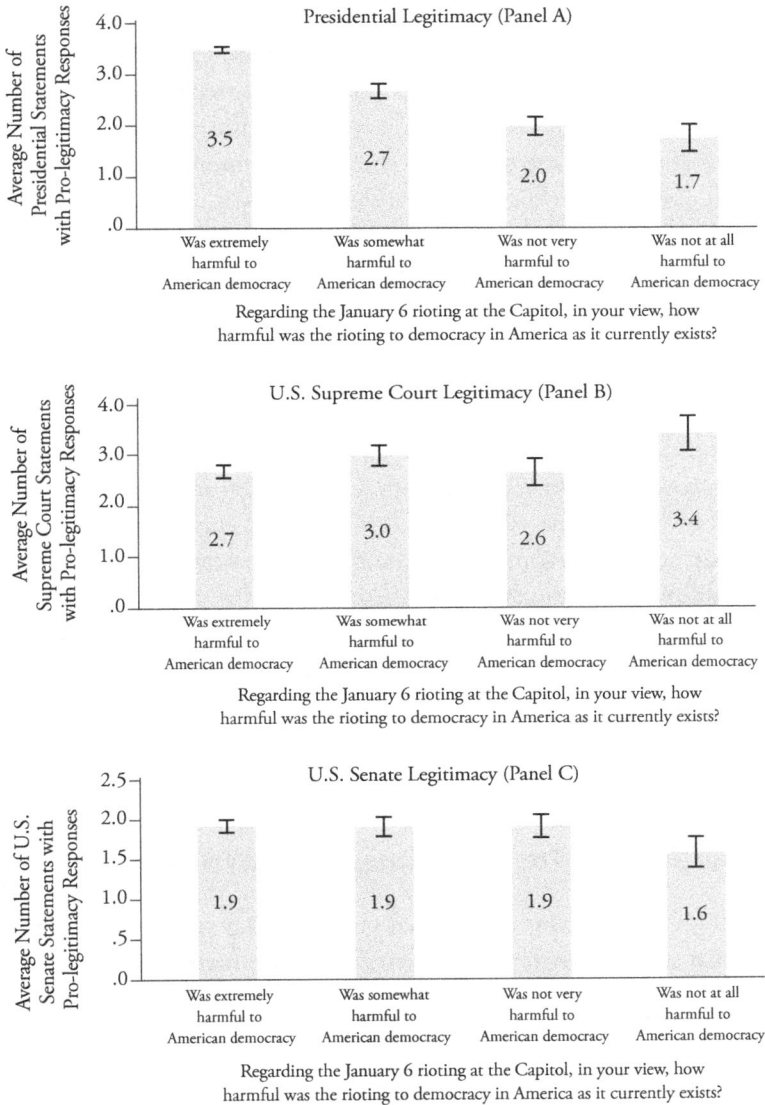

Presidential Legitimacy (Panel A)

Regarding the January 6 rioting at the Capitol, in your view, how harmful was the rioting to democracy in America as it currently exists?

U.S. Supreme Court Legitimacy (Panel B)

Regarding the January 6 rioting at the Capitol, in your view, how harmful was the rioting to democracy in America as it currently exists?

U.S. Senate Legitimacy (Panel C)

Regarding the January 6 rioting at the Capitol, in your view, how harmful was the rioting to democracy in America as it currently exists?

Source: The 2021 Insurrection and Impeachment Survey (t₃), February and March 2021.
Notes:
Panel A: p < .001; r = –0.49; *N* = 2,000.
Panel B: p < .001; r = 0.08; *N* = 1,988.
Panel C: p = .043; r = –0.05; *N* = 1,988.

compared with the Senate. Perhaps most notable is that of the respondents' evaluations of six happenings (counting the two impeachment questions separately), none is substantially related (b > 0.10) to Senate legitimacy. For the court, two coefficients exceed 0.10, and four do not. Indeed, none of the insurrection or impeachment assessments are substantially connected to Supreme Court legitimacy. Perhaps surprisingly, the two assessments that are linked pertain to the Barrett nomination/confirmation and evaluations of the fairness of the election; assessments of older events were more closely related to legitimacy than assessments of more contemporaneous events. (It is perhaps also worth noting that the survey was finished in March 2021, before many of the details of the insurrection became known.)

Perhaps the most important conclusion from this analysis is that broader and more abstract democratic values play the largest role in shaping legitimacy attitudes. Some scholars complain about abstract attitudes, fearing that the answers to our measures represent nothing more than platitudes (or expressive attitudes) with few real-life implications. That seems not to be the case here. Particularly important are attitudes toward the rule of law, the variable with the strongest coefficients across the three legitimacy measures (see figure 5.2). I will have more to say about these attitudes later; here I simply draw the conclusion that legitimacy attitudes are related much more closely to abstract democratic values than to awareness and assessments of the events of the 2020 presidential election, the insurrection, and the impeachment trial of former president Trump.

General Support for U.S. Democratic Institutions

The analysis to this point has focused on institution-specific attitudes and shown that some idiosyncratic content exists in evaluations of the different institutions (especially the presidency). For summary purposes, it is also useful to determine how people feel about U.S. democratic institutions in general. Fortunately, some extant scholarship addresses this issue.

This portion of my analysis is concerned with the degree to which people have faith in American democratic institutions. According to cultural theories of democracy, the views of ordinary people are important.[14] The mass public must have a broad normative and behavioral consensus on the legitimacy of the constitutional system *that cuts across class, ethnicity, nationality, and other cleavages*, however poor or unsatisfying that system's performance may be at any point in time. Consequently, I posed three statements pertaining to overall assessments of the state of American democratic institutions to the respondents in the t_3 national survey. Figure 2.4 reports their replies (with the responses collapsed for illustrative purposes).[15]

Figure 5.5 reveals the results of regressing the support for democratic institutions index on the various predictors used in this chapter.[16] Perhaps the most important finding from the coefficients in the figure has to do with the connections between institutional legitimacy and awareness and assessments of events. None of the coefficients for awareness is of much substantive significance; for assessments, only the election unfairness judgments are connected to legitimacy. Respondents who viewed the 2020 election outcome as more unfair extended less legitimacy to American political institutions.

Figure 5.6 reports the bivariate relationship between fairness perceptions and general institutional legitimacy. The figure shows a nontrivial relationship, but with nuances. The greatest amount of institutional legitimacy was extended by respondents who were very certain that the election was not rigged (46.2 percent of respondents). The least amount of legitimacy is associated with those who were very certain that the election was rigged (13.9 percent of respondents). Interestingly, in the two middle categories (people who are "fairly" uncertain or certain), legitimacy attitudes do not differ. Although the bivariate and multivariate relationships are certainly noteworthy, they are far from overwhelming. And the difference in mean scores between the extremes on assessments is 0.7 on an index that varies from 0 through 3.

I note as well that, while perceptions of the degree to which Democrats threaten democracy are connected to legitimacy, perceptions of the Republican threat are connected in neither the bivariate nor multivariate analyses. Perhaps the most telling conclusion from this analysis is not that assessments that the election was rigged are associated with low levels of legitimacy but that legitimacy scores are relatively low across the board. The bivariate relationship between assessments of the Capitol riots and institutional legitimacy is also revealing. Figure 5.7 reports this analysis.

The reason why this relationship is so weak is easy to discern: practically no difference exists among the legitimacy levels of respondents who saw the riots as somewhat harmful, those who saw them as not very harmful, and

Figure 5.5 Predictors of Support for U.S. Democratic Institutions after the January 6, 2021, Insurrection

Dependent Variable: Support for U.S. Democratic Institutions

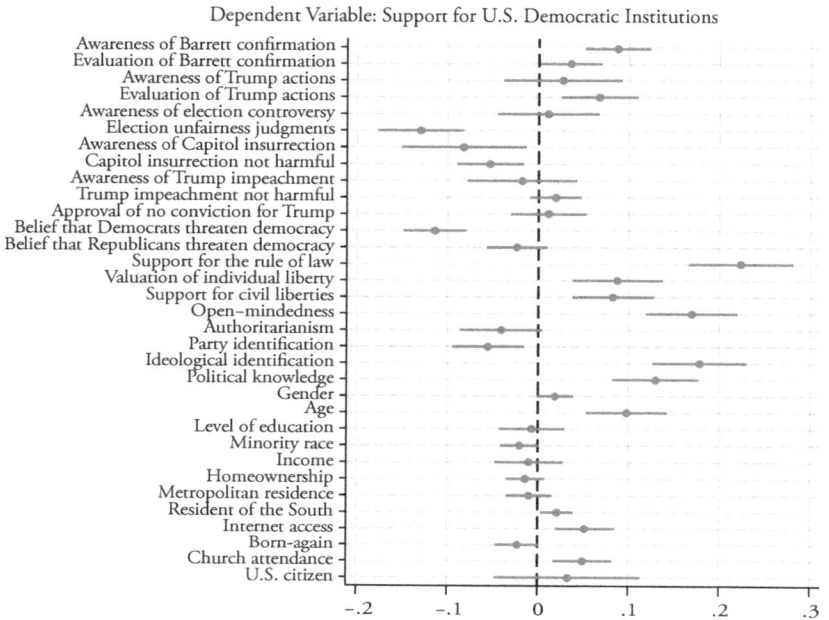

Source: The 2021 Insurrection and Impeachment Survey (t₃), February and March 2021.
Notes: Equation:

$R^2 = 0.35$***

$N = 1,864$

Significance of unstandardized OLS regression coefficients:

* $p \leq .05$

    Evaluation of Barrett confirmation

    Awareness of Capitol insurrection

    Resident of the South

** $p \leq .01$

    Evaluation of Trump actions

    Capitol insurrection not harmful

    Party identification

    Internet access

    Church attendance

*** $p \leq .001$

    Election unfairness judgments

    Belief that Democrats threaten democracy

    Support for the rule of law

    Support for Individual liberty

    Support for civil liberties

    Open-mindedness

    Ideological identification

    Political knowledge

    Age

All variables are scored to range from 0 to 1. For their distributions, see table A.11. For the full regression table from which these results are derived, see table A.10. Shown are the unstandardized regression coefficients and their confidence intervals. For details on the measurement of the predictors, see the appendix.

Figure 5.6 The Bivariate Relationship between Election Unfairness Judgments and Institutional Legitimacy

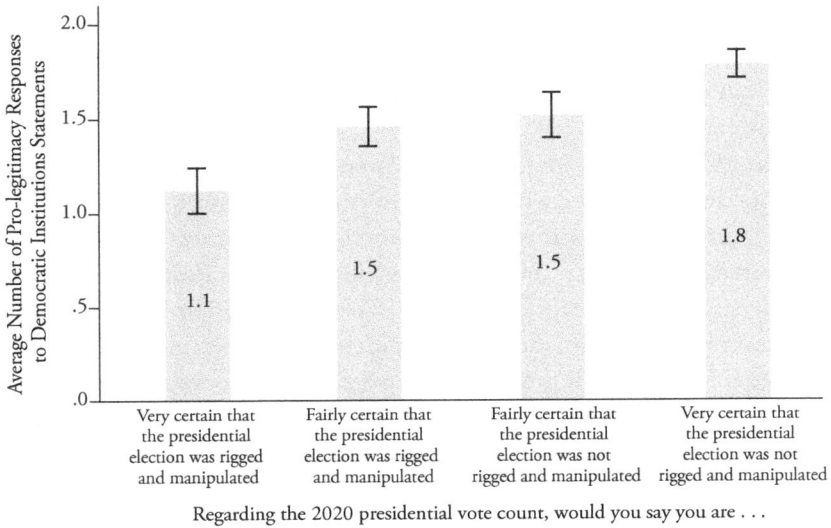

Regarding the 2020 presidential vote count, would you say you are . . .

Source: The 2021 Insurrection and Impeachment Survey (t₃), February and March 2021.
Notes: $p < .001$; $r = 0.23$; $N = 1,995$.

Figure 5.7 The Bivariate Relationship between Assessments of the Capitol Riot and Institutional Legitimacy

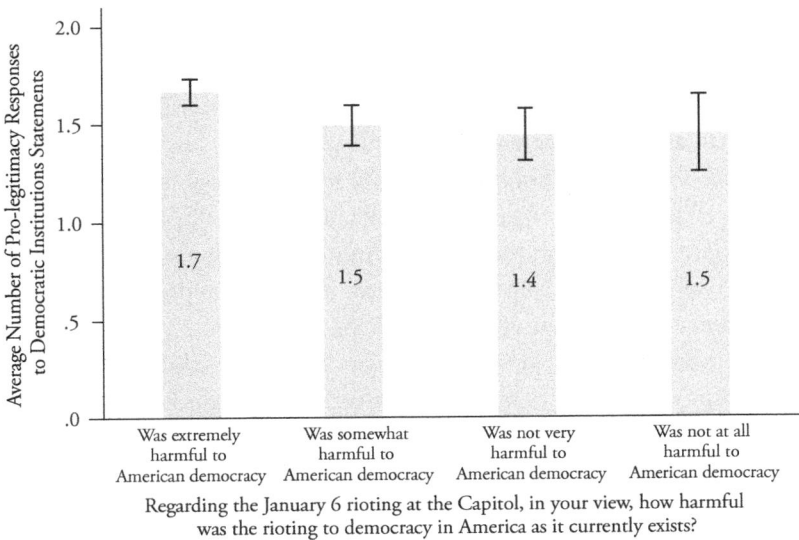

Regarding the January 6 rioting at the Capitol, in your view, how harmful was the rioting to democracy in America as it currently exists?

Source: The 2021 Insurrection and Impeachment Survey (t₃), February and March 2021.
Notes: $p < .001$; $r = -0.10$; $N = 1,998$.

those who saw them as not at all harmful. Only respondents who assessed the riots as extremely harmful extended more legitimacy, though even here the difference in means scores is very small indeed. Generally, these data offer little support for the conclusion that the Capitol riot, as judged by the American people, deteriorated the legitimacy of American democratic institutions.

Two additional considerations should be noted. First, other variables in the equation in figure 5.5 have stronger associations with legitimacy attitudes. Second, while assessments of whether the election was rigged are connected to legitimacy, the other assessments are not: legitimacy does *not* vary by respondents' evaluations of the Barrett nomination, Trump's efforts to overturn the election, the insurrection, or the impeachment trial and its outcome. Indeed, the R^2 from regressing legitimacy on only the events and assessments variables is a mere 0.15 (and, it should be noted, is calculated by assigning *all* the explained variance shared by the awareness and assessments variables with the other variables in the equation to awareness and assessments alone).[17] The relationship is certainly not trivial, but neither is it substantial or dominant.[18]

Figure 5.5 reports notable connections between legitimacy and various democratic values and personality attributes. Indeed, as is so often the case in these analyses, attitudes toward the rule of law are the most strongly connected variable to willingness to extend legitimacy to democratic institutions, a particularly meaningful finding in light of the extensive number of predictors included in the equation. Open-mindedness should be similarly understood. These predictors are far more connected to institutional legitimacy than are awareness and assessments of events.

Partisan identifications have little to do with willingness to extend legitimacy to democratic institutions, but ideological identifications do. In the multivariate case, respondents identifying more strongly as conservative extended *more* legitimacy to U.S. political institutions, probably owing to the tendency of conservatives to defend the status quo.

Respondents who knew more about politics were also more likely to grant legitimacy to U.S. democratic institutions. This finding, although far from strong, seems incompatible with the adage about knowing what goes into the making of the sausage. Those who extended the least legitimacy were those who knew the least about democratic institutions. And general knowledge of politics is more closely connected to legitimacy than is awareness of the election and insurrection events.

Only a single demographic attribute is connected to legitimacy in the multivariate analysis: older respondents were more likely to support democratic institutions. That the demographic indicators generally are of little importance perhaps speaks to the power of the equation's important substantive predictors.

Discussion and Concluding Comments

The purpose of this chapter has been to determine whether people's assessments of the insurrection and riot of January 6, 2021, are associated with any diminution of the legitimacy of American political institutions. The clear answer is that these assessments and legitimacy are mainly (but not entirely) disconnected. Can I thus conclude that the insurrection and the impeachment had no impact on the health of democracy in America? Several caveats are in order before such a conclusion is warranted.

First, events after the conclusion of my survey in March 2021 may well have had a greater impact on public opinion than events in the immediate aftermath of the riot. The congressional investigation, the indictments and convictions of rioters, and the commentary of even some Republican elites may have had more influence in the long term on public views of American institutions than did the actual events of January 6, 2021.

Second, the 2020 presidential election may itself have created a change in public attitudes, such that any further information provided by the insurrection had only a small marginal effect. This seems unlikely, however, given the findings of chapter 4.

Third, many of the predictor variables are intercorrelated, although diagnostic tests (for example, VIF) point to no serious statistical problems. When two variables are competing to explain essentially the same variance in a dependent variable, statistical analysis will almost always favor the independent variable with the strongest bivariate connection to the dependent variable, to the discredit of its competitors. This is as it should be. But cross-sectional data such as those analyzed in this chapter are poorly suited to unraveling complex causal processes. Partisanship, for example, might play a bigger role in these processes than I acknowledge, even though I have tried to give partisanship all the statistical credit it deserves. The most reliable conclusions of the analyses in this chapter pertain to legitimacy's lack of connections to awareness and assessment of the insurrection events, as well as the role of democratic values as a grounding for legitimacy attitudes.

Finally, this chapter, in contrast to chapter 4, is entirely an analysis of cross-sectional data, with no indicators of change in attitudes. My own view, incompletely grounded in the available data, is that little change in legitimacy attitudes took place after January 6, 2021. A more tenable model, for me at least, goes as follows. General democratic values shaped how people paid attention to the insurrection and impeachment events and especially how they evaluated those events. Their evaluations therefore conformed to their preexisting expectations (motivated reasoning). Consequently, their awareness and assessments of events simply tended to confirm their preexisting attitudes and values. As in so many areas of public opinion, change was minimal.

I am impressed and somewhat surprised with how well the summary measure of allegiance to America's democratic institutions has performed in this chapter. I certainly recognize that institution-specific attitudes exist and are meaningful. But analysis of the allegiance index (for example, in figure 5.5) tells very much the same story as does analysis of the institution-specific legitimacy attitudes (with the already acknowledged possible exception of the presidency). Survey researchers are always concerned about the number of items it takes to validly and reliably measure a concept; perhaps the summary indicators I created will prove useful, not only in the next chapter of this book but also in future research.

The analysis reported in this chapter does not consider how different subgroups reacted to the election, the insurrection, and the impeachment. Because the t_3 sample included a large representative sample of African Americans, my next task is to examine inter- and intraracial differences in institutional support. As reported in figure 5.2, whether respondents were of a minority race had no direct consequences for presidential or Supreme Court legitimacy but did have a tiny relationship with Senate legitimacy. Table A.10 reports a significant bivariate relationship with being a member of a minority race and support for American democratic institutions, but the multivariate coefficient is indistinguishable from zero. These findings, which treat Black people, Hispanic people, and those of additional races other than White as minorities, do not necessarily rule out the possibility of Black-White differences (especially in terms of interaction effects) and do not, of course, address intraracial differences. Thus, further analysis of these measures is essential. That is the purpose of chapter 6.

CHAPTER 6

Racial Differences in Support for
Democratic Institutions

> You and I have never seen democracy, all we've seen is hypocrisy.

> —Malcolm X, "The Ballot or the Bullet," *Speech*, April 3, 1964

> The challenge of racial justice is actually the challenge of democracy because we can't make society work unless we can address racial division, distrust, inequality and racism.

> —Ralph Richard Banks and Diane Chin, "For Democracy to Work, Racial Inequalities Must Be Addressed." Quoted in Melissa De Witte, "For Democracy to Work, Racial Inequalities Must Be Addressed," *Stanford Report*, February 16, 2021

THE ANALYSES REPORTED to this point have focused on the American people as a whole. When it comes to law and politics, however, extant research documents vast differences across racial groups.[1] Indeed, as I showed in chapter 2, interracial differences in support for national political institutions after the insurrection were massive.

Consequently, this chapter considers both inter- and intraracial variability in attitudes toward democratic values, institutions, and processes. Because my limited resources did not allow me to field oversamples of all minority groups in the United States—funds were available (despite my efforts) for only a large oversample of African Americans interviewed in the February and March 2021 survey (t_3)—my focus is on Black people, not Hispanic people or those of other races.[2] This does not mean that understanding the reactions of these groups to the 2020 election is any less important than understanding the reactions of Black and White Americans. Furthermore, my analysis draws from the t_3 survey—conducted after the insurrection and the close of the second Trump impeachment trial. Here I

https://doi.org/10.7758/dvkr4409.9752

focus on Black-White differences in levels of regard for America's democratic institutions.

Expectations about Interracial Differences in Support for Democratic Values and Institutions?

Following Jon Kingzette and Michael Neblo's persuasive call for a "multicultural theory of civic culture," I do not presume that democratic polities require or enjoy a uniform political culture.[3] Researchers who study a country's political culture too often assume that a single set of values dominates it. Any such investigation must consider the possibility that support for democratic institutions and processes varies across segments of society. Investigating that variability is a primary purpose of this chapter. Consequently, I first examine the factors that contribute to the hypothesis that African Americans are less likely than White people to support democratic values, institutions, and processes.

Extant Research

Not a great deal of earlier research has investigated interracial differences in democratic attitudes. Some of the earliest work focused on interracial differences in levels of political intolerance.[4] More recently, Christopher Claassen, Joan Barceló, and I have found that, even in a fully specified model of the etiology of political intolerance, Black Americans express less tolerance than White people ($p < .001$), as do Hispanic people ($p < .01$).[5] However, the sizes of the coefficients, while significant, were small; and as with virtually all studies based on nationally representative samples, the numbers of minority respondents were fairly small.

Moving beyond political intolerance, Nelson and I report one of the most recent investigations in *Black and Blue*.[6] This book focuses primarily on explaining the variability in legal attitudes among African Americans, but some important findings on interracial differences emerge as well. In particular:

- White respondents tended to grant considerably more legitimacy to the Supreme Court than Black respondents did. On the most extreme measure of institutional support—whether to do away with the institution altogether if it does not make desirable decisions—about 10 percent of White respondents rejected the court, while the figure nearly doubled for Black people (18 percent).[7] Nearly one in five Black Americans expressed the lowest possible level of institutional commitment to the nation's highest court.

- White respondents were more supportive of the rule of law than Black respondents and tended, in comparison, to favor individual liberty more than social order. White people endorsed an average of 3.7 of 5 statements in support for the rule of law, while Black people endorsed an average of 3.2 such statements. White people supported an average of 1.9 of 3 pro–individual liberty statements, while Black people supported an average of 1.5.[8] However, we also note the *absence* of interracial difference in levels of political tolerance: Black and White respondents expressed similar levels of unwillingness to "put up with" groups with which they disagreed.[9]

- Black respondents who showed the highest levels of support for the rule of law (those who gave five out of five pro-rule-of-law responses) were, on average, less supportive of the Supreme Court than White respondents who expressed the same level of support for the rule of law.[10]

- For White respondents, support for the rule of law, the valuation of individual liberty, and political tolerance were all closely connected to allegiance to the Supreme Court. For Black respondents, these values were generally only weakly connected to their support for the court.[11]

In earlier research specifically focused on the views of African Americans toward the Supreme Court, Caldeira and I also found significant interracial differences in attitudes toward the court's legitimacy, concluding that "blacks are on balance fairly positive toward the Court, but they are decidedly less positive than whites."[12] We also observed strong generational cohort differences in Supreme Court attitudes and ascribed this intraracial variability to the effects of the pro-Black rulings of the Warren Court. Under Chief Justice Earl Warren, African Americans came to view the Supreme Court as an institution friendly to their interests, and as a consequence, their institutional loyalty increased over time. However, loyalty has its limits: as the Supreme Court turned more conservative on racial issues,

Black people, and especially young Black people, started to withdraw their allegiance from the institution.

Rosalee Clawson and Eric Waltenburg report one of the most comprehensive studies of Black attitudes toward the Supreme Court. Using a variety of datasets, they generally conclude that court legitimacy is high among Black people and contributes to the willingness of African Americans to accept Supreme Court decisions, even those with which they disagree.[13]

However, if the attitudes of Black people are being continuously reshaped as the Supreme Court's policies move even further away from their preferences, then the datasets on which Clawson and Waltenburg rely may have become significantly outdated.[14]

Some state-level studies of Black people's attitudes toward the broader judicial system have also been conducted. For instance, Marvin Overby and his colleagues find that Black people in Mississippi tend to judge their state judicial system as significantly less fair than do White Mississippians.[15] Experience with the judicial system has some effect on fairness judgments, with greater experience associated with perceptions of greater fairness, although the effects of experience are not consistent across the various dependent variables they investigate.

Undoubtedly the most far-reaching study of Black-White variation in attitudes toward legal institutions is that of Mark Peffley and Jon Hurwitz. Focusing on both inter- and intraracial differences, they draw several important conclusions: "First, it is difficult to exaggerate the degree to which perceived (and real) bias within the community affects the more global judgments that individuals formulate about the criminal justice system."[16] Second, vicarious experiences matter, and matter greatly, in shaping attitudes. Third, "the different 'realities' of justice between Blacks and Whites could not be more dissimilar. Blacks far more often have encounters with law enforcement officers, see rampant discrimination in their communities, see the legal system as fraught with bias, and attribute the distribution of legal outcomes to inherent bias in the justice system."[17] Their research paints a picture of a vast chasm in the experiences, perceptions, and evaluations of Black and White Americans.

Ernest Dupree and John Hibbing report 2018 survey data on trust in various institutions—which is not the same as legitimacy or diffuse support[18]—and find substantial differences in Black-White trust in most institutions.[19] The largest gap concerns trust in local police: 39.2 percent of

Black people reported trusting the local police, compared with 69.8 percent of White people. The only institution in which White people reported less trust than Black people did was Congress: 30.6 percent of Black respondents reported trusting Congress, compared with 22.2 percent of White respondents. This finding reinforces the conclusion that trust is a concept closer to specific than diffuse support.

Finally, Black people are almost twice as likely as White people, at least in a somewhat different but temporally related context, to endorse rioting as a means of expressing a group's grievances.[20]

Black people thus seem to be less strongly committed to democratic institutions and processes and may be less likely to see the insurrection events as representing an existential threat to America's democracy. If so—and given that a major predictor of support for the Supreme Court (at least) is a commitment to democratic values—we can expect African Americans to extend less diffuse support to the court than do White people.

Profit from the Current Political Dispensation

One might also argue that African Americans have profited less than others from the political system dominant in the United States and therefore have fewer incentives to support the institutional status quo.[21] Certainly, that is the conclusion of the literature on reparations for Black people.[22] One would therefore be unsurprised to find that many African Americans view American political institutions as having failed them.

Experiences with Legal Authorities

One clear way in which African Americans have not profited from the current political dispensation can be seen in their interactions with legal authorities such as the police. Black people in general are more likely than White people to have had run-ins with the police that they judge to have been unfair. According to a Pew survey in 2019, 44 percent of Black people in the United States reported having been "unfairly stopped by the police," compared with only 9 percent of White people, 16 percent of Asians or Asian Americans, and 19 percent of Hispanic people.[23] In reporting similar findings regarding unfair treatment, Nelson and I find that 40 percent of Black people claimed to have been treated unfairly by the police because of their race.[24] Unfair treatment by legal authorities is not likely to build a sense of the legitimacy of those authorities.

Black People, the Insurrection, and the Trump Years

Black people were far less likely than others to have voted for Trump in the 2020 presidential election.[25] In addition, Trump and the Republicans, in their attempts to overturn the election, often (if not typically) sought to disenfranchise Black voters.[26] Relatedly, as signaled by the flying of the Confederate flag during the siege on the Capitol, many insurrectionists were sympathetic to White nationalists.[27] At the same time, however, some limited evidence suggests that Black people and White people (and Hispanic people as well) do not differ in their perceptions of the insurrection.[28]

Thus, for all these reasons, I hypothesize that African Americans are less likely than White people to extend support to national political institutions. Consequently, I next consider whether interracial differences in institutional support emerged in the period following the insurrection and the second Trump impeachment trial.

Research Design and Analytical Approach

The February and March 2021 survey on which this chapter is based was specifically designed to be representative not only of the American people as a whole but also of African Americans as a whole. (For details, see the appendix.) In the general sample, the respondents were White, Black, Hispanic, or of another race, with the last category defined as mixed-race people, people of other non-Hispanic races, and people of Asian ancestry.[29] Despite the overall size of this sample ($N = 2,132$) and the large number of African Americans ($N = 723$), the number of Hispanic people ($N = 269$) and people of another race in the sample is too small to warrant much separate attention.[30] Consequently, nearly all of my analysis focuses on differences between Black people and White people.[31]

General Support for Democratic Institutions

In chapters 2 and 5, I discussed the conceptualization and t_3 measures of generalized support for American democratic institutions. Using that index of support, figure 6.1 reports the substantial interracial differences in allegiance to American democratic institutions; White respondents, for instance, expressed considerably greater faith in these institutions than did respondents of other races.[32] The Black-White comparison in this figure is particularly revealing. On average, White people gave pro-democracy responses to 1.8 of the 3 items; for Black people the comparable figure was only 1.3.[33] The best indicator of the concept (the third item) illustrates well the Black-White difference: while 75 percent of White people did not believe that America's democratic institutions should be scrapped, this was true of only 49 percent of the African American respondents. The index of generalized unwillingness to give up on American political institutions will serve as the dependent variable for this portion of my analysis.

As I have noted, a central objective of this research is to investigate the connections between support for democratic institutions and perceptions of the election, insurrection, and impeachment events. The general hypoth-

Figure 6.1 Interracial Differences in Support for U.S. Political Institutions

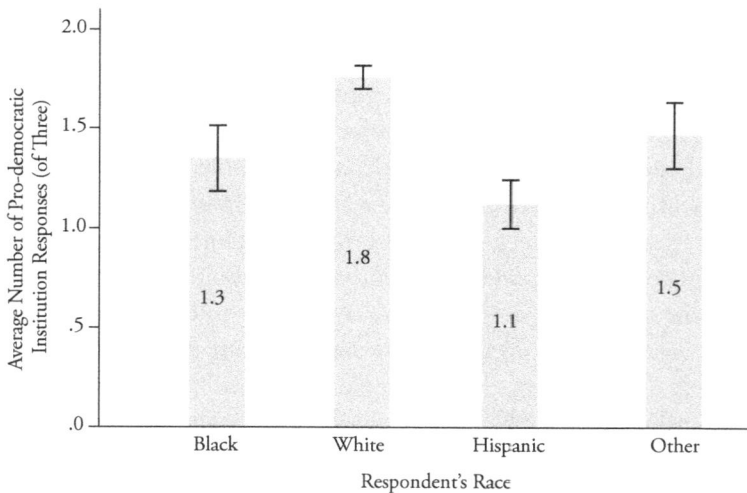

Source: The 2021 Insurrection and Impeachment Survey (t₃), February and March 2021.
Notes: N = 2,018. Cross-race difference in means: $p < .001$. The error bars depict 95 percent confidence intervals. The (unweighted) numbers of respondents are 675 for African Americans, 903 for Whites, 237 for Hispanics, and 197 for other races.

esis guiding this research is that event assessments and support for the institutions of democracy are interconnected.

Perceptions and Evaluations of Events

As in the earlier analyses reported in this book, I do not assume that political events are perceived by everyone in the same way or that, once perceived, they are understood and evaluated in the same way. Consequently, I have focused on measuring awareness and evaluations of five potentially delegitimizing events: (1) allegations that the 2020 presidential election was rigged; (2) President Trump's efforts to get the outcome of the 2020 presidential election overturned; (3) the insurrection of January 6, 2021; (4) the impeachment of President Trump; and (5) the nomination and confirmation of Amy Coney Barrett to the Supreme Court. For all five events, I asked questions about both levels of awareness of the event and assessments of it.[34] Table 6.1 reports the responses of both Black and White respondents to these questions.

Differences between Black and White Americans' reactions to the various events associated with the insurrection of January 6, 2021, were substantial. In general, White people paid considerably more attention to these events, although awareness of all five events was quite high among both Black people and White people, with very large majorities of both groups claiming to have been "very" or "somewhat" aware of them. Attentiveness to these happenings was unsurprisingly widespread; nevertheless, claimed awareness did vary, as incorporated into the analysis that follows.

The chasm between Black and White Americans in their assessments of these events was momentous and extensive. For instance, 12 percent of Black respondents concluded that the election was rigged, compared with 39 percent of White respondents. Only a small percentage of Black people (9 percent) judged the insurrection as not harmful to America's democracy, while nearly one-quarter of White people (24 percent) considered it to have been harmless. While only 15 percent of Black people approved of Trump's acquittal by the Senate, 51 percent of White people held that view.

As with so many aspects of American politics, Black and White assessments of the events surrounding the insurrection differed enormously.[35] These data reinforce a truism in contemporary American politics: reality

Table 6.1 Racial Differences in Awareness and Assessments of Election and Insurrection Events

	Black People	White People
Awareness of events		
Barrett nomination		
Mean (standard deviation)***	0.69 (0.34)	0.80 (0.29)
Very or somewhat aware	73% (679)	87% (1,274)
Trump's efforts to overturn the election		
Mean (standard deviation)***	0.87 (0.26)	0.00
Very or somewhat aware	90% (673)	96% (1,274)
Election rigged		
Mean (standard deviation)***	0.83 (0.29)	0.92 (0.19)
Very or somewhat aware	85% (672)	96% (1,270)
Capitol insurrection		
Mean (standard deviation)**	0.91 (0.21)	0.93 (0.17)
Very or somewhat aware	94% (669)	97% (1,274)
Trump impeachment and trial		
Mean (standard deviation)	0.90 (0.20)	0.91 (0.19)
Very or somewhat aware	94% (672)	95% (1,269)
Assessments of events		
Barrett nomination		
Mean (standard deviation)***	0.37 (0.32)	0.60 (0.39)
Entirely or somewhat appropriate	35% (671)	59% (1,270)
Trump's efforts to overturn election		
Mean (standard deviation)***	0.15 (0.28)	0.40 (0.41)
Entirely or somewhat appropriate	14% (670)	41% (1,261)
Election rigged		
Mean (standard deviation)***	0.17 (0.28)	0.37 (0.38)
Very or fairly certain election was rigged	12% (669)	39% (1,264)
Capitol insurrection		
Mean (standard deviation)***	0.10 (0.23)	0.28 (0.33)
Not harmful to democracy	9% (669)	24% (1,264)
Trump impeachment and trial		
Mean (standard deviation)***	0.65 (0.39)	0.53 (0.38)
Not harmful to democracy	68% (666)	53% (1,264)
Trump not convicted		
Mean (standard deviation)***	0.18 (0.30)	0.50 (0.44)
Strongly or somewhat approve	15% (671)	51% (1,268)

Source: The 2021 Insurrection and Impeachment Survey (t_3), February and March 2021.
Notes: All variables are scored to range from 0 to 1. For their distributions, see the appendix. For the percentages, the numbers shown in parentheses are the total numbers of cases on which the percentages are based.
Significance of the difference of means: * $p \leq .05$; ** $p \leq .01$; *** $p \leq .001$

and perceptions and assessments of that reality often diverge among the American people.

Controlling for Democratic Values

As I have noted, I distinguish in this research between commitments to American democratic institutions and more general democratic values, just as research on institutional legitimacy distinguishes between diffuse support for institutions and democratic values.[36] Consequently, I include as predictors of institutional commitments three widely used scales to measure democratic values: (1) support for the rule of law, (2) the valuation of individual liberty, and (3) willingness to extend civil liberties to a variety of unpopular groups (see the appendix).

Notably, in earlier research, Nelson and I find substantial interracial differences in support for democratic values and processes.[37] In this survey, I also find that Black people were considerably (and significantly) less likely to support the rule of law and less likely to prioritize individual liberty when it conflicted with social order, but they were no more or less willing to grant civil liberties to unpopular groups.

These general attitudes are associated with about 19 percent of the variance in democratic institutional support among White people and about 16 percent of the variance in support among Black people (analysis not shown). With one exception, all the coefficients are significant and substantial. Among Black people, a preference for individual liberty was not related to democratic institutional support. Support for the rule of law is by far the most powerful predictor of attitudes toward democratic institutions for both Black people and White people.

Hypothesis Testing: Allegiance to U.S. Political Institutions

Figure 6.2 reports the results of regressing allegiance to democratic institutions on awareness of the election and post-election events, assessments of those events, three more general democratic values, two personality attributes often found in models of democratic values,[38] ideological and partisan self-identifications, and a variety of demographic attributes of the respondents.[39] Most of the predictors included in this equation are derived from research on the etiology of political tolerance, a crucial democratic value, because the tolerance literature provides one of the most fully articulated models of support for democratic values.[40] For example, in earlier work I provide a basic model of the predictors of tolerance and support for civil liberties that is useful in this context.[41] Similar predictors are used in most research focused on explaining variability in support for the Supreme Court.[42]

The analysis in this figure supports many additional conclusions. First, generally speaking, variation in awareness of the various events seems to have little connection with support for democratic institutions. Among Black Americans, only one of the five awareness measures is connected to attitudes, and the awareness measure that is significantly related (awareness of the Barrett nomination and confirmation) is perhaps the measure least directly relevant to general democratic attitudes.[43] For White Americans, awareness of the insurrection is negatively associated (but not quite significantly, at $p = .055$) with democratic institutional support, meaning that those who were more aware were slightly less supportive. Generally, however, as documented in table 6.1, public awareness of these events was quite high, and therefore the limited variability—nearly everyone reported being aware of the happenings to at least some degree—seems to have only marginal connections (at best) to institutional support.

The findings on assessments of these events, however, differ considerably. Most important, one of the strongest predictors of support for democratic institutions among White respondents was their judgment of the fairness of the election: White people who believed that the election was rigged were considerably less supportive of democratic institutions, indicating that the efforts of Trump and the Republicans to delegitimize the election either met with some success or were embraced by those already weakly committed to democracy. As figure 6.2 reports, the standard deviation of the democratic support variable among White people is 0.22. The effect of assessments of the election therefore approaches almost a full standard deviation.[44]

For Black Americans, however, election assessments were inconsequential (ceteris paribus). Instead, the important event for Black people was the insurrection—although judgments of the insurrection had no consequences for White people. The (relatively few) African Americans who concluded that the insurrection was not harmful to American democracy were decidedly less supportive of American democratic institutions. Over the range of these appraisals, the effect of these assessments is roughly one-half of a standard deviation. For these two event assessments, the data require rejecting the null hypothesis that the Black and White coefficients do not differ.

With the noted exceptions, neither awareness nor assessments of the other events have much connection to support for democratic institutions. Awareness and judgments of the second Trump impeachment, for instance, are entirely disconnected from institutional support. In a hierarchical regression, the eleven awareness and assessment variables alone are associated with considerably less than one-half of the total explained variance reported in figure 6.2, for both Black people and White people (data not shown). Clearly, democratic institutional support reflects much more than how people felt about the election and post-election events.

For both Black and White respondents, assessments of the threat to American democracy posed by Democrats are significantly related to support for democratic institutions, with greater threat perceptions associated with less support.[45] While I observe no comparable relationship with the perceived threat of the Republicans, it seems that for some people, regardless of race, part and parcel of their dissatisfaction with American political institutions was an unwillingness to recognize their political opponents as a legitimate competitor for political power.[46] Relatedly, greater opposition to civil liberties for unpopular groups is also connected to rejection of these democratic institutions.

One of the single best predictors of commitment to democratic institutions among both Black people and White people is support for the rule of law: respondents who valued the rule of law more highly were considerably more likely to express strong allegiance to democratic institutions. For White people, no other predictor was as closely connected to democratic assessments; for Black people, support for the rule of law, open-mindedness, party identification, and ideological self-identification all had coefficients greater than or equal to 0.20. The other democratic values also contribute to democratic commitments, although a preference for individual liberty over social order bears no relationship to such commitments among Black people.[47] Generally, however, respondents' attitudes toward democratic institutions were substantially connected to whether they held more general values congenial to democratic processes.

Figure 6.2 Predictors of Racial Differences in Support for U.S. Democratic Institutions

Dependent Variable: Support for U.S. Democratic Institutions, Black People (Panel A)

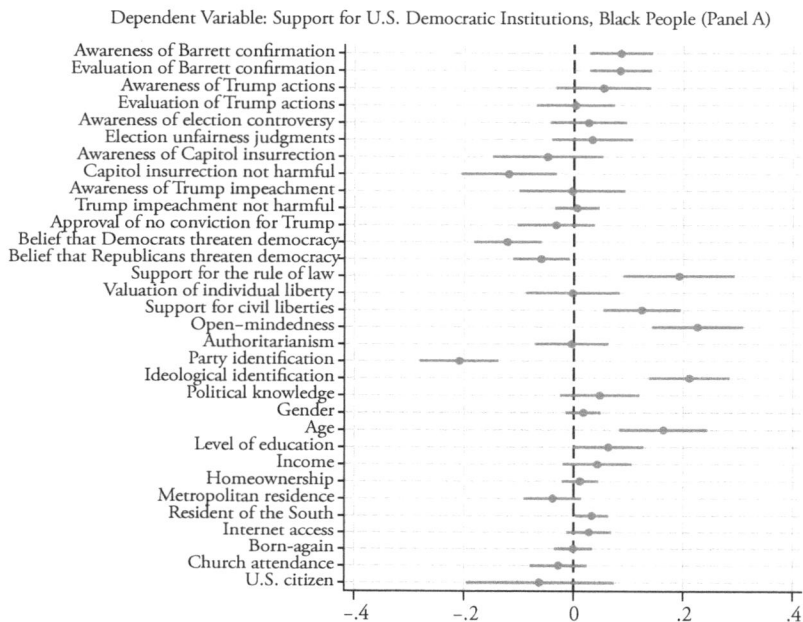

Source: The 2021 Insurrection and Impeachment Survey (t₃), February and March 2021.
Notes:
Panel A: Equation:

    $R^2 = 0.44***$

    $N = 611$

Significance of unstandardized OLS regression coefficients:

$* \ p \leq .05$

    Belief that Republicans threaten democracy

    Resident of the South

$** \ p \leq .01$

    Awareness of Barrett confirmation

    Capitol insurrection not harmful

$*** \ p \leq .001$

    Evaluation of Barrett confirmation

    Belief that Democrats threaten democracy

    Support for the rule of law

    Support for civil liberties

    Open-mindedness

    Party identification

    Ideological identification

    Age

Figure 6.2 (*continued*)

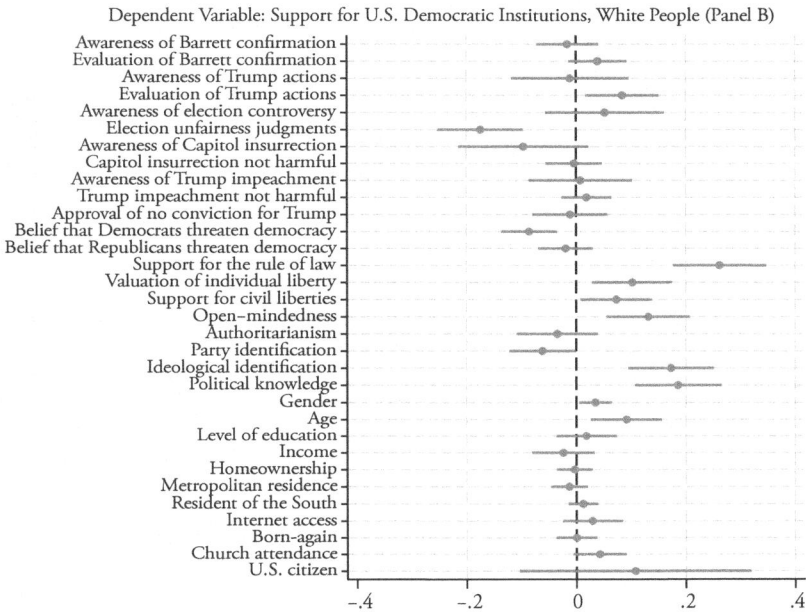

Dependent Variable: Support for U.S. Democratic Institutions, White People (Panel B)

Source: The 2021 Insurrection and Impeachment Survey (t_3), February and March 2021.

Notes:

Panel B: Equation:

  $R^2 = 0.37$***

  $N = 1,193$

Significance of unstandardized OLS regression coefficients:

* $p \le .05$

  Party identification

  Church attendance

** $p \le .01$

  Evaluation of Trump's actions

  Support for civil liberties

  Gender

*** $p \le .001$

  Election unfairness judgments

  Belief that Democrats threaten democracy

  Support for the rule of law

  Valuation of individual liberty

  Open-mindedness

  Ideological identification

  Political knowledge

  Age

All variables are scored to range from 0 to 1. For their distributions, see table A.13. For the full regression table from which these results are derived, see table A.12. Shown are the unstandardized regression coefficients and their confidence intervals.

The coefficients in figure 6.2 suggest that institutional commitments have partisan and ideological components, even if the equation shows that support for democratic institutions is about far more than partisanship and ideology. For both Black people and White people, however, the data revealed some puzzles. In the multivariate equation, Republicans tended to support democratic institutions less than Democrats, which seems consistent with some of the findings already discussed (for example, regarding beliefs that the election was rigged). And even for Black people, among whom variation is more limited, respondents less strongly committed to the Democratic Party were significantly less supportive of American democratic institutions. The relationship for White people is similar, although much weaker (even if barely distinguishable from zero). For White people, even the bivariate correlation of party identification and allegiance to democratic institutions is fairly weak. Of course, with relatively few Black people identifying as Republicans, the overall consequences of party affiliations for democratic support become muted.

Puzzlingly, the sign on the ideological self-identification variable is opposite that of my prediction: Black people and White people who were more conservative tended to express substantially more support for American democratic institutions. And for White people, ideology was *much* more closely related to democratic assessments than partisanship, whereas both ideology and partisanship for Black people had similarly strong connections. This finding may be driven in part by significant multicollinearity among White people, for whom the correlation of party and ideological identifications is 0.74.[48] Among Black people, that correlation is only 0.24, and though those identifying as Democrats tended to also identify as liberals, the tendency is only modest. Republican identification is associated with a tendency to reject democratic institutions, but conservative identification is associated with a tendency to support these institutions. It is not clear why; given Black people's historical attachment to the Democratic Party, respondents' ideology may well have become connected more closely than their party to a variety of substantive preferences.

The regression equation also indicates that open-mindedness is closely related to support for democratic institutions among both Black people and White people, although the coefficient is larger for Black people than it is for White people. Recall that this concept represents the view that the world is divided into friends and foes, that many issues should be understood as either "black or white," and that compromise is dangerous.[49] Noteworthy as well is the complete absence of any relationship between authoritarianism and democratic values. (And this is not a function of excessive correlations between authoritarianism and open-mindedness—for Black people the correlation is –0.35; for White people, it is –0.33.) In addition, variability in political knowledge is significantly related to democratic commitments among White people (as usual, greater knowledge is associated with greater support for democratic institutions), but not among Black people.

With such a fully specified model, the demographic variables unsurprisingly are largely unconnected to support for democratic institutions. Some exceptions, however, do stand out. Both Black and White older people were considerably more supportive of democratic institutions, and the relationship is at least moderately strong for older Black Americans (and is not, of course, attributable to the possibility that older people identified as more conservative). White women were slightly more supportive of democratic institutions than White men, but the relationship was not reproduced among Black people and was actually quite weak among White people. The frequency of church attendance was also barely significant among White people, though not among Black people.

Summary

The central argument of my analysis is that awareness and assessments of the events of the 2020 presidential election and its aftermath did little to structure support for democratic institutions and processes. Instead, support for democratic institutions is grounded in more fundamental democratic values, especially veneration for the rule of law.

The equations I use to support this argument are a bit cumbersome, in that they include several variables, many of which are intercorrelated (but not excessively). Simplifying the analysis therefore may help show if my basic conclusions are still supported.

Table 6.2 reports the results of a hierarchical regression using institutional support as the dependent variable. Using the conceptual categorizations reported in the regression tables (for example, in figure 6.2), I added variables to the equation in item-sets. First, I included the five measures of democratic values and personalities. Then, I added the eleven awareness

Table 6.2 Contributions to Explaining the Variance in Willingness to Extend Legitimacy to U.S. Democratic Institutions

	Black People	White People
Legitimacy of democratic institutions		
Democratic values	0.21***	0.23***
Awareness and assessments of events	0.31***	0.28***
Party threat to democracy	0.34***	0.29***
Demographics	0.44***	0.37***

Source: The 2021 Insurrection and Impeachment Survey (t_3), February and March 2021.

Notes: The entries are the total explained variance in the dependent variable (R^2) for the item-set as entered into a hierarchical regression analysis.

Significance of change in R^2, variable set: * $p \le .05$; ** $p \le .01$; *** $p \le .001$

and assessment measures, followed by the two party-threat indicators and the host of demographic attributes. Reported in the table are the R^2 statistics for each step in the hierarchical analysis for Black and White respondents. Recorded as well is the statistical significance of the change in explained variance (not of the total R^2 itself, each of which is of course significant at $p < .001$). To be as clear as possible, the results of the hierarchical regressions reported in table 6.2 are exactly the results reported in figure 6.2.

The five democratic values measures can account for about one-half of the variance explained in the full equation. Moreover, the addition of the eleven awareness and assessments variables increases the amount of explained variance only marginally. Neither do the measures of perceived party threat to democracy play much of a role in predicting support for democratic institutions. Finally, and somewhat to my surprise, the demographic variables often make a nontrivial contribution to accounting for the variance in legitimacy attitudes.

Hierarchical regression results like those reported in table 6.2 have some obvious limitations. But in conjunction with the results reported earlier in the chapter, at least one substantive conclusion seems entirely warranted: a willingness to extend legitimacy to America's democratic institutions depends much more on citizens' degree of commitment to democratic values, such as reverence for the rule of law, than it does on their awareness and assessments of the events of the 2020 presidential election and its aftermath.

Discussion and Concluding Comments

This portion of my research has vividly documented that a considerable number of Americans, albeit a minority, seem willing to give up on American political institutions. Moreover, and perhaps even more important, the research has shown markedly less support for these institutions among America's racial minorities. I am unwilling to put much stock in my findings for Hispanic people and those of other races, but respondents in the sizable Black oversample included in this research design—one that is reasonably representative of Black people as a whole—expressed notably less support for America's democratic institutions, with the exception of the Biden presidency, than their White counterparts.

That Black people would support democratic institutions less resolutely, given their experiences with those institutions, is unsurprising. Efforts to disenfranchise Black voters played a prominent role in the 2020 presidential election (and Republican efforts at voter suppression are far from concluded); moreover, White supporters of the Confederacy rose to eye-catching prominence in the assault on the Capitol in January 2021. Add to this the George Floyd murder in the summer of 2020 and seemingly weekly reports of legal authorities taking the life of yet another Black person. Indeed, it would be surprising *not* to find that Black Americans express less confidence in American political institutions than White people after the Trump tempest, given that a great many if not nearly all aspects of Trumpism are profoundly racialized.[50]

But whether the 2020 election and 2021 insurrection events played a dominant and independent role in shaping the support that Americans—Black or White—express for democratic institutions is unclear. Perhaps the most fecund finding from this analysis is that the connections between awareness and assessments of the events associated with the 2020 presidential election and its aftermath and support for democratic institutions are generally not especially strong. For example, none of the Trump impeachment judgments were found to bear any relationship to democratic institutional support. White people's assessments of the Capitol insurrection were not linked to their support for democratic institutions, and Black Americans' assessments were only moderately related to such support. Conversely, the election events themselves, particularly whether the election was judged to have been rigged, were somewhat associated with White people's support for democratic institutions. But this was not true of Black people. I cannot determine whether those who extended little support to democracy in America were more responsive to elite claims of election rigging or whether those claims caused people to reassess whether American democracy is worth supporting. But in general, awareness and assessments of the events of January 6, 2021, and their aftermath were not closely interrelated with a willingness to support democratic institutions.

Instead, broader democratic values were found to be far more powerful predictors of support for America's democratic institutions. Particularly noteworthy is the connection, among both Black people and White people, between attitudes toward the rule of law and allegiance to democratic institutions. Other researchers find rule-of-law attitudes to be potent predictors of presidential attitudes, or to play a central role in analyses of political tolerance and of the institutional legitimacy of the Supreme Court.[51] The present study confirms that those general attitudes have consequences for more specific commitments to democratic institutions.

Democratic institutional support's much closer association with democratic values than with event assessments, among both Black people and White people, has many important implications. In a context of affective polarization and information silos and echo chambers, if values are obdurate, mainly reflecting childhood and early adulthood political socialization, and if people are motivated to assess events as confirming rather than disconfirming those values, then even watershed moments in American history are unlikely to have profound consequences for value change.[52] Without discounting the importance of forces *reinforcing* existing values, a reasonable conclusion from this analysis is that it seems more likely that opponents of American democracy were predisposed to believe lies about the electoral process than that the lies changed fundamental commitments to democratic institutions. Undoubtedly, however, this is a question that requires further investigation. (The next chapter follows up by focusing on micro-level change in African Americans' allegiance to democratic institutions.)

Some scholars discount research on citizen attitudes and values; Matthew Graham and Milan Svolik, for example, argue that "conventional direct-questioning measures of support for democracy may be flawed because they fail to account for voters' willingness to trade off democratic principles for partisan interests."[53] No doubt citizens often must play the hand they are dealt and make the trade-offs they must. But elite canards usually try to anticipate public values and preferences but sometimes do so inaccurately.[54] The values held by the mass public therefore can matter greatly, because they may very well determine just what sort of falsehoods elites can sell to the American people. If so, then understanding the causes and consequences of these attitudes and values is a crucial task for future research.

A premise of this chapter is that Black people have not been treated fairly by many of America's institutions and that it therefore makes sense that they would extend less legitimacy to those institutions. Although Dupree and Hibbing analyze trust, which is not diffuse support, they report that one of the best predictors of distrust is having been subjected to discriminatory treatment in the past.[55] In a prior study, Nelson and I also emphasize the importance of unfair treatment by authorities in considering Black people's feelings of legal alienation.[56] Dupree and Hibbing also point to what they term "Black centrality" as an important predictor, a concept synonymous with in-group attachments.

Unfortunately, the t_3 interview did not have sufficient space to include measures of experiences of unfair treatment or measures of group attachments. Fortunately, however, the t_4 interview (of only African Americans) did include these measures. The next chapter therefore continues this consideration of intra-Black variability in institutional support, using a more comprehensive model of that variability and focusing on accounting for individual-level change.

CHAPTER 7

Intra-Black Variability in Legitimacy Attitudes: An Update

THE ANALYSIS IN chapter 6 revealed that African Americans extend considerably less support to U.S. political institutions than do White Americans, with the exception of the Biden presidency, to which Black people are firmly committed. It also revealed that people's willingness to extend legitimacy to political institutions is closely connected to their degree of commitment to more general democratic values, such as reverence for the rule of law. Awareness and assessments of the events of the presidential election and its aftermath, including the insurrection and Trump's second impeachment, play a decidedly smaller role in shaping institutional support. Thus, while Black people are not as committed to American democratic institutions as members of the White majority are, the canards of Trump and his fellow travelers do not seem to be the cause of those weaker commitments.

Causal purists will no doubt harbor many reservations about the analysis reported in chapter 6, because it failed to present or test dispositive evidence on the nature of the causal flows. In some instances, the best the analysis could conclude was "what goes with what," although perhaps the main story of that chapter is "what does not go with what"—that is, awareness and assessments of events are not much connected to evaluations of democratic institutions.

Moreover, the analysis excluded important variables from consideration

https://doi.org/10.7758/dvkr4409.7396

because the t_3 survey did not measure them. Perhaps the most important of these unavailable variables pertained to experiences with discrimination and in-group attachments and consciousness. To remedy these two short-comings, this chapter offers a more complete account of why some Black people extend legitimacy to political institutions and others do not.

One answer to the causal complaints is to analyze changes in support for democratic institutions over time, which is the central purpose of this chapter. The African Americans in the t_3 sample were reinterviewed a few months later, after some of the dust of the election, insurrection, and impeachment had settled. In an analytical strategy much like that used in chapter 4, this t_4 interview—the African American Panel Survey—included some of the t_3 measures of institutional legitimacy in order to consider how these attitudes might have changed.

In addition, because the t_4 interview included several measures of experiences with legal authorities, both personal and vicarious, venerable hypotheses about how experiences shape attitudes could be tested.[1] Moreover, the survey included a variety of measures of in-group attachments. Especially in the aftermath of the Black Lives Matter movement, variation in in-group psychological attachments is expected to shape many assessments of American political institutions. Thus, while the last chapter focused mainly on intergroup variation in support for democratic institutions, this chapter focuses on intragroup variability. As Dupree and Hibbing note:

> An unfortunate tendency in many analyses of race in America is to conduct blanket comparisons of Black and White attitudes, thus leaving the impression that each of those groups is more homogeneous than it actually is. In reality, of course, as is the case with White attitudes, Black attitudes are remarkably diverse, and an important goal of research in this area needs to be accounting for these variations.[2]

Still, even with panel data and a more fully specified analytical model, I must begin this analysis with a discussion of important caveats and limitations. First, data are available only for the African American portion of the sample analyzed in chapter 6. This limitation precludes the sort of intergroup analysis that was presented in that chapter. Second, unlike the earlier analyses, no highly salient democratic or antidemocratic events took place between the t_3 and the t_4 interviews. Chapter 4 focused on the events of the 2020 presidential election, and chapter 5 was concerned with the insurrection and the impeachment; this chapter, by contrast, examines the period between March 2021 and June 2021 (the time period of the t_4 survey), which was something of a standing-down period. I do not contend that no democracy-relevant events took place, but certainly the intensity of the media attention to the election, insurrection, and impeachment events abated. I include in this analysis of change the awareness and assessment variables considered in chapter 6 (and measured at t_3), but the t_4 survey did not measure awareness and assessment of any new events.

The analyses in this chapter, however, include some crucial new predictors. To test a more fully specified model of intra-Black variability in support for democratic institutions, I focus on the influence of past experiences of unfair treatment by legal authorities—both personal and vicarious—as well as on measures of in-group attachments.[3] From the viewpoint of causal certainty, however, I acknowledge up front that many important predictors of support for democratic institutions, including the identity variables, were measured only at t_4, simultaneously with the dependent variables.

Change in Support for America's Democratic Institutions

The items used at t_3 to measure willingness to extend legitimacy to America's democratic institutions were repeated in the t_4 survey, allowing the calculation of indices of individual-level change over the few months between the two interviews. The results are reported in table 7.1.

The upper portion of this table, pertaining to democratic institutions in general, supports several conclusions. First, between March 2021 and June 2021, support for democratic institutions declined, albeit not dramatically. This conclusion is drawn from the change in the average support score and the increase in the number of anti-legitimacy responses to the three items. The average number of anti-democracy replies went from 0.61 to 0.89 (of 3).[4] Moreover, regarding the responses to the individual questions (data not shown), the percentage of respondents who agreed that current institutions should be scrapped and the system started over increased from 18.3 percent to 30.2 percent. In addition, the percentages of respondents who were uncertain about each of the legitimacy questions declined markedly. Change can also be registered in another, more alarming way: at t_3, 25.7 percent of the respondents gave three pro-democracy replies; this percentage slipped at t_4 to only 19.9 percent (data not shown). Even more telling, at t_3, 61.8

Table 7.1 Change in African American Support for Democratic Institutions between the Insurrection and Impeachment Survey and the African American Panel Survey

	Index of Support			Number of Nonsupportive Responses		
	Mean	Standard Deviation	N	Mean	Standard Deviation	N
Democratic institutions in general						
2021 survey (t₃)	0.58	0.23	570	0.61	0.92	570
2021 survey (t₄)	0.55	0.24	570	0.89	1.02	570
Change	−0.03	0.22	570	0.28	0.99	570
Supreme Court						
2021 survey (t₃)	0.51	0.19	568	1.42	1.53	568
2021 survey (t₄)	0.44	0.19	568	2.07	1.70	568
Change	−0.07	0.17	568	0.64	1.53	568

Source: The 2021 Insurrection and Impeachment Survey (t_3), February and March 2021, and the African American Panel Survey (t_4), June 2021.

Notes: Only those t_3 respondents who were also interviewed at t_4 are included in this table. The index of support for democratic institutions is the average response to the three items measuring support for democratic institutions in general and is scored to range from 0 to 1, with higher scores indicating more support. The number of nonsupportive responses is the number of items, out of three, on which the respondent expressed a rejection of institutional support (irrespective of intensity, and with "uncertain" respondents in the denominator). The index of support for the Supreme Court is the average response to the five items measuring support for the court and is scored to range from 0 to 1, with higher scores indicating more support. The number of nonsupportive responses is the number of items, out of five, on which the respondent expressed a rejection of institutional support for the court (irrespective of intensity, and with "uncertain" respondents in the denominator). "Change" is the change at the individual level between responses at t_3 and t_4. Negative change scores on the index represent declines in institutional support. For the text of these items, see the appendix.

percent of African Americans gave no anti-democracy replies; at t_4, the percentage dropped to 46.6 percent. The most tenable conclusion from this analysis is that alienation from America's democratic institutions increased markedly from t_3 to t_4 for the African American sample.[5] Something caused Black alienation from democratic institutions to crystallize between the two interviews.

Two explanations of these findings are possible: either something quite significant took place between the t_3 and t_4 interviews, or the effects of the election, insurrection, and impeachment took a considerable amount of time to fester and be felt in legitimacy attitudes. If the latter is true, as I suspect it might be, then this finding should give pause to those who model the consequences of an event as materializing very quickly after it takes place.

The lower portion of table 7.1 reports the change in African American attitudes toward the Supreme Court from t_3 to t_4. These figures describe a rather dramatic loss of legitimacy by the court between the two interviews. For instance, the number of anti-legitimacy replies rose from 1.42 to 2.07 out of 5. Regarding the individual components of the index, the percentage of African Americans who would support removing judges who rule against the preferences of the majority ballooned from 24.0 percent to 38.3 percent. And at t_4 fully one-fourth of the respondents expressed a willingness to do away with the court for making decisions contrary to the will of the institution's constituents (data not shown). The central message of the data reported in this table is unambiguous: legitimacy-affirming attitudes toward the Supreme Court among Black people slipped markedly over a period of around three months in 2021. Again, either something fairly dramatic happened after March 2021 or the effects of the 2020 election and its aftermath were felt later than many people might have assumed.

My purpose in this chapter is to assess change in the willingness to extend support to America's political institutions in general and to the Supreme Court in particular. At t_3, the two measures of support are correlated at 0.51; at t_4, the relationship declines to 0.36. Perhaps most notably, change in support for democratic institutions is uncorrelated with change in support for the Supreme Court ($r = 0.01$). These findings require me to analyze the two measures of institutional legitimacy separately and independently.

An important contribution of this chapter is its significant expansion of the testable hypotheses about the sources of intra-Black variation in support for democratic institutions. Because experiences and identities are so central to the analyses in this chapter, I begin with an examination of African Americans' interactions with legal authorities and of various in-group attachments. Testing several hypotheses about how these variables, although measured only at t_4, are connected to the willingness to extend legitimacy to America's democratic institutions is essential.

Experiences with the Legal System

I begin this analysis of variability within the nationally representative survey of Black Americans by examining differences in their reported experiences with the legal system. Following the work of Peffley and Hurwitz as well as my earlier work with Nelson, I use a single item to measure personal experience with legal discrimination.[6]

> Some people have had encounters with the police; others have not. Was there any time in the last five years or so when you felt you were treated unfairly in dealing with the police—such as being stopped or followed while driving—just because you are African American? If so, did this happen once, twice, or three times, or more?
>
>> No, haven't been treated unfairly in dealing with the police
>> Have been treated unfairly once in dealing with the police
>> Have been treated unfairly twice in dealing with the police
>> Have been treated unfairly three times in dealing with the police
>> Have been treated unfairly more than three times in dealing with the police[7]

Perhaps some readers will be surprised by the finding that well over half of the respondents (54.2 percent) reported *not* having been treated unfairly by the police at any point in the past five years. That is, a majority had not directly experienced the kind of unequal police treatment so often reported in the news nowadays. Still, that four in ten Black people claimed to have had an unfair encounter with the police is highly significant—both for them and for the legal and political systems. At the other extreme, 10.5 percent of respondents claimed to have been treated unfairly more than three times within the last five years.

Personal experience with unfair legal treatment, however, is not the same thing as understanding that Black people as a group are often treated unfairly by the legal system. Again following work by Peffley and Hurwitz and my work with Nelson, vicarious experiences with unfair treatment by legal authorities were measured in this survey by asking the respondents two questions about the treatment of African Americans by the justice system.[8]

> The following are some statements that some people make about problems with the justice system in their community. Please rate how serious it is in your community on a seven-point scale, where 1 means it is not a problem and 7 means it is a serious problem.
>
>> Police stop and question Blacks far more often than they stop whites.
>> Courts give harsher sentences to African Americans than to whites.

The responses to these items measure perceptions of what other Black people experience. For both items, a considerable majority of the respondents rated unfair treatment as a "serious problem," the highest score on the response set (58.0 percent and 64.2 percent, respectively, for the two statements). Put slightly differently, only a minority of African Americans rated discrimination by the legal system as something less than a "serious problem." Also, only tiny numbers of respondents said that these issues were "not a problem." Clearly, African Americans tend to view their group as being unfairly targeted by criminal justice authorities. Following earlier work, I created a measure of vicarious experiences with unfair treatment by taking the mean of the responses to these two items (which are correlated at 0.67).[9]

Personal and vicarious experiences with discrimination are far from redundant: $r = 0.14$. This weak relationship is perhaps foretold by the frequencies: most African Americans have not personally experienced unfair treatment, while at the same time large a majority of African Americans perceive that Black people as a group are unfairly treated. Indeed, as figure 7.1 reports, perceptions of discrimination against African Americans varied little depending on respondents' own experiences with discrimination. For example, the mean discrimination score for those who had not had any unfair experiences with the police is about the same as that for those who had had one or two unfair experiences. Likewise, the average score for African Americans who had not had any unfair experiences is only slightly smaller than the score for those with more than three such experiences. Perhaps the most important conclusion from this figure is that one need not experience personal discrimination to perceive that Black people in general suffer from discrimination by the legal system. Personal and vicarious experiences with unfair treatment are, simply put, different phenomena.

Group Identification and Linked Fate

Scholars have paid a great deal of attention to investigating the in-group attachments of African Americans. However, these feelings are conceptually complicated. For example, Paula McClain and her colleagues divide group attachments into two subgroups: group identification and group consciousness.[10] Group identification refers generally to individuals' awareness of

Figure 7.1 The Relationship between African Americans' Personal and Vicarious Experiences with Legal System Discrimination

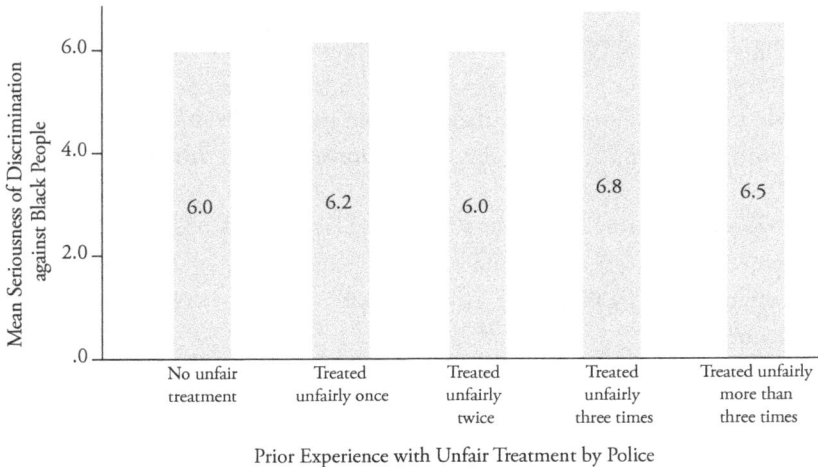

Source: The African American Panel Survey (t_4), June 2021.
Notes: N = 573. The seriousness of discrimination against Black people varies from 1 (not a problem) to 7 (a serious problem). Significance of difference-of-means F test, p = .002; Pearson correlation = 0.14.

their group membership, as well as their level of psychological connection with that group. In this way, group identification fits neatly with social identity theory.[11] Group consciousness, on the other hand, refers to "in-group identification *politicized* by a set of ideological beliefs about one's group's social standing, as well as a view that collective action is the best means by which one can improve its stance and realize its interests."[12] Mc-Clain and her colleagues further note that "as a sophisticated and parsimonious alternative, racial group consciousness may best be operationalized through the measure of linked fate."[13] The sense that one's personal fate is linked to that of one's group is a widely used concept in studies of political attitudes and behavior.

Importantly, group identification and group consciousness are neither theoretically nor empirically synonymous. Some people may identify strongly as African American, for example, but believe that their fate is not tied to the fates of other Black people. For other people, identification as African American may not be personally important, but they may believe that societal structures bind their fate tightly—for better or for worse—to the fates of other Black people. In light of this variability, I examine both concepts here. A major theme of my theory and empirical results is the vast variability in both concepts and their distinct, powerful roles in structuring individual-level attitudes toward democratic institutions and processes.

My measure of group identification is an index based on responses to the following statements (with collapsed responses in parentheses):

> Now, on a different subject, how important is it to think of yourself as African American or Black? Would you say it is very important, somewhat important, not very important, or not important at all? (70.8 percent, very important)
>
> Please indicate whether you agree strongly, agree, are uncertain, disagree, or disagree strongly with each of the following statements:
>
> > Even though I might sometimes disagree with the standpoint/viewpoint taken by other Blacks, it is extremely important to support the Black point of view. (62.8 percent, agree or agree strongly)
> > When it comes to politics, it is important for all Blacks to stand together. (64.6 percent, agree or agree strongly)

On each of these items, the respondents exhibited a fairly distinct lack of unanimity. For example, while 64.6 percent asserted that it is important for Black people to stand together, 24.8 percent disagreed with the statement (and another 10.5 percent were uncertain about their views on this issue). At the same time, a quite sizable majority expressed at least some degree of attachment to Black people as a group.

I created an index of African American in-group identity from the three items.[14] The index was scored from 0 to 1, with high scores indicating stronger group attachments. On this index, only 20.4 percent of the respondents scored at 0.50 (the midpoint on the index) or lower on the measure.

As a measure of group consciousness, the survey asked the respondents to respond to the conventional linked fate measure. As I have noted, linked fate is the belief that, owing to common experiences with discrimination, one's individual circumstances are connected to the status of one's group. The survey asked the respondents the following question:

Do you think what happens generally to Black people in this country has something to do with what happens in your life? Would you say "what happens to Black people in this country has nothing to do with what happens in my life," "what happens to Black people in this country affects what happens in my life very little," "what happens to Black people in this country affects what happens in my life some," or "what happens to Black people in this country affects what happens in my life a lot"?

The data indicate that a strong sense of linked fate is considerably less common than robust African American group identities.[15] For example, while 70.8 percent of the respondents regarded it as very important to think of themselves as Black, only 37.8 percent thought that their fate was tied "a lot" to the fate of Black people as a group. And indeed, the correlation between the linked fate response and the index of group identities is a paltry –0.02. Clearly, a strong sense of group identity does not necessarily translate into the belief that one's fate is tied to the fate of one's group, at least not for African Americans. I therefore include in the analyses both the simple measure of linked fate and the index measuring in-group identification.[16]

Linking Experiences with Identities

It remains to consider how experiences with legal authorities are connected to group attachments. At this point in the analysis, I make no causal claims, given that experiences can form identities, but identities might also lead individuals to interpret encounters with legal authorities differently. After all, the experiential variables include not just reports of facts but also interpretations of those facts (for example, whether a police stop was "unjustified").

Individuals' personal experiences with legal authorities are weakly correlated with their group identification ($r = 0.12$); thus, victims of unfair treatment hold stronger in-group attachments. At the same time, however, the correlation between personal experiences and a sense of linked fate is slightly weaker ($r = 0.08$), such that Black people who have experienced a greater number of unfair police stops are only insignificantly more likely to link their individual fate to the fate of the group (and vice versa). Individuals' vicarious experiences are much more strongly related to their group identifications (r = 0.35). Moreover, vicarious experiences are substantially related to a sense of linked fate (r = 0.23). However, none of these relationships is particularly large, and all the concepts are clearly empirically distinct from one another. I therefore treat each of the four concepts as unique in my subsequent empirical analyses (with few concerns about problems owing to multicollinearity).

Summary

The analysis so far in this chapter has revealed a great deal about Black experiences with the legal system and about Black group identities and attachments. For example, a large minority of Black people reported having contacts with the police that they considered unfair and discriminatory. Similarly, more than a simple majority of Black people regarded discrimination in the legal system as a serious problem for Black people as a group. I am impressed at both how large and how small these figures are. That such a large proportion of African Americans view the American legal system as treating Black people unfairly speaks to the serious problem of the possible lack of legitimacy of these institutions among many Black people. But that the proportions are not larger also speaks to the heterogeneity within the Black community: simply put, Black people differ in their experiences with the legal system.

I have also discovered that personal and vicarious experiences are different phenomena. We might think that those who are personally treated unfairly would view the problem of legal system discrimination as extremely serious, but that is not what the data reveal. Black people who directly experience unfair treatment differ from those who view unfair treatment as an important problem for the Black community. Because personal and vicarious experiences are so different, the analyses that follow develop hypotheses that are idiosyncratic to each type of experience.

My findings on psychological group attachments will likely surprise many readers. Just as with their experiences with legal authorities, Black people are not nearly as homogeneous in how they think about themselves and their group. Almost one-fourth of the Black sample did not think it particularly important to think of themselves as Black. An even larger proportion did not see their own fate as linked to the fate of Black people as a whole.

Most importantly, group identities and linked fate are uncorrelated with each other—a finding contrary to the published literature. My tentative understanding of this lack of correlation is that while, just as Henri Tajfel and John Turner have hypothesized, group identities are indeed grounded in the internal psychology of the individual, Black people's sense of linked fate may be more strongly influenced by the external environmental context in which they find themselves (and which therefore can change over time).[17] For now, my minimalist conclusion is that group identification and linked fate are different phenomena in these data, and I must therefore treat them as such throughout the analyses that follow.

Finally, I examined the interrelationships among both measures of identity and both measures of experience. Here my overwhelming conclusion is that these four concepts—group identification, linked fate, personal experiences, and vicarious experiences—differ empirically just as they do theoretically. Even those correlations that are statistically different from zero are not particularly large. In the analyses to come, I examine the direct and conditional relationships that these four concepts have with individuals' attitudes toward America's democratic institutions and processes.

Analysis

Analytical Strategy

As with the analysis of change in attitudes reported in chapter 4, questions about causality inevitably emerge. One way to ameliorate these concerns is to use panel data, with the predictors of support at t_4 confined to those attributes measured at t_3, including a measure of support at t_3. Consequently, the first portion of my analysis is confined to using t_3 measures to predict levels of support for democratic institutions at t_4.

At the same time, however, some important correlates of support were measured only at t_4, including experiences with unfair treatment by legal institutions (both personal and vicarious) and in-group attachments. So that readers can clearly see the effects of different variables on institutional support, I report the findings in a hierarchical regression, using only t_3 predictors in model 1 and expanding the analysis in model 2 to include t_4 predictors. The results for the correlates of support for America's democratic institutions are reported in table 7.2.

Table 7.2 Predictors of African American Support for Democratic Institutions in the African American Panel Survey

Conceptualization/Predictor	Model 1			Model 2		
	b	s.e.	r	b	s.e.	r
Institutional support						
Institutional support (t_3)	**0.48***	0.05	0.61	**0.45***	0.05	0.61
Events awareness and assessments						
Awareness of Barrett confirmation (t_3)	−0.01	0.03	0.07	0.00	0.03	0.07
Evaluation of Barrett confirmation (t_3)	0.03	0.04	−0.01	0.04	0.04	−0.01
Awareness of Trump actions (t_3)	−0.06	0.05	0.10	−0.06	0.05	0.10
Evaluation of Trump actions (t_3)	0.01	0.04	−0.14	0.00	0.04	−0.14
Awareness of election controversy (t_3)	−0.09*	0.05	0.07	−0.07	0.05	0.07
Election unfairness judgments (t_3)	**−0.14***	0.05	−0.24	**−0.13***	0.05	−0.24
Awareness of Capitol insurrection (t_3)	−0.05	0.07	0.13	−0.02	0.07	0.13
Capitol insurrection not harmful (t_3)	−0.08	0.06	−0.14	−0.09	0.06	−0.14
Awareness of Trump impeachment (t_3)	−0.00	0.06	0.12	0.00	0.06	0.12
Trump impeachment not harmful (t_3)	0.02	0.02	0.11	0.02	0.02	0.11
Approval of Trump not convicted (t_3)	0.07	0.04	−0.08	0.04	0.04	−0.08
Party threat assessments						
Belief that Democrats threaten democracy (t_3)	−0.04	0.03	−0.24	−0.04	0.03	−0.24
Belief that Republicans threaten democracy (t_3)	−0.09***	0.03	−0.10	−0.09**	0.03	−0.10
Democratic values and personality						
Support for the rule of law (t_3)	−0.05	0.06	0.28	−0.05	0.06	0.28
Valuation of individual liberty (t_3)	0.09	0.05	0.23	**0.10***	0.03	0.23
Support for civil liberties (t_3)	0.07	0.04	0.13	0.07	0.04	0.13
Open-mindedness (t_3)	**0.17***	0.05	0.26	**0.19***	0.05	0.26
Authoritarianism (t_3)	0.01	0.04	0.04	0.02	0.04	0.04
Partisanship and ideology						
Party identification (t_3)	**−0.14***	0.04	−0.23	**−0.14***	0.04	−0.23
Ideological identification (t_3)	0.05	0.04	0.02	0.04	0.04	0.02
Political sophistication						
Political knowledge (t_3)	0.03	0.04	0.24	0.03	0.04	0.24
Demographic attributes						
Gender (t_3)	−0.01	0.02	0.08	−0.00	0.02	0.08
Age (t_3)	**0.17***	0.05	0.37	**0.13***	0.05	0.37
Level of education (t_3)	−0.02	0.04	0.06	0.01	0.04	0.06
Income (t_3)	0.05	0.04	0.24	0.04	0.04	0.24
Homeownership (t_3)	−0.01	0.02	0.15	−0.02	0.02	0.15
Metropolitan residence (t_3)	−0.01	0.03	0.02	0.01	0.03	0.02
Resident of the South (t_3)	−0.01	0.02	0.08	−0.01	0.02	0.08
Internet access (t_3)	0.07**	0.02	0.02	−0.07**	0.02	0.02
Born-again (t_3)	0.04	0.02	0.06	0.04*	0.02	0.06
Church attendance (t_3)	0.04	0.03	0.25	0.04	0.03	0.25
U.S. citizen (t_3)	−0.01	0.07	−0.02	0.02	0.07	−0.02

Table 7.2 (*continued*)

Conceptualization/Predictor	Model 1 b	Model 1 s.e.	Model 1 r	Model 2 b	Model 2 s.e.	Model 2 r
Group attachments						
Group identification (t_4)	—	—	—	0.01	0.04	−0.14
Linked fate (t_4)	—	—	—	−0.04	0.03	0.02
Experience with unfair treatment						
Personal experience (t_4)	—	—	—	**−0.10***	0.05	−0.13
Vicarious experience (t_4)	—	—	—	−0.07*	0.03	−0.29
Equation						
Intercept	0.33**	0.11	—	0.36***	0.12	
Standard deviation, dependent variable	0.23			0.23		
R^2 (significance of R^2 change)	**0.50***			**0.52***		
Standard error of estimate	0.18			0.17		
N	505			505		

Source: The African American Panel Survey (t_4), June 2021.

Notes: All variables are scored to range from 0 to 1. For their distributions, see table A.14. b = unstandardized regression coefficient; s.e. = standard error of the unstandardized regression coefficient; r = bivariate correlation coefficient. Regression coefficients greater than or equal to 0.10 are shown in boldface. No variables have a variance inflation factor equal to or exceeding 5.0. In both models 1 and 2, the highest VIF score is 2.9, for the variable "awareness of Capitol insurrection."

Significance of unstandardized OLS regression coefficients: * $p \le .05$; ** $p \le .01$; *** $p \le .001$

Findings

The most unsurprising finding from the coefficients reported in table 7.2 is that support at t_3 is very strongly related to support at t_4, in both the bivariate and multivariate analyses. Were this not the case, doubts would be raised about the quality of the measurement of institutional support.

The second important finding is that the variability among African Americans in support for democratic institutions is quite well accounted for by this equation, with about one-half of the variance explained in model 1.

Many of the earlier findings of my analyses are replicated in this table. For instance, most measures of awareness and assessments of the events of the election and its aftermath (measured at t_3) are *not* significantly related to institutional support. At the same time, one of the best predictors of support at t_4 is assessments of the unfairness of the 2020 election, with respondents judging it to have been more unfair extending less support. The relationship, however, is significant only at $p < .01$, and it is not particularly strong. (Recall that all variables are scored to range from 0 to 1.) None of the variables pertaining to the January riots and the subsequent impeachment are in any way related to institutional support.

Indeed, the two best predictors overall are open-mindedness and age. Open-mindedness has shown itself to be a useful variable throughout my analyses: the respondents less likely to see the world as strictly divided into friend and foe—perhaps a psychological precursor to affective polarization—are more likely to extend allegiance to democratic institutions. Paralleling some important new findings on political tolerance, the data also reveal that democratic support is strongest among older Black Americans.[18] The younger generation of African Americans are the most alienated from America's democratic institutions.

Notably, the stronger respondents' attachments to the Republican Party were, the weaker were their attachments to democratic institutions. The relationship was not stronger because 76.2 percent of the respondents identified as either Democrats or strong Democrats. Still, ceteris paribus in a fairly powerful equation, Black Republicans were more likely to reject America's democratic institutions. Ideological identities were not connected, however, with institutional legitimacy.

The most important failed hypotheses pertain to the connection of democratic values with institutional support: none of the three major attitudes is significantly related to change in support for the institutions. This important finding is consistent with the view, often expressed, that attitudes change for reasons that are not necessarily related to why they formed in the first place.

One of the most important and consistent findings of this book is that willingness to extend legitimacy to America's democratic institutions is closely connected to support for more general democratic values (such as support for the rule of law), as shown in figure 6.2. Taking a step back from the data, I might conclude that one's support for democratic institutions is shaped by one's general commitments to democratic values, but that threats to democracy from one's opponents, especially existential threats, provide the fuel for reconsidering legitimacy and perhaps changing one's beliefs. In this view, values are relatively stable with people normally experiencing little incentive to change them. But perceptions of the world, including threat perceptions, can change, and when they do, they can provoke change. Thus, while democratic values may have produced support for institutions, the impetus for change can arise elsewhere.

Adding Experiences and Identities to the Mix

Model 2 in table 7.2 adds to the basic equation the two measures of experiences with unfair treatment (personal and vicarious) and the two measures of group identity (linked fate and group identification). Recall that these attributes were measured at t_4, the same interview in which the dependent variable was measured.

Although neither of the identity variables is connected to support for democratic institutions, personal experiences with unfair treatment are faintly related to institutional support. Respondents who had had more negative experiences with legal authorities were less likely to extend institutional support. The relationship is certainly not strong, but it does point to the potentially poisonous consequences of being treated badly by legal authorities. The relationship between perceived vicarious unfair treatment and institutional support is even weaker, although the coefficient is significant at $p < .05$. Once more, respondents who understood that Black people are treated more unfairly by the legal system were slightly less likely to extend legitimacy to America's democratic institutions, a finding that is perhaps not very surprising.

Notably, adding the four variables measured only at t_4 to the equation does practically nothing to change the results of model 1, which includes only predictors measured at t_3.

Change in Support for the Supreme Court

The t_4 survey investigated attitudes toward democratic institutions in general and attitudes toward the Supreme Court in particular (but not attitudes toward the presidency nor the Senate). The descriptive data on attitudes toward the court at t_3 and t_4 are reported in table 7.1. Recall that African Americans became dramatically less supportive of the court over the course of the few months between the two interviews. Table 7.3 reports the results from regressing support for the court at t_4 on the t_3 predictors (model 1) and the t_4 measures of identifies and experiences (model 2).

Table 7.3 Predictors of African American Support for the U.S. Supreme Court in the African American Panel Survey

Conceptualization/Predictor	Model 1			Model 2		
	b	s.e.	r	b	s.e.	r
Institutional support						
Institutional support (t_3)	**0.56***	0.05	0.60	**0.55***	0.05	0.60
Events awareness and assessments						
Awareness of Barrett confirmation (t_3)	0.04	0.03	0.07	0.05	0.03	0.07
Evaluation of Barrett confirmation (t_3)	0.04	0.03	0.15	0.04	0.03	0.15
Awareness of Trump actions (t_3)	−0.02	0.04	0.05	−0.02	0.04	0.05
Evaluation of Trump actions (t_3)	−0.05	0.04	−0.01	−0.04	0.04	−0.01
Awareness of election controversy (t_3)	−0.01	0.04	0.07	−0.01	0.04	0.07
Election unfairness judgments (t_3)	−0.06	0.04	−0.09	−0.05	0.04	−0.09
Awareness of Capitol insurrection (t_3)	−0.09	0.05	0.07	−0.08	0.05	0.07
Capitol insurrection not harmful (t_3)	−0.08	0.05	−0.05	−0.07	0.05	−0.05
Awareness of Trump impeachment (t_3)	0.01	0.05	0.06	0.01	0.05	0.06
Trump impeachment not harmful (t_3)	0.00	0.02	0.10	0.00	0.02	0.10
Approval of Trump not convicted (t_3)	0.05	0.03	0.01	0.03	0.03	0.01
Party threat assessments						
Belief that Democrats threaten democracy (t_3)	0.07**	0.03	−0.01	0.08**	0.03	−0.01
Belief that Republicans threaten democracy (t_3)	−0.02	0.02	−0.08	−0.01	0.02	−0.08
Democratic values and personality						
Support for the rule of law (t_3)	0.01	0.05	0.29	0.00	0.05	0.29
Valuation of individual liberty (t_3)	−0.07	0.04	0.21	−0.07	0.04	0.21
Support for civil liberties (t_3)	0.04	0.03	0.12	0.05	0.03	0.12
Open-mindedness (t_3)	**0.14***	0.04	0.39	**0.12**	0.04	0.39
Authoritarianism (t_3)	−0.01	0.03	−0.09	−0.00	0.03	−0.09
Partisanship and ideology						
Party identification (t_3)	0.02	0.03	0.03	0.01	0.03	0.03
Ideological identification (t_3)	0.01	0.04	−0.02	0.02	0.04	−0.02
Political sophistication						
Political knowledge (t_3)	0.02	0.03	0.24	0.01	0.03	0.24
Demographic attributes						
Gender (t_3)	0.00	0.02	0.21	0.01	0.02	0.21
Age (t_3)	0.04	0.04	0.12	0.02	0.04	0.12
Level of education (t_3)	−0.04	0.03	0.20	−0.04	0.03	0.20
Income (t_3)	0.03	0.03	0.23	0.02	0.03	0.23
Homeownership (t_3)	−0.03	0.02	0.08	−0.03	0.02	0.08
Metropolitan residence (t_3)	−0.02	0.02	0.05	−0.01	0.02	0.05

Table 7.3 (*continued*)

Conceptualization/Predictor	Model 1			Model 2		
	b	s.e.	r	b	s.e.	r
Resident of the South (t_3)	0.01	0.01	0.05	0.01	0.01	0.05
Internet access (t_3)	0.01	0.02	0.07	0.01	0.02	0.07
Born-again (t_3)	–0.04*	0.02	–0.08	–0.03*	0.02	–0.08
Church attendance (t_3)	0.04	0.03	0.12	–0.04	0.03	0.12
U.S. citizen (t_3)	–0.06	0.04	–0.07	–0.05	0.06	–0.07
Group attachments						
Group identification (t_4)	—	—	—	–0.09**	0.04	–0.25
Linked fate (t_4)	—	—	—	0.01	0.02	0.16
Experiences with unfair treatment						
Personal experience (t_4)	—	—	—	–0.01	0.04	–0.05
Vicarious experience (t_4)	—	—	—	–0.02	0.02	–0.09
Equation						
Intercept	0.22**	0.09		0.29**	0.09	
Standard deviation, dependent variable	0.19			0.19		
R^2 (significance of R^2 change)	**0.45***			**0.46**		
Standard error of estimate	0.14			0.14		
N	505			505		

Source: The African American Panel Survey (t_4), June 2021.

Notes: All variables are scored to range from 0 to 1. For their distributions, see table A.14. b = unstandardized regression coefficient; s.e. = standard error of the unstandardized regression coefficient; r = bivariate correlation coefficient. Regression coefficients greater than or equal to 0.10 are shown in boldface. No variables have a variance inflation factor equal to or exceeding 5.0. For model 1, the highest VIF score is 2.8, for the variable "awareness of Capitol insurrection." For model 2, the same variable registers the highest VIF score, at 2.9.

Significance of unstandardized OLS regression coefficients: * $p \leq .05$; ** $p \leq .01$; *** $p \leq .001$

In model 1, only two variables stand out as substantial predictors of Supreme Court support at t_4: support at t_3 and open-mindedness. In this sense, the results for the Supreme Court are similar to the results reported earlier for democratic institutions in general.[19] The coefficient for the open-mindedness variable indicates that those respondents who were more closed-minded, and hence more likely to perceive existential threats from their enemies, were less likely to support the court at t_4 (controlling for support at t_3). None of the awareness or assessment variables is significantly related to Supreme Court support.

Adding the experience and identity variables in model 2 does practically nothing to alter the findings from model 1. It does, however, reveal a weak but significant ($p < .01$) relationship between group identification and institutional support: the respondents more closely attached to Black people as a group withdrew support from the court. At the same time, the measure of linked fate was not related to court support. Echoing a finding from earlier work, experiences, which tend to reflect interactions with local legal authorities, seem not to contaminate attitudes toward the Supreme Court.[20] Thus, African Americans do not seem to generalize from the local to the national level when it comes to their attitudes toward legal institutions.[21]

An interesting story about partisanship seems to emerge from the findings reported here and in chapter 6. Because Black Americans overwhelmingly identify as Democrats, I did not expect partisanship to play much of a role in changing institutional attitudes. Although table 7.3 documents the irrelevance of partisanship (and of ideological identification as well) for changes in attitudes toward the Supreme Court, table 7.2 provides evidence of a relationship between partisanship and changes in attitudes toward democratic institutions in general: Black Republicans became more alienated from these institutions between March 2021 and June 2021. Recall as well that figure 6.2 reports a relationship between partisanship and support for democratic institutions at t_3 among Black people (although not among White people). Thus, as of March 2021, Black Republicans were more likely to reject democratic institutions *and*, as of June 2021, they had become even more likely to abandon those institutions.

This finding seems to indicate that the effect of the election imbroglio was felt among Black people as long as six months after the balloting and the period when the results were being disputed. It appears that, by June 2021, more Black Republicans had become convinced by arguments that the election was unfair (see table 7.2) and that democratic institutions were therefore not worthy of support. This seems not to have happened with attitudes toward the Supreme Court (which may serve as a mini-robustness check, as the court faded from salience in the early part of 2021). And although the available data are not as dispositive (because no White people were interviewed at t_4), White Republicans' attitudes toward the court seem not to have changed. If this speculation is correct, then a reasonable conclusion is that the consequences of events can indeed take some considerable amount of time to materialize. Finally, these findings must be placed in the context of a quite small proportion of Black people who identify as

Table 7.4 Bivariate Correlations of African Americans' Institutional Support and Democratic Values

Democratic Values at t_3	Support for Democratic Institutions			Support for the Supreme Court		
	t_3	t_4	Change	t_3	t_4	Change
Support for the rule of law	0.40***	0.28***	−0.12**	0.46***	0.29***	−0.21***
Valuation of individual liberty	0.27***	0.23***	−0.04	0.34***	0.21***	−0.16***
Support for civil liberties	0.11*	0.13**	0.02	0.13**	0.12	−0.02

Source: The African American Panel Survey (t_4), June 2021.

Notes: Entries are bivariate correlation coefficients. $N = 505$.

Significance of Pearson correlation coefficient: * $p \leq .05$; ** $p \leq .01$; *** $p \leq .001$

Republicans and an equally small proportion of African Americans who rated Trump's efforts to overturn the election as acceptable (see table 6.1).

Here I return for a moment to the finding that democratic values have few consequences for change in institutional support, a finding that, with the exception of open-mindedness, characterizes both support for democratic institutions in general and support for the Supreme Court. I argued earlier that the factors creating change in any given attitude are not necessarily the same as the factors that led to the formation of the attitude in the first place. Table 7.4 reports data relevant to that speculation. It shows the correlations of support for the institutions at t_3, at t_4, and for change in support from t_3 to t_4. The predictor variables are the same measures of democratic values that I have used throughout this book, all measured at t_3.

The pattern revealed in this table is familiar.[22] Support for the rule of law is a strong predictor of institutional attitudes, followed by the valuation attached to individual liberty.[23] The strongest support for the argument that the causes of change can differ from the causes of the formation of attitudes can be found in the contemporaneous correlations of democratic values and institutional attitudes, which are all stronger than the correlations of values and the measure of change. For instance, respondents who valued liberty more than order were more likely to extend legitimacy to institutions (r = 0.27 and 0.34), but they were not more likely to change their views of democratic institutions (r = −0.04) and were only slightly more likely to withdraw support from the Supreme Court (r = −0.16). The driving force for change in institutional support is clearly not support for democratic values. Turning back to the results reported in tables 7.2 and 7.3, the driving force instead may be that closed-minded people are predisposed to perceive existential threats from their opponents and thus to withdraw support from these institutions. Pursuing these conjectures further, however, is certainly beyond the scope of this project.

Discussion and Concluding Thoughts

Perhaps the most eye-catching finding of this chapter is the dramatic decline in African Americans' support for America's democratic institutions, and especially the Supreme Court, over just a few short months between the t_3 and t_4 interviews. Indeed, the 26.1 percent of African Americans who agreed that, "if the U.S. Supreme Court started making a lot of decisions that most people disagree with, it might be better to do away with the Court altogether" likely represents the highest level of rejection of the Supreme Court's authority that any survey has ever reported. The statement is, of course, hypothetical and conditional. But by most scholarly accounts, the court is very close to satisfying the condition of "making a lot of decisions that most people disagree with."[24] Moreover, 41.7 percent of the Black respondents said that they had lost faith in American political institutions, with 30.2 percent agreeing that the institutions ought to be scrapped and that we should just start over. These findings are worrisome.

I have not succeeded, however, in pinpointing the sources of the change in support for America's democratic institutions among African Americans. I expected that the institutional alienation would reflect the unfair treatment of Black people by legal authorities—both personal and vicarious—and at least some support for that expectation is provided by the data. But the relationships are modest at best. The causes of institutional alienation seem to be far broader than personal or vicarious experiences.

Nor do in-group attachments play much of a role in accounting for changing support. Attitudes toward democratic institutions do not seem to be tied up in factors such as the degree to which Black people see their fates as being affected by their group membership or even by the degree to which they identify with Black people as a group. The rejection of the legitimacy of these institutions does not require a strong sense of in-group solidarity among Black people.

Like White Americans, Black Americans derive their views of political institutions from their more general commitments to democratic values. As I have shown, African Americans are less strongly committed to those values, and therefore it follows that they would extend less support to the institutions.

But democratic values cannot explain the changes the data have uncovered. Nor do I see much evidence that the changes occurred in response to the events of the election, the insurrection, and the impeachment. As chapter 6 reveals, Black people and White people certainly saw and judged those events differently, but Black people's awareness and assessments of those events do not account for much variation in support for institutions (chapter 6) and play an even smaller role in change in support for institutions (this chapter). It may be that perceptions of events must fester for some amount of time in order to induce change. But I have no statistical evidence directly supporting that conclusion.

Instead, the most powerful predictor of change in support for democratic institutions, including support for the Supreme Court, is open-mindedness; specifically, closed-minded Black people tend to become less willing to grant legitimacy to the institutions. Recall that one indicator of this concept is agreement with the statement: "To compromise with our political opponents is dangerous because it usually leads to the betrayal of our own side." Respondents agreeing with this sentiment were those who extended less support to political institutions, though not necessarily because they saw threats to democracy emanating from either the Democrats or the Republicans. Instead, I have referred to this tendency as a propensity to perceive existential threats that leads people who do not feel protected by the existing institutions to not support them.

Without a doubt, researchers have much more to unravel and test here. Nevertheless, I am confident that seeing the opposition as the enemy seems to undermine the willingness to commit to the U.S. institutions of democracy. Change, of course, is about more than open-mindedness, and additional thought, inquiry, and testing are certainly required. And obviously the findings of this chapter pertain only to Black Americans; additional research on White attitude change, as well as change among minority groups other than African Americans, is also essential.

CHAPTER 8

Destroying Democracy?

I think the next four years will determine whether, 50 years from now, people will look back on this as a bad moment in American history, the way you might [have] looked at the Civil War as a bad moment in American history, or look back on it as the moment when America's democracy perished.

> —Harvard Law School professor Lawrence Lessig, quoted in Melissa Gismondi, "American Democracy Is at a Precipice, Experts Say. And Time Is Ticking." CBC, September 29, 2022

The U.S. still has a chance to fix itself before 2024. But when democracies start dying—as ours already has—they usually don't recover.

> —Brian Klaas, "America's Self-Obsession Is Killing Its Democracy," *Atlantic*, July 21, 2022

The United States faces a serious risk that the 2024 presidential election, and other future U.S. elections, will not be conducted fairly, and that the candidates taking office will not reflect the free choices made by eligible voters under previously announced election rules.

> —Election law expert and professor Rick Hasen, "Identifying and Minimizing the Rise of Election Subversion and Stolen Elections in the Contemporary United States, *Harvard Law Review Forum* 135

THE PRIMARY MOTIVATION for conducting this research and writing this book was to determine whether the events of the 2020 presidential election and its aftermath did lasting damage to three American political institutions. After traversing a great deal of theoretical, conceptual, and empirical terrain, I believe I have discovered a relatively simple answer to

https://doi.org/10.7758/dvkr4409.4693

that question: try as they might (and did), Trump and his Republicans did not in fact succeed in undermining the three American national political institutions investigated in this book.

I have developed some understanding as to why this was the case. First, for many people, alienation from American political institutions likely predated the 2020 election. Many Americans did not withdraw support from the institutions because of the 2020 election, but because they had already withdrawn support *before* the election. The election events may well have simply reconfirmed their alienation rather than produced it. By the time of the 2020 events, many Americans were already alienated and polarized.

Many Americans heard Trump's whines about the election[1] but did not accept them (that is, in addition to the eighty-six judges who ruled against Trump's various election objections),[2] just as Nelson and I found regarding Trump's attack on judges, and as in Kalmoe and Mason's discovery that Trump's exhortations to violence fell on deaf ears.[3] Even many of his supporters concluded that the charges of a fraudulent election did not originate from a credible source.[4] That wild allegations from a noncredible source, with most credible sources making contrary arguments, failed to persuade many Americans of the bankruptcy of American political institutions should not be surprising.

Controversial issues do not always create a backlash, but the Trump-led assault on American democracy may have done so.[5] Some people who previously took the American system for granted mobilized in its defense.[6] Whatever democratic alienation Trump and the Republicans were able to stoke may well have been counterbalanced by the efforts of those who rose for the first time to the defense of American democracy.

Public opinion is notably difficult to change. Many models of public opinion identify two main sources of resistance to change. The first is being tuned out: people who are oblivious to public affairs are unlikely to be changed by those events. I have shown in this research, however, that the election events, the January riot, and the impeachment were all highly salient to Americans, so this part of the model is an unlikely source of resistance to change.

The second source of resistance to change, and a major mechanism, is motivated reasoning. People who hold well-formed attitudes and ideological commitments are unlikely to be influenced by information that is disruptive to or inconsistent with those views. Attitude change is most likely to take place when new information arrives "under the radar." Visible contrary information is typically subject to counterargumentation, which can undo its effect on attitude change. The events of the 2020 election and its aftermath certainly did not evade most people's radars, even as, for many, they most likely did little more than reinforce preexisting beliefs, values, and attitudes.

Some readers may be puzzled that I draw essentially the same conclusions about the effects of the election imbroglio and the insurrection. Despite Trump and his MAGA-ites' ("make America great again") efforts to create boldfaced lies about the attack on the Capitol, the January 6 events seem to have proved less ambiguous and less subject to prevarication than the election events—or at least so it seems as I write this in late 2022 in the midst of the exhaustive House of Representatives investigation of the insurrection.[7] Perhaps the full effects of those events materialized slowly and were therefore not captured in my February and March 2021 survey; perhaps the insurrection needed more time to simmer to reach its full potency. The findings from my sample of African Americans (who were last interviewed in June 2021) certainly indicate that this is possible. Still, substantial material differences exist between challenging an election outcome in a court (even if entirely baselessly) and mounting an assault on the Capitol and the American government in front of a multitude of television cameras. Nevertheless, I draw essentially the same conclusion from my findings about the events before and after January 6: few consequences for the legitimacy of these three institutions seem to have emerged. This conclusion is surprising and unexpected. In the end, support for these democratic institutions did not look too different after the election and its aftermath from how it had looked prior to November 2020.

Because it is reasonable to expect Black people to respond differently to the events of the 2020 election and its aftermath, I invested heavily in African American oversamples in my surveys. The investment seems to have been worthwhile, because many if not most of these results differ when it comes to African Americans. All too often, scholars of public opinion in the United States pay little attention to the views of subgroups. Indeed, an important contribution of this book is its sustained focus on Black public opinion.

Hypothesizing that Black people and White people reacted differently to the 2020 presidential election and its aftermath turned out to be prescient.[8] I not only discovered that African Americans extend less support to these democratic institutions but also made some progress in understanding why. Black people are far more likely than others to have been unfairly treated by legal authorities, and even those who have not experienced such treatment themselves perceive Black people as a group that is typically treated unfairly. This sense of vicarious victimization most likely became more widespread after the George Floyd murder in Minnesota, by way of strengthening in-group attachments and identities. In addition, Black people tend to express less support for basic democratic values (such as support for the rule of law) compared with others; when weakened allegiance to democratic values is coupled with enhanced intergroup threat perceptions, their withdrawal of support for democratic institutions is an understandable consequence. So, while I conclude that the events of the 2020 election and its aftermath had few consequences for Americans as a whole, the effect on Black Americans was more substantial and more worrisome. When allegiance to these democratic institutions becomes polarized by race and ethnicity in ways it has not been polarized by partisanship or ideology, highly unwelcome consequences may follow.

This somewhat simplified view of the consequences of the 2020 presidential election and its aftermath is not without its limitations and will undoubtedly be resisted by some observers for several reasons (perhaps including motivated reasoning). I therefore anticipate, as the final step in my analyses, some of the unanswered questions about my evidence and conclusions and offer some defenses and rejoinders (as well as a handful of concessions and admissions). I offer this in the time-honored scientific tradition of making explicit some of the limitations of my research.

Unanswered Questions and Challenges to My Conclusions

Thus far in this concluding chapter I have described what I know about the effects of the election and insurrection on the health of these democratic institutions. Much remains, however, that I do not know. Therefore, in the rest of this chapter, I address what I anticipate being some of the most burning unanswered questions about the findings reported here.

*Why Do My Conclusions Run Counter to Those of
Many Other Observers of American Politics?*

I am not the first to consider the question whether the events of the Trump era have damaged American democracy. As Thomas Meaney put it in the somewhat different context of a book review, now is a "time when professional doom-mongering about democracy has become one of the most inflationary sections of the American economy."[9] But with only some exceptions (discussed later), not many observers are as sanguine about democracy's resilience as I may seem to be. Can my relatively optimistic findings on the legitimacy of these three institutions be reconciled with the views of doomsayers?

My theoretical and conceptual focus in this research is on the legitimacy of democratic institutions in the United States. Legitimacy, simply put, is recognition of an institution's right to make authoritative decisions for a polity, irrespective of whether those decisions are approved of by its constituents. This definition goes to the heart of the distinction between diffuse and specific support, concepts embedded in legitimacy theory for decades. Diffuse support and legitimacy are equivalent to loyalty; specific support is the same thing as performance approval. A constituent can be disappointed in the performance of an institution in the short term but still be loyal to that institution (the analogy to interpersonal loyalty is quite apposite). I acknowledge that *sustained* disappointment with the performance of an institution can undermine its legitimacy.[10] So long as constituents "win" some of the time, however, many are willing to continue to support the authority of the institution. Of course, diffuse support and specific support are interconnected to at least some degree, but the entire point of legitimacy theory is that constituents will continue to support an institution even when they are "losers," that is, they will accept decisions of which they disapprove.

My analysis focuses primarily on legitimacy, not on performance evaluations. My basic finding is that even when people embraced the assault by Trump and Republicans on the election and on the Capitol, they did not seem to withdraw much support from these three political institutions. At the same time, those who condemned the assaults on the election and the Capitol did not differ much in their levels of support from those embracing the "Big Lie." Perhaps both sides in the conflagration wanted American political institutions to function fairly and effectively.

I acknowledge that perhaps other aspects of democratic infrastructure (including institutions other than the three investigated here) and culture (for example, levels of polarization) can be damaged even while leaving these institutions intact. Thus, this book may tell only part of the story of the overall health of American democracy.

Nevertheless, my research is noteworthy for its commitment to transparency about the items I used to measure institutional legitimacy and the methodological basis on which I reached my conclusions. At least some observers who draw the most dire and alarmist conclusions about the future of American democracy are far less specific about the empirical bases of their conclusions. For better or for worse, I am not.

In the same vein, some scholars have argued that the evidence of democracy's demise in the United States is not nearly as strong as is typically assumed. For instance, Amel Ahmed concludes that "the question of whether the American public is truly turning away from democracy could not be more pressing. The explosion of research on this question, however, has yielded no clear answers, as various studies have produced mixed and contradictory findings."[11] More specifically, and as a prime example, Ahmed takes issue with the influential research of Graham and Svolik:

> Importantly, the study reports the strongest findings for items considered least threatening and the weakest findings for items posing the greatest threat: "Respondents most severely punish candidates who want to prosecute journalists (16.1%) and ignore court rulings (14.1%). Respondents are least sensitive to candidates who endorse gerrymandering (by 2 [seats], 10.6%) and suggest that the governor ban protests or rule by executive order (10.2 and 10.5%, respectively)" (Graham and Svolik 2020, 402). While there is a positive finding for all items, this suggests that the overall threat represented in these findings may not be as severe as it would appear based on an undifferentiated view of transgressions.

Perhaps even more seriously, Ahmed argues that the larger literature addresses such different aspects of democratic backsliding that no uniform conclusions are possible: "The problem here is not that these studies are measuring different things but that they all purport to be measuring the same thing, which can lead to misleading interpretations, exaggerating the threat in some areas and downplaying it in others."[12] My study is focused specifically on the legitimacy of three democratic institutions. On that singular aspect of democracy, I find little compelling evidence of backsliding.

Can a Representative Survey of the Preferences of Americans Really Tell Us Much about the Well-being of America's Democratic Institutions?

Without any doubt whatsoever, this book is about what legal scholars refer to as sociological legitimacy. That is, this is a study of the willingness of ordinary people to extend legitimacy to America's democratic institutions. Although many observers believe that democracies require constituents on the whole to see their courts and other political institutions as legitimate, I am not required in an empirical study to make normative judgments about whether current levels of legitimacy are good or bad.[13]

Being the author of a study of a representative sample of ordinary people, I must acknowledge two important points. First, it could easily take far less than a majority of Americans to overthrow the current democratic system. After all, the rioters in Washington, D.C., on January 6, 2021, were small in number and in no sense a representative sample of the American people. Allegiance from 60 percent—or 70, 80, or even 90 percent—of a sample may not be enough to protect democratic institutions from a determined antidemocratic minority, even if the malcontents constitute no more than 10 percent of the population. Political scientists are in broad agreement that a political culture supportive of democratic institutions and processes is essential to the viability of democracy but have reached no consensus about how widespread opposition to democracy must be to threaten democratic institutions.

Second, the views of elites may be more important than the views of regular people. No student of public opinion would argue that public policies are shaped simply by what the majority of the people want. Institutions are undoubtedly important—the absence of a system of one person/one vote in the United States (and the presence of institutions such as federalism, the Electoral College, and the filibuster) profoundly influences American politics. The so-called elitist theory of democracy places much more weight on the preferences of elites than on the preferences of the mass public.[14] No political scientists seriously argue that the majority in the United States "rules."

On the other hand, without some support from a sizable proportion of

Americans, an overthrow attempt by antidemocratic canards would struggle to succeed. This is true in two senses. First, and most obviously, elections can only be said to be rigged when the voting outcome is close. (Even the most ardent MAGA adherents cannot believe that voter fraud affected the outcome of the 2020 presidential vote in Vermont, where about two-thirds of the voters voted for Biden!) Second, elites routinely make appeals to their constituents; some gain traction, and others do not. Marc Howard and I advance this argument regarding anti-Semitism in the former Soviet Union.[15] Around the time of the breakup of the Soviet Union, right-wing elites made anti-Jewish appeals to the Soviet people; those appeals fell on deaf ears because anti-Semitism was not a strong motivating force for most of the Soviet people. All political scientists believe in elite leadership of mass opinion, but few believe that public opinion can be reshaped easily, quickly, or profoundly. As I say, elites place many offers before the American people, and some are accepted but others are rejected. We should not concede that elites always—or even often—necessarily get what they want.

Still, no political scientist would argue that a majority of the people in the United States routinely get the policies they want.[16] Some combination of the preferences of the mass public, the aggressiveness and leadership of elites, and the frailty of institutions must exist for democracy to be cast aside.

Does What People Say in Survey Interviews Represent Their True Beliefs and Do True Beliefs Actually Matter?

This book is based on the responses of people who sat down in front of their computer or their phone and answered my questions. That these questions were based on topics they may not have thought about a great deal is a critique pertinent to all survey research. And even if some respondents may lie about whether they support Trump, few scholars have advanced the view that people lie about how they feel about the Supreme Court.

Another frequently heard complaint is that attitudes do not in fact predict behavior. It turns out that this criticism is empirically false. The overall conclusion of a variety of published meta-analyses of the relationship between attitudes and behaviors is that attitudes are moderately related to behavior, although the relationship is often moderated and mediated (context matters).[17] Unquestionably, research rejects the view that attitudes are irrelevant to actual behavior, even if they are far from perfect predictors of behavior. Attitudes toward the legitimacy of American political institutions clearly have consequences for the political activities of many Americans.[18] The complaint that people misrepresent views that have no actual political consequences is one of the least trenchant criticisms of this research.

Have My Measures of Institutional Support "Stacked the Deck" against Finding an Effect of the 2020 Election and Insurrection?

The measures of institutional legitimacy reported in this book that have been in the widest and longest use by scholars pertain to the Supreme Court. Generally, voluminous research has found that institutional support changes at a snail's pace and not by much; the "poster child" for this conclusion is the impact of the Supreme Court's 2001 ruling in *Bush v. Gore* (which awarded the presidency to the Republican candidate, George W. Bush). Scholars have debated the magnitude of the impact of rulings in individual cases (for example, challenges to Obamacare), but the bulk of the evidence indicates that change among the dissatisfied is small (at most). And whether short-term changes in legitimacy in fact persist is unclear. Most findings examining change in Supreme Court support therefore conclude that legitimacy is obdurate and resistant to change (but see chapter 7 on change among African Americans). However, some observers may be skeptical about whether the measures of legitimacy are capable of registering change when it does in fact occur; they may wonder whether the measures are too coarse or too abstract to be capable of capturing meaningful attitudinal change.

I present important new evidence on this score in a recent article examining the impact of the Supreme Court's ruling in *Dobbs v. Jackson Women's Health Organization* (2022), the case overturning the abortion and privacy rights first announced by the court in *Roe v. Wade* (1973).[19] I find what I describe as the largest impact on the court's legitimacy of dissatisfaction with any individual decision that has been studied. By abrogating abortion and privacy rights, the court substantially undermined its own legitimacy. In that analysis, I provide unequivocal evidence that Supreme Court support can be responsive to unwanted rulings in at least some issue domains, and that the measures commonly adopted to measure legitimacy can in fact register changes in institutional legitimacy.

My *Dobbs* study is based in small part on the survey data reported in this book. The analysis makes note of the contrast in institutional support from before and after the Barrett nomination and confirmation and support from before and after *Dobbs*. The findings from that research are shown in figure 8.1.

Figure 8.1 Pre- to Post-*Dobbs* Change in Indicators of U.S. Supreme Court Legitimacy

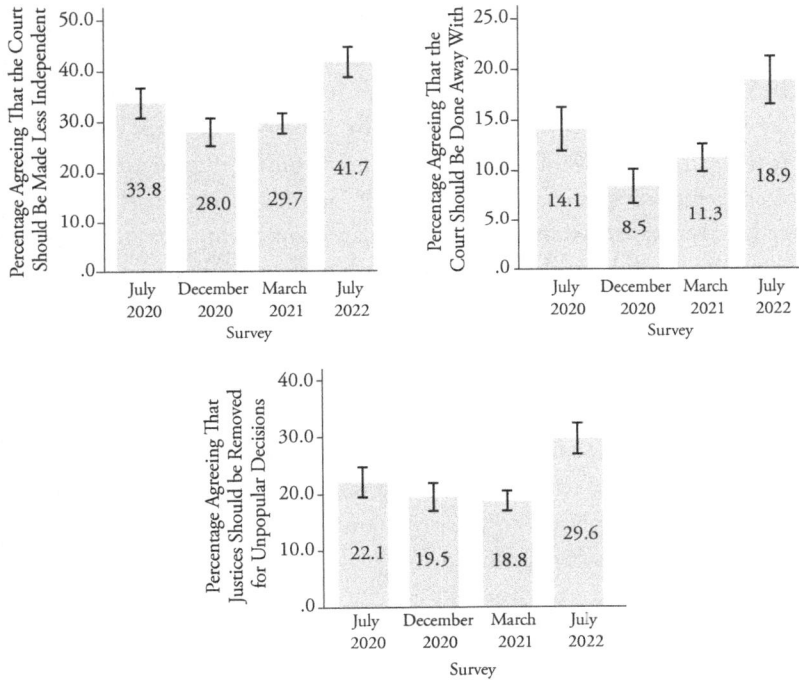

Sources: The 2020 Freedom and Tolerance Survey (t$_1$), July 2020; The 2020 Pre-insurrection Survey (t$_2$), December 2020 and January 2021; The 2021 Insurrection and Impeachment Survey (t$_3$), February and March 2021; NORC AmeriSpeak, 2022 Post-*Dobbs* Survey (t$_5$), July 2022.
Notes: The items posed (with a five-point Likert response set) were:

(*The court should be made less independent*): The U.S. Supreme Court ought to be made less independent so that it listens a lot more to what the people want.
(*The court should be done away with*): If the U.S. Supreme Court started making a lot of decisions that most people disagree with, it might be better to do away with the Court altogether.
(*Justices should be removed for unpopular decisions*): Justices on the U.S. Supreme Court who consistently make unpopular decisions should be removed from their position as justice.

The differences of means across surveys of the uncollapsed responses are all statistically significant at *p* < .001.

The results from four surveys are reported in this figure: t_1 through t_3 are the surveys analyzed in this book; t_5 is a nationally representative survey conducted (also by NORC) after the Supreme Court overturned *Roe v. Wade*. The t_5 survey was able to ask only three institutional support questions, so the comparison is limited to the responses to those items.

From July 2020 until March 2021 practically no change in support for the court seems to have taken place; indeed, whatever change occurred seems to have enhanced its legitimacy. After the *Dobbs* decision, change clearly appears to have detracted from its legitimacy. The change in support from before the Barrett confirmation to after it (from t_1 to t_2) is particularly striking when juxtaposed with the change from before the *Dobbs* ruling to after it (from t_3 to t_5). While my *Dobbs* study produced no evidence that the loss of legitimacy persisted over time,[20] this research clearly confirms that under some circumstances legitimacy can be undermined and that the indicators used in this book are indeed capable of registering change.

But what of the institutional legitimacy of the presidency and the Senate? Unfortunately, since this project invented new measures of support for these institutions, I can adduce no evidence supporting the conclusion that the indicators change when actual legitimacy changes. However, the similarity in the items used to measure the legitimacy of the Supreme Court and the Senate strongly suggests that the Senate items can in fact register change when it actually takes place. For the presidency measures, I have no empirical basis for drawing a conclusion.

Does the Empirical Analysis Reported in This Book Accurately Describe the Causal Structures of the Various Attitudes?

The simple and honest answer to this question is, no, it may not.

All research based on surveys of public attitudes faces at least two major obstacles: internal validity and external validity. Internal validity refers to the degree of confidence in causal inferences, a continuum ranging from 0 to 100 percent certainty. External validity refers to the generalizability of the conclusions and is affected not just by factors influencing the representativeness of the sample (and factors such as "total survey error") but also by the "mundane realism" of the questions asked.[21] External validity can also be seen as a continuum of certainty ranging from complete uncertainty about the generalizability of the findings to complete certainty.

Social scientists today are greatly concerned about internal validity, which they typically privilege over external validity.[22] My responses to the challenges of internal validity in the analyses in this book have been multi-faceted. First, relatively fixed attributes of the respondent (for example, gender) are highly unlikely to be affected by external events and attitudes toward politics. How individuals' attitudes toward the Supreme Court could affect their genders, for instance, is difficult for me to understand. Other demographic attributes may not be fixed (for example, homeowner-ship), but they too are unlikely to be influenced by a willingness to extend legitimacy to America's democratic institutions.

In some portions of this research, I am able to marshal panel data to measure the independent variables prior to the dependent variables. Panel surveys have become popular with social scientists, but of course panel data do not by themselves allow causal inferences of perfect certainty, even if they definitely "move the needle" on certainty. Using independent variables measured at t_1 to predict dependent variables measured at t_{1+1} is a time-honored means of increasing the internal validity of conclusions.

A fair amount of the research reported here relies on cross-sectional data, with the independent and dependent variables measured at the same point in time. For one of the central concerns of this research—assessing the im-pact of awareness and assessment of the 2020 election and insurrection events—no alternative with two-wave panel data was possible: I could not ask at t_1 about events that had not yet happened. An expensive but not very practical solution in most instances would have been to measure indepen-dent variables at t_1, perceptions of events at t_2, and the dependent variables at t_3.[23] In situations like the 2020 election and insurrection of January 6, 2021, in which events were fast moving and seemingly ever more shocking, such a research design would have been very difficult to implement (al-though my analysis in chapter 7 takes a stab at implementing a variant of this approach).

I have responded to the limitations of analyzing cross-sectional data in several ways, most commonly by asserting the caveat that what my statisti-cal analysis shows is "what goes with what." This is unlikely to satisfy causal purists. Importantly, when I observe no relationship between two variables, I can conclude that one does not cause the other with at least a moderate degree of certainty. I use this argument often with regard to the impact of awareness and assessments of election events.

I must acknowledge, of course, that the lack of correlation between two variables has more than a single explanation. The first and most favored explanation in this research is truth. The second is random measurement error, although I am careful throughout to report evidence on the validity and reliability of my measures and am typically able to conclude that the measurement error is not a likely culprit for weak relationships.[24] The third explanation is heterogeneity: that the overall relationship is zero on average does not necessarily mean that the relationship is zero for all subgroups in the population. Finally, suppression is a form of spuriousness that can undermine the conclusion that two variables are not causally related. Nevertheless, when repeated analyses of cross-sectional surveys all show that X and Y are not connected (for example, X = awareness and assessments of events, and Y = legitimacy), then researchers can be reasonably certain about the conclusion that X does not cause Y.

My research does not suffer much from external validity concerns. Some observers certainly believe that what respondents type on their computer or phone about the legitamacy of institutions has little relationship to political action in the real world. I am a bit sympathetic to that argument, although I have long subscribed to the theory that attitudes cause behavioral intentions and, in the right context, behavioral intentions cause actual behavior. My surveys seem to suffer from no greater threat to external validity than the usual studies of public opinion, especially given the quality of the NORC surveys that generated the data I analyze here.

Different research projects ascribe different degrees of importance to external and internal validity. As I noted, the trend in the social sciences today is to worry a great deal about internal validity and not so much about external validity. That trend is punctuated by the use of inexpensive opt-in samples, which have proliferated to such an unimaginable degree that the social sciences sought to find a way to justify the use of such flawed, if quite inexpensive, samples (often by some sort of weighting scheme). Researchers who fret about external validity are currently in the minority in the social sciences.[25]

The dominant approach to the internal validity issue involves experiments; thus, if experiments are embedded in representative surveys, researchers kill two birds with one stone. I have been an early and frequent advocate of the use of experiments implemented within representative samples. Experiments inevitably use hypothetical scenarios.

Survey respondents, no doubt, have limits to their imaginations. A survey might ask me to imagine that I shot someone on Fifth Avenue, or that I owned a Lamborghini, and I would undoubtedly answer that I could do so. Whether these imagined scenarios are too unreal to be useful for saying anything about the real world, as opposed to the survey world, is unclear to me in many circumstances.[26]

In the end, assessments of both the internal and external validity of research findings are highly subjective. Does weighting fully repair unrepresentative opt-in samples, as required by the assumption, for instance, that young people who take surveys are the same as young people who do not take surveys? Do panel surveys provide foolproof evidence of causality, even though, for some variables, the time at which they are measured is not of much relevance? Do the tasks we ask subjects to perform in experiments parallel tasks in real life, especially when a great many subjects fail the checks of comprehension of the manipulations? Are events in any meaningful sense exogenous, and what are the consequences of falsely assuming that they are? What should we make of the evidence that so many important social science research findings cannot be replicated? These are all questions with no clear answers, either for my research or for that of others, but are nevertheless essential for all researchers to acknowledge.

Do the Surveys Actually Show That African Americans Are Less Willing to Extend Legitimacy to U.S. Democratic Institutions?

Perhaps they do, in the sense that African Americans extend less support to these contemporary political institutions (with the important exception of the presidency and the president) and are less supportive of basic democratic values such as the rule of law. The answer is no, however, when we acknowledge that African Americans seem to lack the political power to have much impact on the persistence and efficacy of those institutions.

That Black people are less likely to extend support to the political institutions considered here is, of course, unsurprising. About 40 percent of most Black samples report having been treated unfairly by legal authorities, and such experiences undoubtedly do not enhance the legitimacy respondents extend to the authorities meting out such treatment. The thrust of my research with Nelson on Black attitudes toward legal authorities is that local experiences and institutions do *not* generalize to attitudes toward national institutions, but those findings are certainly dated, having been based on a 2014 survey conducted in a pre–George Floyd world.[27] The evidence reported in chapters 6 and 7 suggests that experiences with unfair treatment by legal authorities, both personal and vicarious, are important predictors of alienation from America's democratic institutions. Being treated unfairly has taken its toll; were other groups treated the way Black Americans have been, their allegiance to democracy in America would surely have faltered as well.

What Do This Study's Findings Imply about Future Threats to America's Democratic Institutions?

This is perhaps the most important question unanswered by my research.

My answer to whether Trump and his allies undermined these democratic institutions is succinct: Not yet!

At the time of this writing in the fall of 2022, Americans have been preparing and organizing for the 2024 presidential election. Many fear that the assault on U.S. democratic institutions has only just begun. Perhaps the greatest apprehension of the protectors of American democracy is that Trump and his Republicans have learned some important lessons from the 2020 election and its aftermath: they now know that not all Republicans (including Republican judges) can be trusted to help subvert democracy; that low-level election functionaries perform many tasks crucial to a fair counting of the votes; that voter suppression is essential to Republican electoral victories; and that state legislatures (especially those adroitly gerrymandered) are a possible mechanism for subverting the will of the voters. I have no doubt whatsoever that antidemocratic Republicans are not stupid, and I strongly suspect that as I write this sentence, they are devising schemes to more effectively subvert the next presidential election.

They may even learn something from this book! In some (quite limited) sense, this book may be an example of the Heisenberg Principle, which, simply put, is that the very act of measuring and describing something changes the fundamental characteristics of the thing being measured and described. The commanding conclusion of this book is that these institutions are resilient. If that is so, then perhaps punches in the future do not need to be pulled. While Russia may not care that defeating Ukraine may require destroying that country, the MAGA-ites probably do not want to eviscerate entirely the Senate, the Supreme Court, or even the power of the presidency. The lesson of this book is that to undo institutional legitimacy is difficult indeed. I hope that that lesson does not somehow contribute to the further endangerment of democracy in the United States.

Last Thoughts

In the final analysis, perhaps a democracy needs to face some threats from time to time if citizens are to fully appreciate its value as a form of self-governance.[28] As Boris Yeltsin once said: "We don't appreciate what we have until it's gone. Freedom is like that. It's like air. When you have it, you don't notice it."[29] Or as Joni Mitchell once sang:

> Don't it always seem to go
> that you don't know what you got 'til it's gone
> they paved paradise and put up a parking lot.[30]

Such tests of democratic commitments, however, can be harrowing and foreboding. And the current test of American democracy is far from over.

APPENDIX

Chapter 1

A summary of the survey data used in this book is provided in table A.1. Details on each of the individual surveys follow.

The 2020 Freedom and Tolerance Survey (t_1), July 2020

The fieldwork for the 2020 Freedom and Tolerance Survey was conducted by NORC. Funded and operated by NORC at the University of Chicago, AmeriSpeak is a probability-based panel designed to be representative of the U.S. household population. Randomly selected U.S. households are sampled using area probability and address-based sampling, with a known, nonzero probability of selection from the NORC National Sample Frame. These sampled households are then contacted by U.S. mail, through telephone calls, and by field interviewers (face-to-face). The panel provides sample coverage of approximately 97 percent of the U.S. household population. People excluded from the sample include those with a PO box–only address or an address not listed in the USPS Delivery Sequence File, as well as some who live in a newly constructed dwelling. Most AmeriSpeak households participate in surveys by web, but households without internet access can participate in AmeriSpeak surveys by telephone. Households that lack conventional internet access but have web access via smartphones are allowed to participate in AmeriSpeak surveys by web. AmeriSpeak panelists participate in NORC studies or studies conducted by NORC on behalf of

https://doi.org/10.7758/dvkr4409.1907

Table A.1 Survey Work Completed for This Study's Analyses

Survey	Population	Date	N	Funding
Freedom and Tolerance Survey (t_1)	Nationally representative	July 2020	1,006	Washington University in St. Louis
Post-election Survey (t_2)	Reinterview of July 2020 respondents	December 2020 through	689 reinterviews	Washington University in St. Louis
	Nationally representative	January 5, 2021	337 new respondents	
			1,026 (total)	
Post-insurrection Survey (t_3)	Nationally representative	February and March 2021	2,019 (total)	Russell Sage Foundation
	African American oversample		680 African Americans	Washington University in St. Louis
	Active college student oversample		316 active college students	Foundation for Individual Rights in Education
African American Panel Survey (t_4)	Reinterview of Post-insurrection Survey Black respondents	June 2021	579	Washington University in St. Louis

Source: Author's compilation.

a variety of governmental agencies, academic researchers, and media and commercial organizations.

A general population sample of U.S. adults ages eighteen and older was selected from NORC's AmeriSpeak Panel for this study. This survey was offered only in English and was administered on the web and over the phone. Invitations to participate in the survey were initiated on July 1, 2020, and the last interviews were completed on July 24, 2020. In total, NORC collected 1,006 interviews, 950 in web mode and 56 in phone mode.

To encourage study cooperation, NORC sent five email reminders to sampled web-mode respondents. Panelists were offered the cash equivalent of $5 for completing the study. Interviewed respondents took twenty-nine minutes (median) to complete the survey.[1] NORC applied cleaning rules to the survey data for quality control by removing responses in the main study from ineligible respondents. Because their responses indicated that they had sped through the survey and skipped questions, they were not included in the final dataset.

The data are weighted, with various factors going into the construction of the final study weight: (1) panel base sampling weights, (2) final panel weights, (3) study-specific base sampling weights, and (4) non-response-adjusted survey weights. The weighted American Association for Public Opinion Research (AAPOR) Response Rate #3 recruitment rate was 23.6 percent, with a weighted household retention rate of 84.8 percent and a survey completion rate of 28.4 percent. A weighted AAPOR Response Rate #3 cumulative response rate of 5.7 percent was achieved. The survey has a margin of error of 4.17 percent and a design effect of 1.82.

This research was approved by the Washington University in St. Louis Institutional Review Board, which judged this project to be in the "exempt" category given that participation in the survey was voluntary, no harm was afflicted on the respondents, and no identifiers were connected to the database generated, among other factors.

The 2020 Pre-insurrection Survey (t_2), December 2020 and January 2021

The t_2 survey for this project was based on a hybrid survey design: a portion of the respondents from the July 2020 t_1 survey were reinterviewed and their responses combined with those of another portion of the AmeriSpeak panel who had not participated in the t_1 survey. A total of 689 respondents of the 1,006 in the July 2020 survey were reinterviewed. In addition, 337 new respondents were included in the sample.

PANEL ATTRITION

Not all the respondents in the July 2020 AmeriSpeak survey were reinterviewed in the December 2020 panel survey. As a consequence, the 72.5 percent of respondents successfully reinterviewed possibly differed systematically from those we were unable to reinterview.

To assess panel attrition bias, I investigated whether the July 2020 respondents who completed the December 2020 interview differed systematically from those who did not. For this analysis, I considered the following variables: gender, age, minority race, level of education, household internet access, metropolitan area residence, homeownership, whether the respondent was born-again, party identification, ideological identification, and level of diffuse support for the Supreme Court. In a multivariate logit equation, only a single variable achieves statistical significance: the respondent's age. The effects of none of the other predictors, including diffuse support, even approach achieving statistical significance.

The effect of the respondent's age on participating in the t_2 survey is exactly as predicted. Figure A.1 reports the bivariate relationship. Younger people were considerably more likely not to be reinterviewed; those age sixty-five and older were considerably more likely to participate in the 2020–2021 survey.

Unfortunately, the respondent's age is related to several variables of interest in this research. The bivariate correlation with diffuse support for the Supreme Court is 0.18, for instance. One consequence is that all analyses of change between t_1 and t_2 must include these control variables.

REACTIVITY

To consider the differences between panel respondents and new respondents in the 2020–2021 survey, I focus on diffuse support for the Supreme Court.

In the December 2020 survey, the respondents were presented with six items concerning the legitimacy of the court. For five of the six, no significant difference was found in the responses between panelist respondents

Figure A.1 Age and Attrition of Respondents from July to December 2020

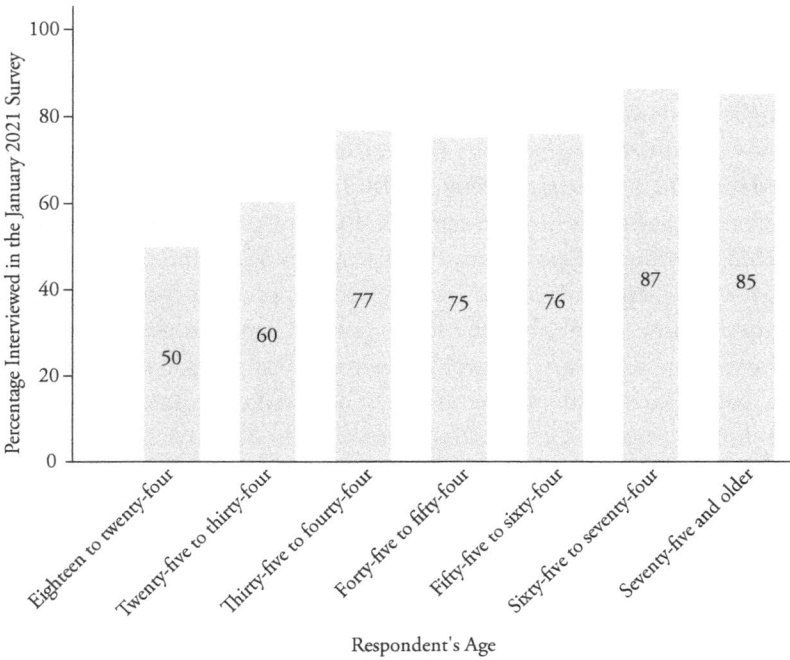

Source: The 2020 Freedom and Tolerance Survey (t_1), July 2020, and the 2020 Pre-insurrection Survey (t_2), December 2020 and January 2021.

and those who were freshly interviewed. The item about removing justices who rule against the majority differed significantly ($p = .009$, $N = 1,022$), but the degree of association is weak indeed (eta = 0.08), with new respondents expressing slightly less support for the court than the panelists. For the indices of Supreme Court support, the differences are entirely insignificant. Thus, the results of this analysis justify blending together the responses of the panelists and the new respondents in the 2020 t_2 cross-sectional analysis.

The 2021 Insurrection and Impeachment Survey (t_3), February and March 2021

The fieldwork for the 2021 Insurrection and Impeachment Survey was conducted by NORC, also using the AmeriSpeak panel. A general population sample of U.S. adults ages eighteen and older was selected from NORC's AmeriSpeak Panel for this study. Included as well were oversamples of African Americans (resulting in 680 completed interviews) and active college students (resulting in 316 completed interviews). This survey was offered only in English and was administered on the web. Invitations to participate in the survey were initiated on February 18, 2021, and the last interviews were completed on March 10, 2021. In total, NORC collected 2,027 interviews.

To encourage study cooperation, NORC sent three email reminders to sampled web-mode respondents. Panelists were offered the cash equivalent of $5 for completing the study. Interviewed respondents took a median of twenty minutes to complete the survey. NORC applied cleaning rules to the survey data for quality control by removing responses in the main study from ineligible respondents. Because their responses indicated that they had sped through the survey and skipped survey questions, they were not included in the final dataset.

The data are weighted, with various factors going into the construction of the final study weight: (1) panel base sampling weights, (2) final panel weights, (3) study-specific base sampling weights, and (4) non-response-adjusted survey weights. The weighted AAPOR Response Rate #3 recruitment rate was 19.5 percent, with a weighted household retention rate of 75.0 percent and a survey completion rate of 20.1 percent. A weighted AAPOR Response Rate #3 cumulative response rate of 2.9 percent was achieved. The survey has a margin of error of 3.77 percent, and an average design effect of 2.99.

This research was approved by the Washington University in St. Louis Institutional Review Board, which judged this project to be in the "exempt" category given that participation in the survey was voluntary, no harm was afflicted on the respondents, and no identifiers were connected to the database generated, among other factors.

The African American Panel Survey (t_4), June 2021

NORC attempted to reinterview all African American respondents in the t_3 survey. Fieldwork commenced on June 2, 2021, and when it concluded on June 24, 2021, interviews were completed with 579 respondents, with a response rate of 85.3 percent. The median interview length was twenty-one minutes.

This research was approved by the Washington University in St. Louis Institutional Review Board, which judged this project to be in the "exempt" category given that participation in the survey was voluntary, no harm was afflicted on the respondents, and no identifiers were connected to the database generated, among other factors.

PANEL ATTRITION

Not all the Black respondents in the February and March 2021 (t_3) Ameri-Speak survey were reinterviewed in the June 2021 panel survey (t_4). As a consequence, the 85.3 percent of respondents who were reinterviewed possibly differed systematically from those we were unable to reinterview.

To assess panel attrition bias, I investigated whether the t_3 respondents who completed the t_4 interview differed systematically from those who did not. For this analysis, I considered the following variables: gender, age, income, level of education, household internet access, metropolitan area residence, homeownership, whether the respondent was born-again, party identification, ideological identification, and level of diffuse support for the Supreme Court. In a multivariate logit equation, only a single variable achieves statistical significance: the respondent's age. The effects of none of the other predictors, including diffuse support, even approach statistical significance.

The effect of the respondent's age on participating in the t_4 survey is exactly as predicted. Figure A.2 reports the bivariate relationship. Younger people were considerably more likely not to be reinterviewed; those who were age sixty-five and older were considerably more likely to participate in the June survey. These and other incidental imbalances are corrected via t_4 sample weights.

Chapter 2

Validating the Measure of Presidential Legitimacy

Because so little work exists on developing empirical indicators of presidential legitimacy, it is difficult to know exactly what would constitute evidence of the validity of the measures presented in this research. A couple of limited tests, however, are obvious and possible.

Figure A.2 Age and Attrition of African American Respondents from February to June 2021

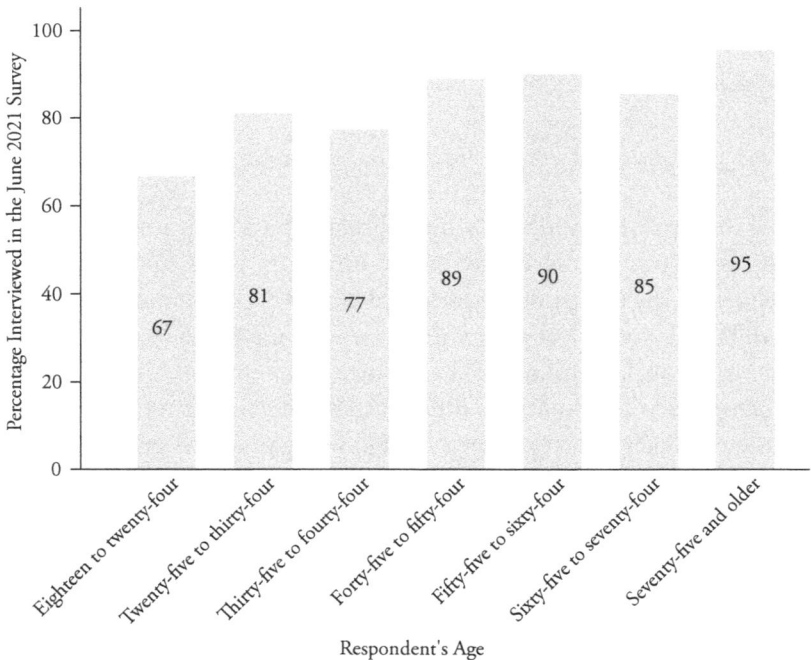

Source: The 2021 Insurrection and Impeachment Survey (t₃), February and March 2021, and the African American Panel Survey (t₄), June 2021.

Based on feeling thermometer scores for Democrats and Republicans, presidential legitimacy is clearly something more than pure partisanship. Affect toward the Democrats is correlated with presidential legitimacy at 0.59; for affect toward the Republicans, the correlation is –0.53. The correlation of party identification and presidential legitimacy is –0.58. Perhaps we would welcome measures of legitimacy that are less strongly correlated with partisan affect, but the reality of the matter is that many people, though far from all, probably conflate their views of the office and the incumbent. Still, as Reeves and Rogowski assert: "Our argument implies that Americans view the institution of the presidency through different lenses relative to how they evaluate the occupants of that office."[2]

The survey also asked whether Biden legitimately won the election (a dichotomy). The correlation between responses to this question and presidential legitimacy is more substantial: r = 0.69, providing additional validation of my presidential legitimacy measures.

The presidential legitimacy items were also asked in the t_2 survey. No feeling thermometer question was asked about Biden at t_2. However, a seven-point Biden thermometer was asked in the t_1 interview. The correlation of positive affect for Biden and the legitimacy index is 0.55. Those feeling more warmly toward Biden extended more legitimacy to the presidency. Obviously, while strong, this correlation is not overwhelming—as it should not be.

Figure A.3 reports the relationship between Biden affect and agreement with the statement to the effect that Biden will "never be my president." Even among respondents holding the most anti-Biden sentiments, less than a majority rejected Biden as their president. This figure clearly suggests that this presidential legitimacy item measures more than incumbent affect.

Figure A.3 Incumbent Affect and Presidential Legitimacy

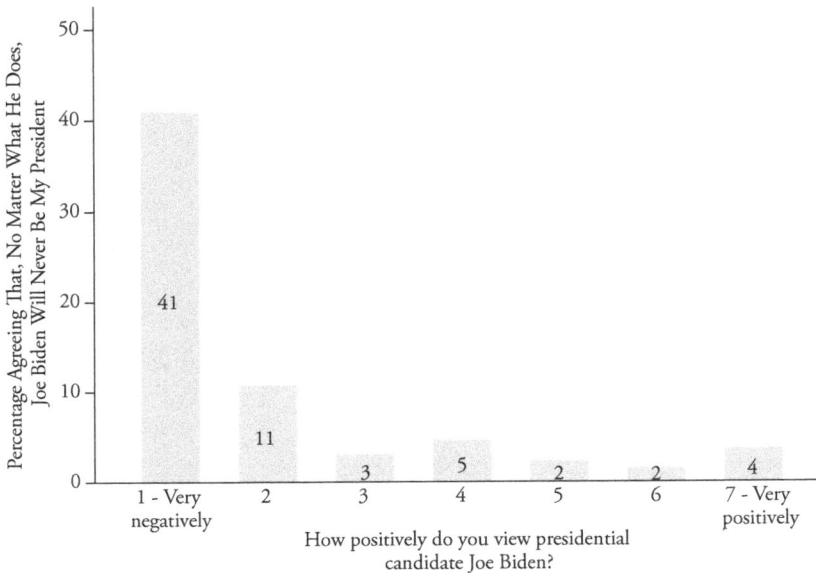

Source: The 2021 Insurrection and Impeachment Survey (t_3), February and March 2021.

Validating the Measure of Senate Legitimacy

As I have observed, one conclusion from the voluminous literature on institutional support is that diffuse support and specific support should not, of course, be uncorrelated, but also should not be excessively correlated. If diffuse support is to have any substantive meaning, it must represent something beyond performance satisfaction.

When the respondents were asked to judge how well the Senate does its job, only about one-third (36 percent) said that it did at least a pretty good job. The relationship between respondents' performance evaluations and the measure of institutional legitimacy is shown in figure A.4.

The important conclusion that can be drawn from this figure is that a willingness to extend legitimacy to the Senate is not closely connected to performance evaluations ($r = -0.07$). The clear indication in these data that diffuse support and specific support for the Senate are not the same adds confidence to the validity of the legitimacy index.

The survey also used a feeling thermometer to measure affect toward the Senate. The correlation between the thermometer scores and institutional support is only 0.15. Clearly, diffuse support for the institution is something more than just positive affect for the institution.

Figure A.4 The Relationship of Performance Evaluations and U.S. Senate Legitimacy

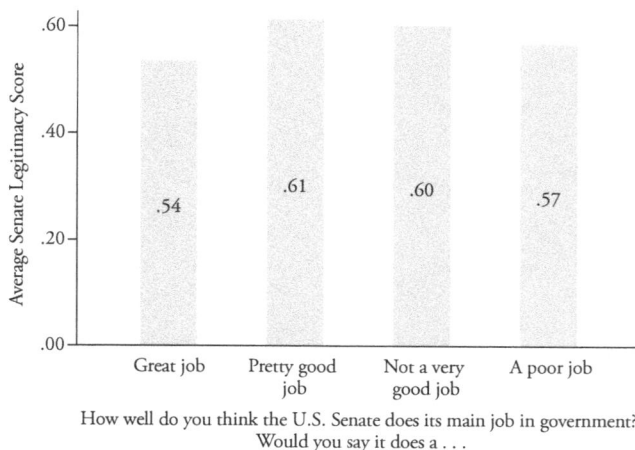

Source: The 2021 Insurrection and Impeachment Survey (t_3), February and March 2021.
Notes: Difference of means (F-test): $p < .001$; $r = -0.07$. $N = 2,011$. The Senate legitimacy index varies from 0 to 1.

The respondents were also asked to rate the Senate in terms of whether it is too liberal or too conservative. The relationship to diffuse support, while statistically significant, is only 0.04. When this measure is "folded" so as to vary from ideological satisfaction to dissatisfaction, the correlation, at −0.04, barely moves.

Finally, diffuse support contributes to acquiescence but is not the same thing, either conceptually or empirically.[3] As a result, the correlation of diffuse support and responses to a statement about accepting actions taken by the Senate even when one disagrees with them is 0.29, which is just about as expected.

The overall conclusion of these various tests is that the measure of Senate institutional legitimacy performs very much as predicted by the theory of institutional support. Diffuse support is weakly related to performance evaluations, but not so much that the validity of the diffuse measure is called into question.

Validating the Measure of Support for Democratic Institutions

Some observers may wonder whether the responses to these items are driven by the belief that the current institutional arrangement is antidemocratic (for example, one person/one vote is not uniformly used) and that reforms making these institutions more democratic would be appropriate. One way to address this conjecture is to examine the relationship between the general democratic institutions index and support for the Supreme Court, the Senate, and the presidency. Table A.2 reports the bivariate correlations among these four indices.

The correlations in table A.2 provide considerable validation of the index

Table A.2 Intercorrelations of Institutional Attitudes: 2021 Insurrection and Impeachment Survey

Support for . . .	Democratic Institutions	The Supreme Court	The Senate	The Presidency
Democratic institutions	1.00			
The Supreme Court	0.53	1.00		
The Senate	0.57	0.63	1.00	
The presidency	0.31	0.16	0.32	1.00

Source: The 2021 Insurrection and Impeachment Survey (t₃), February and March 2021.

Notes: N = 1,864.

of general support for democratic institutions. In every instance, the correlations are positive, and the relationships between the general measures and a willingness to extend legitimacy to the Supreme Court and the Senate are quite substantial. As I have already noted, attitudes toward the presidency are more distinct, no doubt because some respondents find it difficult to separate their views of the office from their views of the incumbent.[4]

Measures of Specific Support

To evaluate job performance, we asked:

How well do you think the U.S. Supreme Court does its main job in government? Would you say it does . . .

a great job (4.2 percent)
a pretty good job (64.5 percent)
not a very good job (26.5 percent)
a poor job (4.9 percent)

To measure satisfaction with the court's rulings, we asked:

In general, would you say that the U.S. Supreme Court is . . .

too liberal (21.1 percent)
too conservative (35.3 percent)
about right in its decisions (43.7 percent)

Gallup reports findings remarkably similar to mine from a survey it conducted August 31–September 13, 2020, when 42 percent of Americans said that the court's policies are "about right," 21 percent rated it as "too liberal," and 35 percent believed it to be "too conservative."[5]

Figure A.5 shows that, while diffuse support and performance evaluations are indeed correlated, even respondents with the lowest levels of diffuse support expressed considerable satisfaction with the performance of the court.

Measure of Ideological Distance from the Supreme Court

I measure respondents' ideological distance from the Supreme Court using the absolute value of the difference between respondents' own ideological

Figure A.5 Evaluations of the U.S. Supreme Court's Performance at Varying Levels of Diffuse Support

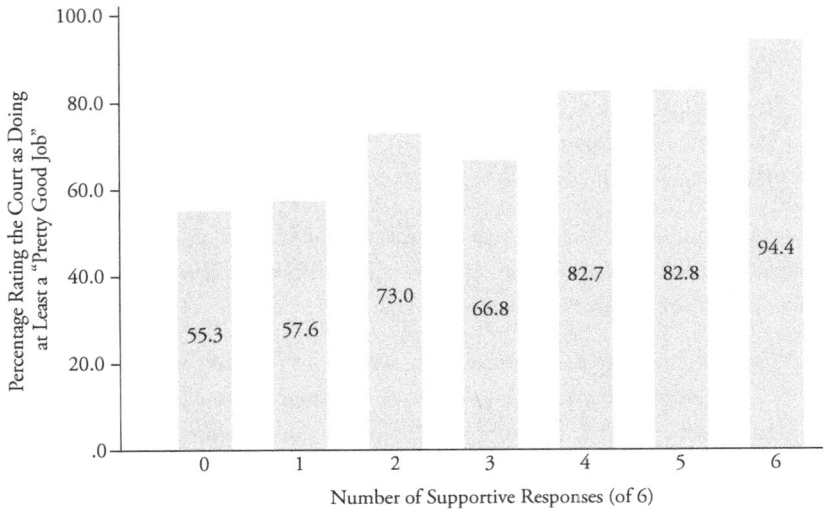

Source: The 2020 Freedom and Tolerance Survey (t₁), July 2020.
Notes: Entries are the percentages of respondents at each level of diffuse support who judge the Supreme Court to be doing at least a "pretty good job." Weighted N = 932. p < .001; r = 0.31.

self-identification and their perception of the ideological location of the Supreme Court. The correlation between this measure and respondents' ideological self-identification is only −0.34.

Measures of Political Knowledge

We measured knowledge about institutional politics with five items (correct answers are shown in italics):[6]

Do you happen to know who has the last say when there is a conflict over the meaning of the Constitution—the U.S. Supreme Court, the U.S. Congress, or the President?

U.S. Supreme Court (85 percent correct)
U.S. Congress
The president

In the case of a tied vote in the U.S. Senate, is the deciding vote cast by the vice president, the president, the Senate majority leader, or the Senate parliamentarian?

> *The vice president* (64 percent correct)
> The president
> The Senate majority leader
> The Senate parliamentarian

As you might know, there are two chambers in the U.S. Congress—the U.S. Senate and the House of Representatives. Which of the following describes how people are represented in the two chambers?

> *Each state has two U.S. Senators; the number of members of the House of Representatives depends on the state's population.* (85 percent correct)
> The number of U.S. Senators and the number of members of the House of Representatives is the same for each state.
> For each state, the number of members of the House of Representatives is twice the number of Senators.

When the U.S. Supreme Court decides a case, would you say that . . .

> *the decision is final and cannot be further reviewed* (69 percent correct)
> the decision can be appealed to another court
> Congress can review the decision to see if it should become the law of the land

Which of the following women was recently confirmed to serve on the U.S. Supreme Court?

> *Amy Coney Barrett* (91 percent correct)
> Condoleezza Rice
> Nikki Haley

Partisan and Ideological Identifications

People sometimes think (or assume) that party and ideological attachments are essentially the same thing. Because they are not, I investigate the relationship between the two variables more carefully in this appendix.

Figures A.6 and A.7 provide the average values of ideological identification and party identification (respectively) as the other type of political identification varies. Figure A.6 shows a fairly strong relationship between partisanship and ideological identification, even if there is a slight deviation from monotonicity at the most Democratic end of the scale.

Figure A.7 illustrates well why the relationship between partisan and ideological self-identifications is not stronger. The figure shows the average score on the seven-point ideology scale (high = extremely conservative) according to respondent's party identification. The reason why the statistical relationship is not stronger is entirely obvious: conservative ideologies among the three types of Republicans (from leaners to strong Republicans) vary insignificantly. At the opposite side of the party identification scale, respondents who leaned toward the Democrats were just as liberal as mod-

Figure A.6 Average Party Identification, by Ideological Identification

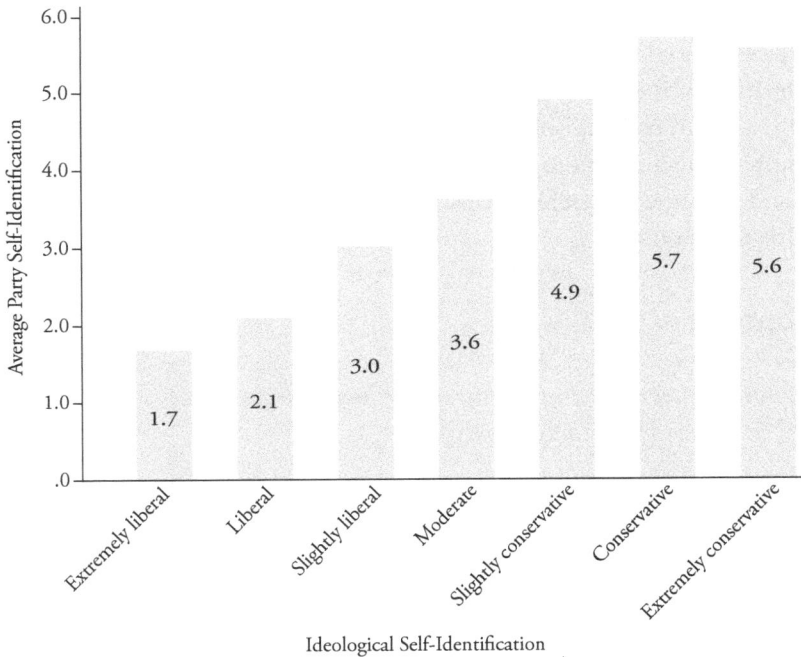

Ideological Self-Identification

Source: The 2020 Freedom and Tolerance Survey (t_1), July 2020.
Notes: Partisanship ranges from (1) strong Democrat to (7) strong Republican. $N = 879$; $r = 0.64$; $p < .001$.

Figure A.7 Average Ideological Identification, by Party Identification

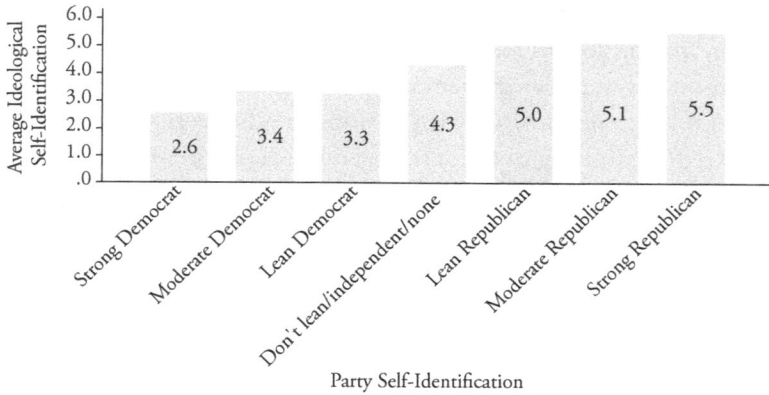

Source: The 2020 Freedom and Tolerance Survey (t_1), July 2020.
Notes: Ideology ranges from (1) extremely liberal to (7) extremely conservative. $N = 879$; $r = 0.64$; $p < .001$.

erate Democrats. These deviations from strict monotonicity drive down the correlation of the two measures.

I draw two conclusions from this analysis. First, party and ideological identifications are not the same thing even if they are fairly strongly related. Second, we should therefore examine separately their effects on support for political institutions.

Chapter 3

Measures of Awareness and Assessments of Events in the 2020 Pre-insurrection Survey (t_2)

NORC asked the following questions to measure respondents' awareness and assessments of the events associated with the 2020 election and the subsequent insurrection:

> Are you aware that there is some disagreement over how the latest addition to the U.S. Supreme Court, Amy Coney Barrett, was nominated and confirmed so quickly, in the run-up to the presidential election? Would you say you are . . .

very aware of the disagreement
somewhat aware of the disagreement
not very aware of the disagreement
not aware of the disagreement

Regarding the Barrett nomination, some say the president and the U.S. Senate should have waited until after the presidential election to fill the vacant seat on the Supreme Court, while others say that the president and the U.S. Senate had every right to fill the seat before the election. Would you say that the nomination and confirmation process for Amy Coney Barrett was . . .

entirely appropriate for a democracy like ours
somewhat appropriate for a democracy like ours
not very appropriate for a democracy like ours
entirely inappropriate for a democracy like ours

Are you aware that there is some disagreement over whether the 2020 presidential election was rigged or somehow manipulated so that it did not represent the actual votes of the American people? Would you say you are . . .

very aware of the disagreement
somewhat aware of the disagreement
not very aware of the disagreement
not aware of the disagreement

Regarding the 2020 presidential vote-count, some say that the election was generally fair and that the outcome ought to be accepted by the American people, while others say that the election was rigged and manipulated and that the outcome ought not to be accepted by the American people. Would you say you are . . .

very certain that the presidential election was rigged and manipulated
fairly certain that the presidential election was rigged and manipulated
fairly certain that the presidential election was not rigged and manipulated
very certain that the presidential election was not rigged and manipulated

Are you aware that there is some discussion over President Trump's efforts to get the outcome of the 2020 presidential election overturned and reversed? Would you say you are . . .

very aware of the discussion
somewhat aware of the discussion
not very aware of the discussion
not aware of the discussion

Regarding President Trump's efforts to overturn the outcome of the 2020 presidential election, some say that Trump has every right to try to overturn and reverse the outcome in any way that he can, while others say that Trump's refusal to accept the outcome of the election is bad for democracy. Do you consider President Trump's efforts to get the outcome of the 2020 presidential election overturned and reversed . . .

entirely appropriate for a democracy like ours
somewhat appropriate for a democracy like ours
not very appropriate for a democracy like ours
entirely inappropriate for a democracy like ours

Supporting Analyses

Table A.3 Predictors of Assessment of Events at the December 2020 and January 2021 Survey, Using Predictors from the 2020 Freedom and Tolerance Survey

Predictor	Barrett Nomination		Efforts to Overturn the 2020 Election		2020 Election Was Rigged	
	b	s.e.	b	s.e.	b	s.e.
Party identification (t_1)	0.35***	0.05	0.37***	0.06	−0.38***	0.05
Ideological identification (t_1)	0.51***	0.07	0.42***	0.07	−0.42***	0.07
Institutional support (t_1)	0.21**	0.07	0.00	0.08	−0.06	0.07
Performance satisfaction (t_1)	0.08	0.07	0.01	0.07	0.05	0.07
Ideological satisfaction (t_1)	0.05	0.04	−0.03	0.04	0.04	0.04
Ideological proximity to the Court (t_1)	0.07	0.06	0.14*	0.06	−0.18**	0.06
Political knowledge (t_1)	−0.05	0.06	−0.21***	0.06	0.19***	0.05
Support for the rule of law (t_1)	0.20**	0.07	0.31***	0.08	−0.19***	0.07
Valuation of individual liberty (t_1)	−0.10	0.05	−0.14*	0.07	0.09	0.06
Support for civil liberties (t_1)	−0.07	0.05	−0.06	0.05	0.09	0.05
Open-mindedness (t_1)	0.02	0.07	−0.21**	0.08	0.24***	0.07
Gender (t_1)	0.05*	0.02	0.03	0.03	0.02	0.02
Age (t_1)	−0.09	0.06	−0.09	0.06	0.09	0.06
Minority race (t_1)	−0.06*	0.03	−0.08**	0.03	0.10***	0.03

Table A.3 (*continued*)

Predictor	Barrett Nomination		Efforts to Overturn the 2020 Election		2020 Election Was Rigged	
	b	s.e.	b	s.e.	b	s.e.
Level of education (t_1)	−0.01	0.05	−0.03	0.06	0.04	0.05
Income (t_1)	0.05	0.05	−0.01	0.05	−0.01	0.05
Homeownership (t_1)	−0.03	0.03	0.01	0.03	0.03	0.03
Metropolitan residence (t_1)	−0.01	0.03	0.03	0.03	−0.01	0.03
Resident of the South (t_1)	−0.01	0.02	−0.02	0.03	0.00	0.02
Internet access (t_1)	0.00	0.04	−0.03	0.05	0.02	0.04
Born again (t_1)	0.00	0.03	0.03	0.03	0.01	0.03
Church attendance (t_1)	0.05	0.04	0.06	0.04	−0.09*	0.04
Equation						
Intercept	**−0.10**	0.09	**0.16**	0.09	**0.74*****	0.08
Standard deviation, dependent variable	0.39		0.41		0.39	
R^2	**0.49*****		**0.48*****		**0.50*****	
Standard error of estimate	0.28		0.30		0.28	
N	634		634		634	

Source: The 2020 Freedom and Tolerance Survey (t_1), July 2020, and the 2020 Pre-insurrection Survey (t_2), December 2020 and January 2021.

Notes: All variables are scored to range from 0 to 1. For their distributions, see table A.4. b = unstandardized regression coefficient; s.e. = standard error of the unstandardized regression coefficient. For details on the measurement of the predictors, see table A.4. Regression coefficients greater than or equal to ±0.10 are shown in boldface.

Significance of unstandardized OLS regression coefficients: * $p \le .05$; ** $p \le .01$; *** $p \le .001$

Table A.4 The Distributions of the Variables Used in the Analyses (Table A.3)

Variable	Range	Mean	Standard Deviation	N
Barrett nomination (t_2)	0 → 1	0.55	0.39	634
Efforts to overturn (t_2)	0 → 1	0.38	0.41	634
Election was rigged (t_2)	0 → 1	0.54	0.39	634
Party identification (t_1)	0 → 1	0.47	0.33	634
Ideological identification (t_1)	0 → 1	0.52	0.27	634
Institutional support (t_1)	0 → 1	0.58	0.21	634
Performance satisfaction (t_1)	0 → 1	0.57	0.20	634
Ideological satisfaction (t_1)	0 → 1	0.60	0.40	634
Ideological proximity to the Court (t_1)	0 → 1	0.41	0.24	634

(*continued*)

Table A.4 (*continued*)

Variable	Range	Mean	Standard Deviation	N
Political knowledge (t_1)	$0 \rightarrow 1$	0.79	0.26	634
Support for the rule of law (t_1)	$0 \rightarrow 1$	0.71	0.19	634
Valuation of individual liberty (t_1)	$0 \rightarrow 1$	0.65	0.21	634
Support for civil liberties (t_1)	$0 \rightarrow 1$	0.54	0.25	634
Open-mindedness (t_1)	$0 \rightarrow 1$	0.50	0.20	634
Gender (t_1)	$0 \rightarrow 1$	0.48	0.50	634
Age (t_1)	$0 \rightarrow 1$	0.43	0.22	634
Minority race (t_1)	$0 \rightarrow 1$	0.29	0.45	634
Level of education (t_1)	$0 \rightarrow 1$	0.60	0.25	634
Income (t_1)	$0 \rightarrow 1$	0.60	0.27	634
Homeownership (t_1)	$0 \rightarrow 1$	0.70	0.46	634
Metropolitan residence (t_1)	$0 \rightarrow 1$	0.84	0.37	634
Resident of the South (t_1)	$0 \rightarrow 1$	0.34	0.47	634
Internet access (t_1)	$0 \rightarrow 1$	0.92	0.28	634
Born-again (t_1)	$0 \rightarrow 1$	0.29	0.45	634
Church attendance (t_1)	$0 \rightarrow 1$	0.47	0.35	634

Source: The 2020 Freedom and Tolerance Survey (t_1), July 2020, and the 2020 Pre-insurrection Survey (t_2), December 2020 and January 2021.

Chapter 4

Threat to Democracy from Political Parties

Research on political intolerance, a key democratic value, repeatedly shows that a perception of threat from one's political enemies powerfully structures attitudes.[7] Consequently, the survey also asked:

> How much of a threat to democracy in America do you think the Democrats and Republicans currently present?
>
> First, the Democrats: would you say that . . . / And then the Democrats: would you say that . . .
>
> > the Democrats present a large threat to American democracy
> > the Democrats present some threat to American democracy
> > the Democrats present a small threat to American democracy
> > the Democrats present no threat to American democracy

the Democrats present no threat to American democracy
the Democrats present a small threat to American democracy
the Democrats present some threat to American democracy
the Democrats present a large threat to American democracy

First, the Republicans: how much of a threat to democracy in America do you think the Republicans currently present?/ And then the Republicans: would you say that . . .

the Republicans present a large threat to American democracy
the Republicans present some threat to American democracy
the Republicans present a small threat to American democracy
the Republicans present no threat to American democracy

the Republicans present no threat to American democracy
the Republicans present a small threat to American democracy
the Republicans present some threat to American democracy
the Republicans present a large threat to American democracy

Support for the Rule of Law (t₂): Results

When the five items are factor-analyzed, a single dominant factor emerges (eigenvalue$_2$ = 0.88). The best indicator of the concept is the second statement (ignore the law and solve problems); all indicators load on the first unrotated factor at 0.40 or higher. The item-set is quite reliable, with a Cronbach's alpha of 0.79 and a mean inter-item correlation of 0.43.[8]

I created a measure of support for the rule of law (universalism) that is simply the average response to the five statements. This index correlates with the factor score from the factor analysis at 0.98. For some descriptive purposes, I also used an index indicating the number of pro-rule-of-law responses to the five items. On this measure, 29 percent of the respondents at t₂ gave pro-rule-of-law responses to all five items; 10 percent gave no pro-rule-of-law responses.

Valuation of Individual Political Liberty (t₂): Results

When the three items are factor-analyzed, a single dominant factor emerges (eigenvalue$_2$ = 0.71). The best indicator of the concept is the last statement (free speech is just not worth it). The item-set is at least somewhat reliable (especially for a scale with only three indicators), with a Cronbach's alpha of 0.63 and a mean inter-item correlation of 0.37.

I created a measure of the valuation of individual political liberty that is simply the average response to the three statements. This index correlates with the factor score from the factor analysis at 0.98. For some descriptive purposes, I also used an index indicating the number of pro-liberty responses to the three items. On this measure, 29 percent of the respondents at t_2 gave pro-liberty responses to all three items; 21 percent gave no pro-liberty responses.

Support for Civil Liberties (t_2): Results

When the responses to these four items are analyzed using common factor analysis (CFA), a single dominant factor emerges, with an eigenvalue of 2.4. The second extracted factor has an eigenvalue of 0.70. The strongest loading on the factor is from the item regarding demonstrations by atheists; the weakest is for White nationalists. The item-set is reasonably reliable, with a Cronbach's alpha of 0.74 and a mean inter-item correlation of 0.42.

I created a measure of support for civil liberties that is simply the average response to the four statements. This index correlates with the factor score from the factor analysis at 0.99. For some descriptive purposes, I also used an index indicating the number of tolerant responses to the four items. On this measure, 34 percent of the respondents at t_2 gave tolerant responses to all four of the items; 15 percent gave no tolerant responses.

Open-Mindedness (t_2): Results

CFA produces a single significant factor (eigenvalue$_2$ = 0.64) for the three-item-set. The scale is to some degree reliable: Cronbach's alpha = 0.72 (mean inter-item correlation of 0.41). The correlation between the factor scores from this analysis and a simple summated index constructed from the items is 0.99.

Supporting Analyses

Table A.5 Cross-panel Predictors of Institutional Support for the U.S. Supreme Court

Conceptualization/Predictor	Supreme Court Support (t_2)		
	b	s.e.	r
Institutional support (t_1)	0.54***	0.04	0.73
Events awareness and assessments			
Awareness of Barrett confirmation (t_2)	0.04	0.03	0.31
Evaluation of Barrett confirmation (t_2)	0.06**	0.02	0.22
Awareness of Trump actions (t_2)	–0.03	0.05	0.22
Evaluation of Trump actions (t_2)	0.02	0.03	–0.02
Awareness of election controversy (t_2)	–0.00	0.05	0.19
Election fairness judgments (t_2)	0.05	0.03	0.06
Party threat assessments			
Belief that Republicans threaten democracy (t_2)	–0.03	0.02	–0.12
Belief that Democrats threaten democracy (t_2)	–0.05*	0.02	–0.04
Specific support			
Performance satisfaction (t_1)	0.02	0.03	0.36
Ideological satisfaction (t_1)	0.01	0.02	0.18
Ideological proximity to the Court (t_1)	0.01	0.03	–0.07
Democratic values and personality			
Support for the rule of law (t_1)	0.04	0.04	0.37
Valuation of individual liberty (t_1)	0.08**	0.03	0.38
Support for civil liberties (t_1)	0.03	0.02	0.22
Open-mindedness (t_1)	0.04	0.03	0.35
Partisanship and ideology			
Party identification (t_1)	0.05	0.03	0.11
Ideological identification (t_1)	0.00	0.03	0.07
Political sophistication			
Political knowledge (t_1)	0.01	0.03	0.40
Demographic attributes			
Gender (t_1)	0.02	0.01	0.11
Age (t_1)	0.06*	0.03	0.22
Minority race (t_1)	0.01	0.01	–0.16
Level of education (t_1)	0.05	0.03	0.29
Income (t_1)	–0.04	0.03	0.22
Homeownership (t_1)	0.03	0.01	0.24
Metropolitan residence (t_1)	–0.01	0.02	0.00
Resident of the South (t_1)	–0.00	0.01	0.00

(continued)

Table A.5 (*continued*)

Conceptualization/Predictor	Supreme Court Support (t_2)		
	b	s.e.	r
Internet access (t_1)	0.03	0.02	0.14
Born-again (t_1)	−0.02	0.02	−0.01
Church attendance (t_1)	0.03	0.02	0.12
U.S. citizen (t_2)	0.01	0.04	0.06
Equation			
Intercept	−0.02	0.07	
Standard deviation, dependent variable	0.20		
R^2	0.60***		
Standard error of estimate	0.13		
N	622		

Source: The 2020 Freedom and Tolerance Survey (t_1), July 2020, and the 2020 Pre-insurrection Survey (t_2), December 2020 and January 2021.

Notes: All variables are scored to range from 0 to 1. For their distributions, see table A.6. b = unstandardized regression coefficient; s.e. = standard error of the unstandardized regression coefficient; r = bivariate correlation coefficient.

Significance of unstandardized OLS regression coefficients: * $p \le .05$; ** $p \le .01$; *** $p \le .001$

Table A.6 The Distributions of the Variables Used in the Analyses (Table A.5)

Variable	Range	Mean	Standard Deviation	N
Institutional legitimacy (t_1)	0 → 1	0.58	0.21	622
Institutional legitimacy (t_2)	0 → 1	0.61	0.20	622
Awareness of Barrett confirmation	0 → 1	0.81	0.26	622
Evaluation of Barrett confirmation	0 → 1	0.55	0.39	622
Awareness of Trump actions	0 → 1	0.90	0.20	622
Evaluation of Trump actions	0 → 1	0.38	0.41	622
Awareness of election controversy	0 → 1	0.92	0.19	622
Election fairness judgments	0 → 1	0.64	0.39	622
Belief that Democrats threaten democracy	0 → 1	0.43	0.39	622
Belief that Republicans threaten democracy	0 → 1	0.55	0.26	622
Performance satisfaction	0 → 1	0.57	0.21	622
Ideological satisfaction	0 → 1	0.60	0.40	622
Ideological proximity to the Court	0 → 1	0.41	0.24	622
Support for the rule of law	0 → 1	0.71	0.19	622
Valuation of individual liberty	0 → 1	0.65	0.21	622
Support for civil liberties	0 → 1	0.54	0.25	622

Table A.6 (*continued*)

Variable	Range	Mean	Standard Deviation	N
Open-mindedness	0 → 1	0.50	0.20	622
Party identification	0 → 1	0.47	0.33	622
Ideological identification	0 → 1	0.52	0.27	622
Political knowledge	0 → 1	0.79	0.26	622
Gender	0 → 1	0.49	0.50	622
Age	0 → 1	0.43	0.22	622
Minority race	0 → 1	0.29	0.45	622
Level of education	0 → 1	0.50	0.25	622
Income	0 → 1	0.60	0.27	622
Homeownership	0 → 1	0.70	0.46	622
Metropolitan residence	0 → 1	0.84	0.37	622
Resident of the South	0 → 1	0.34	0.47	622
Internet access	0 → 1	0.92	0.28	622
Born-again	0 → 1	0.28	0.45	622
Church attendance	0 → 1	0.37	0.35	622
U.S. citizen	0 → 1	0.98	0.15	622

Source: The 2020 Freedom and Tolerance Survey (t_1), July 2020, and the 2020 Pre-insurrection Survey (t_2), December 2020 and January 2021.

The U.S. Supreme Court's Involvement in the 2020 Presidential Election

The Supreme Court played a much more diminished role in the 2020 presidential election than it did in the 2000 election. Still, in 2020 the court made a few important summary rulings:

- A request for injunctive relief in a case challenging the constitutionality of the new voting laws in Pennsylvania, *Kelly, Mike, et al. v. Pennsylvania et al.*, was thrown out on December 8, 2020, in a one-sentence statement from the Supreme Court: "The application for injunctive relief presented to Justice Alito and by him referred to the Court is denied."[9]
- *Texas v. Pennsylvania, et al.* was thrown out by the court on December 11, 2020. The case argued that Pennsylvania, Wisconsin, Georgia, and Michigan, using COVID-19 as an excuse to do so, unconstitutionally changed their voting laws. The Supreme Court responded: "The State of Texas's motion for leave to file a bill of complaint is denied for lack of standing under Article III of the Constitution. Texas has not

demonstrated a judicially cognizable interest in the manner in which another State conducts its elections. All other pending motions are dismissed as moot." Justice Alito, joined by Justice Clarence Thomas, added the note: "In my view, we do not have discretion to deny the filing of a bill of complaint in a case that falls within our original jurisdiction. See *Arizona v. California*, 589 U.S. ___ (February 24, 2020) (Thomas, J., dissenting). I would therefore grant the motion to file the bill of complaint but would not grant other relief, and I express no view on any other issue."[10]

- Expedited consideration was denied to several other election cases.[11]

Regression Results and the Distributions of the Variables

Table A.7: Predictors of Support for Institutional Legitimacy before the January 6, 2021, Insurrection

Conceptualization/Predictor	Presidential Legitimacy		Supreme Court Legitimacy		Senate Legitimacy	
	b	s.e.	b	s.e.	b	s.e.
Events awareness and assessments						
Awareness of Barrett confirmation	0.09***	0.03	0.08***	0.02	0.06**	0.02
Evaluation of Barrett confirmation	0.05*	0.02	0.09***	0.02	0.10***	0.02
Awareness of Trump's actions	0.04	0.04	0.03	0.03	−0.01	0.03
Evaluation of Trump's actions	−0.09***	0.03	−0.01	0.03	−0.02	0.02
Awareness of election controversy	−0.06	0.03	−0.02	0.03	0.01	0.03
Election fairness judgments	.30**	0.03	−0.01	0.03	0.04	0.03
Party threat assessments						
Belief that Democrats threaten democracy	−0.08***	0.02	−0.05*	0.02	−0.03	0.02
Belief that Republicans threaten democracy	0.07***	0.02	−0.03	0.02	−0.06***	0.02
Democratic values and personality						
Support for the rule of law	0.17***	0.04	0.16***	0.03	0.16***	0.03
Valuation of individual liberty	−0.02	0.03	0.17***	0.03	0.12***	0.03
Support for civil liberties	0.07*	0.03	0.05*	0.03	0.06**	0.03
Open-mindedness	0.24***	0.03	0.30***	0.03	0.19***	0.03
Partisanship and ideology						
Party identification	−0.06	0.03	0.02	0.03	0.03	0.03
Ideological identification	0.04	0.03	0.02	0.03	−0.08**	0.03
Political sophistication						
Political knowledge	0.07*	0.03	0.02	0.03	0.07**	0.03

Table A.7 (*continued*)

Conceptualization/Predictor	Presidential Legitimacy		Supreme Court Legitimacy		Senate Legitimacy	
	b	s.e.	b	s.e.	b	s.e.
Demographic attributes						
Gender	0.03*	0.01	−0.02	0.01	0.01	0.01
Age	−0.07*	0.03	0.06*	0.03	0.13***	0.03
Minority race	0.01	0.01	0.00	0.01	−0.01	0.01
Level of education	0.03	0.02	0.09***	0.02	0.07***	0.02
Income	0.02	0.02	0.01	0.02	0.01	0.02
Homeownership	−0.00	0.01	0.01	0.01	0.01	0.01
Metropolitan residence	0.04*	0.02	−0.01	0.01	−0.02	0.01
Resident of the South	0.01	0.01	0.00	0.01	−0.00	0.01
Internet access	0.05**	0.02	−0.01	0.02	−0.03*	0.02
Born-again	−0.02	0.01	−0.01	0.01	−0.01	0.01
Church attendance	0.03	0.02	0.04*	0.02	0.08***	0.02
U.S. citizen	0.07*	0.04	−0.03	0.03	0.01	0.03
Equation						
Intercept	0.05	0.06	0.03	0.06	0.07	0.05
Standard deviation, dependent variable	0.28		0.20		0.20	
R^2	0.69***		0.44***		0.44***	
Standard error of estimate	0.16		0.15		0.15	
N	958		958		958	

Source: The 2020 Pre-insurrection Survey (t_2), December 2020 and January 2021.
Notes: All variables are scored to range from 0 to 1. For their distributions, see table A.8. b = unstandardized regression coefficient; s.e. = standard error of the unstandardized regression coefficient. All variables were measured at t_2.
Significance of unstandardized OLS regression coefficients: * $p \leq .05$; ** $p \leq .01$; *** $p \leq .001$

Table A.8 The Distributions of the Variables Used in the Analyses (Table A.7)

Variable	Range	Mean	Standard Deviation	N
Institutional legitimacy—presidency	0 → 1	0.76	0.28	958
Institutional Legitimacy—Supreme Court	0 → 1	0.58	0.20	958
Institutional legitimacy—Senate	0 → 1	0.58	0.20	958
Awareness of Barrett confirmation	0 → 1	0.77	0.29	958
Evaluation of Barrett confirmation	0 → 1	0.53	0.39	958
Awareness of Trump actions	0 → 1	0.88	0.21	958
Evaluation of Trump actions	0 → 1	0.39	0.41	958

(*continued*)

Table A.8 (*continued*)

Variable	Range	Mean	Standard Deviation	N
Awareness of election controversy	0 → 1	0.88	0.23	958
Election fairness judgments	0 → 1	0.62	0.38	958
Belief that Democrats threaten democracy	0 → 1	0.45	0.38	958
Belief that Republicans threaten democracy	0 → 1	0.54	0.37	958
Support for the rule of law	0 → 1	0.70	0.18	958
Valuation of individual liberty	0 → 1	0.64	0.21	958
Support for civil liberties	0 → 1	0.55	0.21	958
Open-mindedness	0 → 1	0.53	0.21	958
Party identification	0 → 1	0.48	0.33	958
Ideological identification	0 → 1	0.51	0.26	958
Political knowledge	0 → 1	0.76	0.25	958
Gender	0 → 1	0.51	0.50	958
Age	0 → 1	0.36	0.58	958
Minority race	0 → 1	0.36	0.48	958
Level of education	0 → 1	0.51	0.29	958
Income	0 → 1	0.56	0.28	958
Homeownership	0 → 1	0.65	0.48	958
Metropolitan residence	0 → 1	0.82	0.38	958
Resident of the South	0 → 1	0.37	0.48	958
Internet access	0 → 1	0.90	0.30	958
Born-again	0 → 1	0.30	0.46	958
Church attendance	0 → 1	0.35	0.34	958
U.S. citizen	0 → 1	0.97	0.16	958

Source: The 2020 Pre-insurrection Survey (t_2), December 2020 and January 2021.

Chapter 5

Question Wording and Measurement: Perceptions and Assessments of Events, the Insurrection and Impeachment Events

How aware are you of the rioting[12] at the U.S. Capitol in Washington, D.C., on January 6, when, following a protest earlier in the day, supporters of Donald Trump broke into the Capitol building while the Senate and House were in the process of certifying Electoral College votes? Would you say you are . . .

very aware of the riot at the U.S. Capitol
somewhat aware of the riot at the U.S. Capitol

not very aware of the riot at the U.S. Capitol
not aware of the riot at the U.S. Capitol

Regarding the January 6 rioting at the Capitol, in your view, how harmful was the rioting to democracy in America as it currently exists?

Was extremely harmful to American democracy
Was somewhat harmful to American democracy
Was not very harmful to American democracy
Was not at all harmful to American democracy

And how aware are you that former President Donald Trump was impeached by the U.S. House of Representatives and tried before the U.S. Senate on charges of inciting an insurrection in Washington, D.C. on January 6?

Very aware of the impeachment and trial
Somewhat aware of the impeachment and trial
Not very aware of the impeachment and trial
Not aware of the impeachment and trial

Regarding the impeachment trial of former President Donald Trump for inciting an insurrection, how harmful would you say the impeachment trial is to democracy in America as it currently exists?

Was extremely harmful to American democracy
Was somewhat harmful to American democracy
Was not very harmful to American democracy
Was not at all harmful to American democracy

As you might know, former President Trump was not convicted at his impeachment trial in the U.S. Senate because fewer than the required two-thirds of the Senators voted to convict him. What is your opinion of this outcome? Would you say that you. . .

strongly approve of former President Trump not being convicted for his role in the January 6 insurrection
somewhat approve of former President Trump not being convicted for his role in the January 6 insurrection
somewhat disapprove of former President Trump not being convicted for his role in the January 6 insurrection
strongly disapprove of former President Trump not being convicted for his role in the January 6 insurrection

Support for the Rule of Law, Individual Political Liberty, and Civil Liberties (t_3): Results

See chapter 2.

Open-Mindedness (t_3): Results

CFA of the three-item-set produces a single significant factor (eigenvalue$_2$ = 0.62). The scale is to some degree reliable: Cronbach's alpha = 0.69 (mean inter-item correlation of 0.42). The correlation between the factor scores from this analysis and a simple summated index constructed from the items is 0.99.

Authoritarianism (t_3): Results

Authoritarianism was measured using the following items:[13]

> We are interested in your views about the attributes it is important for children to have. Which of the following do you think is more important for a child to have:
>> Independence or respect for elders?
>
>> Strongly prefer that children be independent
>> Somewhat prefer that children be independent
>> Somewhat prefer that children respect elders
>> Strongly prefer that children respect elders
>
> Which one do you think is more important for a child to have:
>> Obedience or self-reliance?
>
>> Strongly prefer obedience
>> Somewhat prefer obedience
>> Somewhat prefer self-reliance
>> Strongly prefer self-reliance
>
> Which one do you think is more important for a child to have:
>> Being orderly or imaginative?
>
>> Strongly prefer that children be orderly
>> Somewhat prefer that children be orderly

Somewhat prefer that children be imaginative
Strongly prefer that children be imaginative

Support for Democratic Institutions (t₃): Results

See chapter 2.

Supporting Analyses

Table A.9 Predictors of Support for Institutional Legitimacy after the January 6, 2021, Insurrection

Conceptualization/Predictor	Presidential Legitimacy		Supreme Court Legitimacy		Senate Legitimacy	
	b	s.e.	b	s.e.	b	s.e.
Events awareness and assessments						
Awareness of Barrett confirmation	0.02	0.01	0.04**	0.01	0.06***	0.01
Evaluation of Barrett confirmation	0.03**	0.01	**0.12*****	0.01	0.05***	0.01
Awareness of Trump actions	0.02	0.03	−0.04	0.03	0.01	0.03
Evaluation of Trump actions	−0.09***	0.02	0.01	0.02	0.04**	0.02
Awareness of election controversy	0.03	0.02	−0.01	0.02	−0.04	0.02
Election unfairness judgments	**−0.20*****	0.02	**−0.10*****	0.02	−0.06**	0.02
Awareness of Capitol insurrection	0.00	0.03	−0.03	0.03	−0.01	0.03
Capitol insurrection not harmful	−0.07***	0.01	−0.00	0.02	−0.05**	0.01
Awareness of Trump impeachment	−0.01	0.02	0.07**	0.02	−0.04	0.02
Trump impeachment not harmful	0.00	0.01	0.04***	0.01	0.04***	0.01
Approval of no conviction for Trump	−0.02	0.02	0.05**	0.02	0.03	0.02
Party threat assessments						
Belief that Democrats threaten democracy	**−0.12*****	0.01	−0.03*	0.01	−0.07***	0.01
Belief that Republicans threaten democracy	0.05***	0.01	−0.05***	0.01	0.01	0.01
Democratic values and personality						
Support for the rule of law	0.08***	0.02	**0.21*****	0.02	**0.20*****	0.02
Valuation of individual liberty	0.00	0.02	**0.16*****	0.02	**0.11*****	0.02
Support for civil liberties	0.06***	0.02	**0.13*****	0.02	0.06***	0.02
Open-mindedness	**0.19*****	0.02	**0.15*****	0.02	**0.11*****	0.02
Authoritarianism	−0.01	0.02	−0.02	0.02	−0.05**	0.02
Partisanship and ideology						
Party identification	−0.05**	0.02	−0.04*	0.02	−0.02	0.02
Ideological identification	0.01	0.02	**0.10*****	0.02	0.06**	0.02

(continued)

Table A.9 (*continued*)

Conceptualization/Predictor	Presidential Legitimacy		Supreme Court Legitimacy		Senate Legitimacy	
	b	s.e.	b	s.e.	b	s.e.
Political sophistication						
Political knowledge	**0.10*****	0.02	0.06***	0.02	0.06**	0.02
Demographic attributes						
Gender	−0.01	0.01	0.02*	0.01	0.01	0.01
Age	−0.05**	0.02	0.07***	0.02	0.08***	0.02
Minority race	−0.01	0.01	−0.02	0.01	−0.04***	0.01
Level of education	0.04**	0.01	0.07***	0.01	0.05***	0.01
Income	0.00	0.01	−0.01	0.02	0.03*	0.02
Homeownership	0.02*	0.01	0.01	0.01	0.00	0.01
Metropolitan residence	0.02*	0.01	−0.01	0.01	−0.01	0.01
Resident of the South	0.01	0.01	−0.01	0.01	0.00	0.01
Internet access	0.00	0.01	−0.01	0.01	0.02	0.01
Born-again	0.00	0.01	−0.01	0.01	−0.02*	0.01
Church attendance	0.00	0.01	0.00	0.01	0.01	0.01
U.S. citizen	−0.01	0.03	0.05	0.03	0.02	0.03
Equation						
Intercept	0.58***	0.04	−0.04	0.05	0.16**	0.05
Standard deviation, dependent variable	0.25		0.20		0.18	
R^2	0.69***		0.49***		0.41***	
Standard error of estimate	0.14		0.15		0.14	
N	1,864		1,864		1.864	

Source: The 2021 Insurrection and Impeachment Survey (t_3), February and March 2021.

Notes: All variables are scored to range from 0 to 1. For their distributions, see table A.11. b = unstandardized regression coefficient; s.e. = standard error of the unstandardized regression coefficient. Regression coefficients greater than or equal to 0.10 are shown in boldface. No variables have a variance inflation factor (VIF) equal to or exceeding 5.0. In this instance, the highest VIF score is 4.4, for the variable "approval of no conviction for Trump." Only three variables have a VIF of ≥ 3.0. See also the appendix on question wording and measurement. Significance of unstandardized OLS regression coefficients: * $p \le .05$; ** $p \le .01$; *** $p \le .001$

Table A.10 Predictors of Support for U.S. Democratic Institutions after the January 6, 2021, Insurrection

Conceptualization/Predictor	b	s.e.	r
Events awareness and assessments			
Awareness of Barrett confirmation	0.02	0.02	0.19
Evaluation of Barrett confirmation	0.04*	0.02	0.03
Awareness of Trump actions	0.03	0.03	0.19
Evaluation of Trump actions	0.07**	0.02	−0.12
Awareness of election controversy	0.01	0.03	0.19
Election unfairness judgments	**−0.13***	0.02	−0.23
Awareness of Capitol insurrection	−0.08*	0.04	0.18
Capitol insurrection not harmful	−0.05**	0.02	−0.10
Awareness of Trump impeachment	−0.02	0.03	0.18
Trump Impeachment not harmful	0.02	0.02	0.13
Approval of no conviction for Trump	0.01	0.02	−0.05
Party threat assessments			
Belief that Democrats threaten democracy	**−0.11***	0.02	−0.19
Belief that Republicans threaten democracy	−0.02	0.02	−0.01
Democratic values and personality			
Support for the rule of law	**0.22***	0.03	0.36
Valuation of individual liberty	**0.09***	0.03	0.26
Support for civil liberties	**0.08***	0.02	0.24
Open-mindedness	**0.17***	0.03	0.36
Authoritarianism	−0.04	0.02	−0.09
Partisanship and ideology			
Party identification	−0.06**	0.02	−0.07
Ideological identification	**0.18***	0.03	0.04
Political sophistication			
Political knowledge	**0.13***	0.02	0.34
Demographic attributes			
Gender	0.02	0.01	0.18
Age	**0.10***	0.02	0.29
Minority race	−0.02	0.01	−0.17
Level of education	−0.01	0.02	0.19
Income	−0.01	0.02	0.16
Homeownership	−0.01	0.01	0.12
Metropolitan residence	−0.01	0.01	0.04
Resident of the South	0.02*	0.01	−0.02
Internet access	0.05**	0.02	0.12
Born-again	−0.02	0.01	−0.09

(*continued*)

Table A.10 (*continued*)

Conceptualization/Predictor	b	s.e.	r
Church attendance	0.05**	0.02	0.07
U.S. citizen	0.03	0.04	0.06
Equation			
Intercept	0.12	0.06	
Standard deviation, dependent variable	0.23		
R²	0.35***		
Standard error of estimate	0.19		
N	1,864		

Source: The 2021 Insurrection and Impeachment Survey (t_3), February and March 2021.
Notes: All variables are scored to range from 0 to 1. For their distributions, see table A.11. b = unstandardized regression coefficient; s.e. = standard error of the unstandardized regression coefficient. Regression coefficients greater than or equal to ±0.10 are shown in boldface. No variables have a variance inflation factor equal to or exceeding 5.0. In this instance, the highest VIF score is 4.4, for the variable "Approval of Trump not being convicted." Only three variables have a VIF of ≥ 3.0.
Significance of unstandardized OLS regression coefficients: * $p \leq .05$; ** $p \leq .01$; *** $p \leq .001$

Table A.11 The Distributions of the Variables Used in the Analyses (Tables A.9 and A.10)

Variable	Range	Mean	Standard Deviation	N
Institutional legitimacy—presidency	0 → 1	0.78	0.25	1,864
Institutional legitimacy—Supreme Court	0 → 1	0.59	0.20	1,864
Institutional legitimacy—Senate	0 → 1	0.60	0.18	1,864
Support for democratic institutions	0 → 1	0.63	0.23	1,864
Awareness of Barrett confirmation	0 → 1	0.76	0.31	1,864
Evaluation of Barrett confirmation	0 → 1	0.55	0.38	1,864
Awareness of Trump actions	0 → 1	0.89	0.21	1,864
Evaluation of Trump actions	0 → 1	0.35	0.40	1,864
Awareness of election controversy	0 → 1	0.88	0.23	1,864
Election unfairness judgments	0 → 1	0.34	0.37	1,864
Awareness of Capitol insurrection	0 → 1	0.92	0.18	1,864
Capitol insurrection not harmful	0 → 1	0.23	0.31	1,864
Awareness of Trump impeachment	0 → 1	0.90	0.20	1,864
Trump impeachment not harmful	0 → 1	0.54	0.39	1,864
Approval of no conviction for Trump	0 → 1	0.42	0.43	1,864
Belief that Democrats threaten democracy	0 → 1	0.42	0.38	1,864
Belief that Republicans threaten democracy	0 → 1	0.53	0.36	1,864
Support for the rule of law	0 → 1	0.71	0.18	1,864
Valuation of individual liberty	0 → 1	0.66	0.21	1,864
Support for civil liberties	0 → 1	0.55	0.21	1,864

Table A.11 (*continued*)

Variable	Range	Mean	Standard Deviation	N
Open-mindedness	0 → 1	0.53	0.22	1,864
Authoritarianism	0 → 1	0.49	0.24	1,864
Party identification	0 → 1	0.45	0.34	1,864
Ideological identification	0 → 1	0.49	0.27	1,864
Political knowledge	0 → 1	0.80	0.24	1,864
Gender	0 → 1	0.51	0.50	1,864
Age	0 → 1	0.41	0.25	1,864
Minority race	0 → 1	0.36	0.48	1,864
Level of education	0 → 1	0.51	0.28	1,864
Income	0 → 1	0.56	0.28	1,864
Homeownership	0 → 1	0.67	0.47	1,864
Metropolitan residence	0 → 1	0.85	0.36	1,864
Resident of the South	0 → 1	0.39	0.49	1,864
Internet access	0 → 1	0.92	0.28	1,864
Born-again	0 → 1	0.25	0.43	1,864
Church attendance	0 → 1	0.33	0.32	1,864
U.S. citizen	0 → 1	0.99	0.11	1,864

Source: The 2021 Insurrection and Impeachment Survey (t_3), February and March 2021.

Chapter 6

Supporting Analyses

Table A.12 Predictors of Racial Differences in Support for U.S. Democratic Institutions

Conceptualization/Predictor	Black People			White People		
	b	s.e.	r	b	s.e.	r
Events awareness and assessments						
Awareness of Barrett confirmation**	0.09**	0.03	0.29	−0.02	0.02	0.22
Evaluation of Barrett confirmation	0.09***	0.03	−0.06	0.04	0.02	0.03
Awareness of Trump actions	0.05	0.04	0.30	−0.01	0.05	0.16
Evaluation of Trump actions	0.00	0.04	−0.21	0.08**	0.03	−0.15
Awareness of election controversy	0.03	0.04	0.28	0.05	0.05	0.17
Election unfairness judgments**	0.03	0.04	−0.23	−0.18***	0.03	−0.06
Awareness of Capitol insurrection	−0.05	0.05	0.29	−0.10	0.05	.016
Capitol insurrection not harmful*	−0.12**	0.05	−0.21	−0.00	0.02	−0.23
Awareness of Trump impeachment	−0.00	0.05	0.22	0.01	0.04	0.18
Trump impeachment not harmful	0.01	0.02	0.12	0.02	0.02	0.14
Approval of no conviction for Trump	−0.03	0.04	−0.18	−0.01	0.03	−0.10

Table A.12 (*continued*)

Conceptualization/Predictor	Black People b	s.e.	r	White People b	s.e.	r
Party threat assessments						
Belief that Democrats threaten democracy	−0.12***	0.03	−0.20	−0.09***	0.02	−0.19
Belief that Republicans threaten democracy	−0.06*	0.03	−0.03	−0.02	0.02	0.02
Democratic values and personality						
Support for the rule of law	0.19***	0.05	0.37	0.26***	0.04	0.36
Valuation of individual liberty	−0.00	0.04	0.21	0.10***	0.03	0.26
Support for civil liberties	0.13***	0.04	0.16	0.07**	0.03	0.26
Open-mindedness	0.23***	0.04	0.30	0.13***	0.03	0.33
Authoritarianism	−0.00	0.03	0.01	−0.03	0.03	−0.08
Partisanship and ideology						
Party identification***	−0.21***	0.04	−0.23	−0.06*	0.03	−0.12
Ideological identification	0.21***	0.04	0.09	0.17***	0.03	0.02
Political sophistication						
Political knowledge**	0.05	0.04	0.33	0.19***	0.03	0.39
Demographic attributes						
Gender	0.02	0.02	0.19	0.04**	0.01	0.23
Age	0.16***	0.04	0.38	0.09***	0.03	0.31
Level of education	0.06	0.03	0.25	0.02	0.02	0.17
Income	0.04	0.03	0.33	−0.02	0.02	0.15
Homeownership	0.01	0.02	0.27	−0.00	0.01	0.12
Metropolitan residence	−0.04	0.03	−0.01	−0.01	0.01	0.07
Resident of the South	0.03*	0.02	0.12	0.01	0.01	−0.00
Internet access	0.03	0.02	0.20	0.03	0.02	0.10
Born-again	0.00	0.02	−0.05	0.00	0.02	−0.04
Church attendance*	−0.03	0.03	0.13	0.04*	0.02	0.08
U.S. citizen	−0.06	0.07	0.00	0.11	0.09	0.08
Equation						
Intercept	0.11	0.10		−0.01	0.11	
Standard deviation—dependent variable	0.23			0.22		
R²	0.44***			0.37***		
Standard error of estimate	0.18			0.18		
N	611			1,193		

Source: The 2021 Insurrection and Impeachment Survey (t₃), February and March 2021.
Notes: All variables are scored to range from 0 to 1. For their distributions, see table A.13. b = unstandardized regression coefficient; s.e. = standard error of the unstandardized regression coefficient; r = bivariate correlation coefficient. Variables for which the interaction term with the race dichotomy is statistically significant are shown in boldface, along with the indication of the level of statistical significance of the interaction term in a single integrated equation. N = 1,804.
Significance of unstandardized OLS regression coefficients: * $p \leq .05$; ** $p \leq .01$; *** $p \leq .001$

Table A.13 The Distributions of the Variables Used in the Main Analysis (Table A.12)

Variable	Black People Mean	Black People Standard Deviation	White People Mean	White People Standard Deviation
Support for U.S. democratic institutions***	0.60	0.23	0.66	0.22
Awareness of Barrett confirmation***	0.71	0.34	0.80	0.28
Appropriateness of Barrett confirmation***	0.37	0.32	0.60	0.39
Awareness of Trump actions***	0.88	0.25	0.92	0.19
Appropriateness of Trump actions***	0.15	0.28	0.39	0.41
Awareness of election controversy***	0.84	0.28	0.93	0.18
Election was rigged***	0.16	0.27	0.36	0.37
Awareness of Capitol insurrection**	0.91	0.21	0.94	0.15
Capitol insurrection not harmful ***	0.09	0.23	0.27	0.32
Awareness of Trump impeachment	0.91	0.20	0.92	0.19
Trump impeachment not harmful ***	0.65	0.39	0.54	0.39
Approval of Trump not convicted***	0.17	0.29	0.49	0.44
Belief that Democrats threaten democracy***	0.17	0.27	0.47	0.38
Belief that Republicans threaten democracy***	0.72	0.32	0.50	0.36
Support for the rule of law***	0.68	0.17	0.74	0.17
Valuation of individual liberty***	0.58	0.20	0.69	0.21
Support for civil liberties	0.55	0.21	0.56	0.22
Open-mindedness***	0.46	0.21	0.57	0.21
Authoritarianism***	0.62	0.26	0.46	0.23
Party identification (Republican)***	0.21	0.24	0.49	0.35
Ideological identification (conservative) ***	0.42	0.22	0.50	0.28
Political knowledge***	0.73	0.27	0.84	0.21
Gender (female)***	0.43	0.50	0.54	0.50
Age	0.42	0.23	0.44	0.25
Level of education**	0.50	0.29	0.54	0.27
Income***	0.44	0.30	0.59	0.27
Homeownership***	0.46	0.50	0.73	0.44
Metropolitan residence***	0.91	0.29	0.81	0.39
Resident of the South***	0.57	0.50	0.34	0.48
Internet access***	0.84	0.37	0.94	0.24
Born-again***	0.45	0.50	0.20	0.40
Church attendance***	0.43	0.34	0.31	0.32
U.S. citizen*	0.99	0.11	1.00	0.06
Supreme Court legitimacy***	.52	0.18	0.63	0.20
Senate legitimacy***	0.55	0.18	0.64	0.17
Presidency legitimacy***	0.86	0.19	0.77	0.25

Source: The 2021 Insurrection and Impeachment Survey (t$_3$), February and March 2021.

Notes: All variables range from 0 through 1. Black N = 611; White N = 1193.

Significance of difference of means across race (student's t-test): * $p \le$ .05; ** $p \le$ .01; *** $p \le$ .001

Chapter 7

Supporting Analyses

Table A.14 The Distributions of the Variables Used in the Analyses (Tables 7.2 and 7.3)

Variable	Range	Mean	Standard Deviation	N
Institutional support (t_3)	0 → 1	0.58	0.23	505
Institutional support (t_4)	0 → 1	0.55	0.24	505
Supreme Court support (t_3)	0 → 1	0.51	0.19	505
Supreme Court support (t_4)	0 → 1	0.44	0.19	505
Awareness of Barrett confirmation (t_3)	0 → 1	0.72	0.32	505
Evaluation of Barrett confirmation (t_3)	0 → 1	0.34	0.31	505
Awareness of Trump actions (t_3)	0 → 1	0.87	0.25	505
Evaluation of Trump actions (t_3)	0 → 1	0.14	0.26	505
Awareness of election controversy (t_3)	0 → 1	0.86	0.26	505
Election unfairness judgments (t_3)	0 → 1	0.15	0.27	505
Awareness of Capitol insurrection (t_3)	0 → 1	0.91	0.20	505
Capitol insurrection not harmful (t_3)	0 → 1	0.08	0.20	505
Awareness of Trump impeachment (t_3)	0 → 1	0.90	0.20	505
Trump impeachment not harmful (t_3)	0 → 1	0.63	0.40	505
Approval of Trump not convicted (t_3)	0 → 1	0.16	0.29	505
Belief that Democrats threaten democracy (t_3)	0 → 1	0.19	0.28	505
Belief that Republicans threaten democracy (t_3)	0 → 1	0.72	0.32	505
Support for the rule of law (t_3)	0 → 1	0.67	0.18	505
Valuation of individual liberty (t_3)	0 → 1	0.56	0.20	505
Support for civil liberties (t_3)	0 → 1	0.54	0.22	505
Open-mindedness (t_3)	0 → 1	0.45	0.19	505
Authoritarianism (t_3)	0 → 1	0.63	0.25	505
Party identification (t_3)	0 → 1	0.20	0.25	505
Ideological identification (t_3)	0 → 1	0.42	0.22	505
Political knowledge (t_3)	0 → 1	0.73	0.26	505
Gender (t_3)	0 → 1	0.41	0.49	505
Age (t_3)	0 → 1	0.43	0.23	505
Level of education (t_3)	0 → 1	0.48	0.29	505
Income (t_3)	0 → 1	0.43	0.30	505
Homeownership (t_3)	0 → 1	0.43	0.50	505
Metropolitan residence (t_3)	0 → 1	0.89	0.32	505
Resident of the South (t_3)	0 → 1	0.58	0.49	505
Internet access (t_3)	0 → 1	0.84	0.37	505
Born-again (t_3)	0 → 1	0.45	0.50	505
Church attendance (t_3)	0 → 1	0.42	0.34	505
U.S. citizen (t_3)	0 → 1	0.99	0.12	505
Group identification (t_4)	0 → 1	0.74	0.21	505
Linked fate (t_4)	0 → 1	0.64	0.36	505
Personal experience (t_4)	0 → 1	0.23	0.33	505
Vicarious experience (t_4)	0 → 1	0.86	0.21	505

Source: The African American Panel Survey (t_4), June 2021.

NOTES

Preface

1. Nelson and Gibson 2019.
2. "The Lost Legitimacy of American Political Institutions? The Consequences of the 2020 Presidential Election." Russell Sage Foundation. Grant number G-2101-30330.
3. "Is America's Democracy at Risk? Inter-Racial and Intra-Racial Differences in Support for Democratic Institutions and Processes." Washington University in St. Louis, Center for the Study of Race, Ethnicity, and Equity and Weidenbaum Center.
4. "College Students and the Insurrection of January 6, 2021: Support for America's Political Institutions." Foundation for Individual Rights in Education.
5. Gibson and Howard 2007.

Chapter 1: The Consequences of Elections

1. Kelley-Romano and Carew 2018.
2. Michaels 2018.
3. Jones and Sun 2017.
4. Revesz 2017; Tobias 2019.
5. Roose 2021.
6. My references to the election of 2020 include the events prior to the election (for example, Trump saying that he would not accept losing), the election itself (which I count as a period of about four weeks to include the recounts and court challenges), and the aftermath (roughly the period after the Electoral College certified the election), during which the loser regularly attacked the election's validity and schemed about ways to overturn its outcome.
7. For his efforts in this coup, Trump's attorney, Rudy Giuliani, has been suspended from practicing law in the state of New York as well as in the District of Columbia,

and the process that may result in his being disbarred by the New York Bar Association is underway. Giuliani also faces several ethics charges, most recently from the Office of Disciplinary Counsel of the District of Columbia Bar (Hong, Rashbaum, and Protess 2021; Neumeister, Hays, and Tucker 2022; see also "Matter of Giuliani," Supreme Court of the State of New York, Appellate Division, First Judicial Department, Motion No. 2021-00491, Case No. 2021-00506, May 3, 2021.

8. These various efforts have been referred to as an "attempted coup," a "putsch," or, more specifically, a "self-coup" (for example, Hill 2021; see also Levitsky and Ziblatt 2018; Lieberman et al. 2019).

9. See, for example, Carey et al. 2019.

10. For example, Fallon 2018.

11. Many law professors and legal commentators worried that Trump's public attacks on the judiciary could have deleterious if not disastrous consequences for judicial legitimacy (Woodruff 2017). In one illustrative exchange, Professor Charles Geyh told the *Washington Post*: "Presidents have disagreed with court rulings all the time. What's unusual is he's essentially challenging the legitimacy of the court's role. And he's doing that without any reference to applicable law. . . . That they are blocking his order is all the evidence he needs that they are exceeding their authority. . . . That's worse than wrong. . . . On some level, that's dangerous" (quoted in Phillips 2017).

12. Kromphardt and Salamone 2021; Nelson and Gibson 2019; but see Armaly 2018.

13. For example, Gibson, Caldeira, and Spence 2003a; Kritzer 2001; Nicholson and Howard 2003; Price and Romantan 2004; Yates and Whitford 2002. Philip Abbott, Lyke Thompson, and Marjorie Sarbaugh-Thompson (2002) provide a useful and thorough review of contested American presidential elections.

14. But see Reeves and Rogowski 2023.

15. For example, Dupree and Hibbing 2022; Mondak et al. 2007.

16. For example, Gibson 1989.

17. Braman 2021.

18. Sniderman 1993.

19. For useful reviews of legitimacy theory, see Gibson 2015; Gibson and Nelson 2014a; Gordon and Huber 2019; Nelson and Gibson 2018; Smyth 2021; Tyler 2006. Because the legitimacy literature has been so often and so thoroughly reviewed, I here provide only a summary explication of the theory.

20. Easton 1965, 1975.

21. Tyler 2006, 375.

22. For recent applications of legitimacy theory, see, for example, Dietsch 2019 (banks); Lanis and Richardson 2012 (corporate social responsibility); Chapman 2007 (international affairs); Tankebe 2013 and Gibson 2024b (police); Martin and Waldman 2022 (algorithms). Many additional citations and subject matters could be listed.

23. For example, Wells 2007; Fallon 2018. Although modern interest in legitimacy is typically said to have begun with the work of Max Weber, the contemporary version of the theory (on which I rely) can be directly traced back to the work of David Easton

(1965), who essentially began the present-day study of sociological legitimacy. For a review of the Weberian and Eastonian roots of contemporary legitimacy theory, see Gordon and Huber 2019, 334–35.

24. Fallon 2018, 22–23.

25. For some thoughts about whether it is possible for an institution to have *too much* legitimacy, see Gibson and Nelson 2014b. Useful studies of normative legitimacy abound; see, for example, the collection of essays in Knight and Schwartzberg 2019. The philosophical literature addressing legitimacy without focusing on public opinion evidence is of little direct relevance to my study, so I follow nearly all empirical studies of institutional legitimacy in paying little attention to that body of work. For those who would like "A Quick Frolic through the Literature," see Levi 2019, 369. As I document later, interest in sociological legitimacy is widespread among scholars, policymakers, and even politicians and judges.

26. Diamond 1999, 162, emphasis added.

27. Easton 1965.

28. Caldeira and Gibson 1992, 658; Easton 1965.

29. Gibson and Caldeira 1992, 1126.

30. Gibson 2015.

31. Friedman 1977, 141.

32. Europeans sometimes refer to this as the "competence" to make a decision.

33. For example, Cann and Yates 2016.

34. For example, Gibson 2012, 2016; Gibson, Caldeira, and Baird 1998.

35. Farganis 2012, 207.

36. Gerstein 2022.

37. For example, Hurley 2022. Legitimacy has become such a hot topic that scholars have also made an effort to summarize legitimacy theory and its implications for lay audiences. See, for example, Ura and Hall 2022.

38. See, for example, Kelley-Romano and Carew 2018. While awkward, I will tend to refer to the office of the president as the "presidency/president" out of concern that, unlike most other political institutions, many Americans have difficulty distinguishing between the office (the presidency) and the incumbent (the president).

39. For a review, see Tyler and Trinkner 2018.

40. For example, Gibson and Nelson 2015.

41. Gibson and Caldeira 1992; see also Gibson and Nelson 2018; Haglin et al. 2021.

42. For example, Gibson and Caldeira 2011.

43. See Gibson and Nelson 2017; Krewson 2022; Krewson and Schroedel 2020, 2023.

44. See Nelson and Gibson 2019.

45. For example, Doherty and Wolak 2012; Mutz and Mondak 1997.

46. On elite leadership of public opinion, see Bullock 2011.

47. See, for example, Chatagnier 2012; Groeling and Baum 2008; Hetherington and Nelson 2003.

48. But see Bishin et al. 2021.

49. For example, Chatagnier 2012.

50. The key events of the election period are enumerated in chapter 3, and the key events of the insurrection period are enumerated in chapter 5.

51. Cantor 2017; Bloomberg 2020.

52. See Rutenberg et al. 2021.

53. Some rightly describe "exposure" to Supreme Court decisions as whether the respondent could have heard about and understood them (Christenson and Glick 2019, 647), but of course, "could have" is not at all a valid indicator of "did." Similarly, Dino Christenson and David Glick (2019, 638) properly refer to court decisions as "immediately observable," not "immediately observed."

54. In the context of judicial research, Michael Unger (2008) is particularly insistent on the need to measure not just exposure to Supreme Court decisions but understandings of them as well. In one of the few analyses of awareness of court decisions, Matthew Hitt, Kyle Saunders, and Kevin Scott (2019) document considerable variability in public awareness of rulings across court decisions, types of people, and the degree of coverage by the mass media (see also Malhotra and Jessee 2014).

55. For example, Althaus 2011.

56. Perhaps one of the most egregious such attempts was Trump's telephone call to the Georgia secretary of state on January 2, 2021. For a full accounting of these efforts, see Rutenberg et al. 2021.

57. Monmouth University Polling Institute 2020. The poll's total sample size, however, was only 807 respondents, so its findings regarding racial differences are unlikely to be very stable or precise.

58. In the same 2020 poll (Monmouth University Polling Institute 2020), 44 percent of Black people reported that they or an immediate family member had been harassed by the police. Gibson and Nelson (2018, 52) report that 40 percent of Black people claimed to have been treated unfairly by police because of their race.

59. Writing about the 2020 survey, the Monmouth poll analyst concluded: "Compared to five years ago, though, overall satisfaction with local police has increased among black Americans (from 50% at least somewhat satisfied in 2015 to 72% now), while it has held more steady among other minority groups (from 65% to 68%) and among whites (from 78% to 72%)" (but see Dupree and Hibbing 2022).

60. Gibson and Nelson 2018, 37–39.

61. About 8 percent of Black people voted for Trump (NPR Staff 2021). Furthermore, in 2019, only 5 percent of registered voters were Black Republicans, according to a Pew study (Gramlich 2020).

62. Summers 2020.

63. Cramer 2021. Rogers Smith and Desmond King (2021) argue that, while Trump has not explicitly endorsed White nationalism, he might at least be thought of as one who advocates "White Protectionism."

64. Gibson and Nelson 2018. For example, on the most extreme measure of institutional support—whether to do away with the institution altogether if it does not make desirable decisions—about 10 percent of White respondents rejected the Court. For

Black people, the figure nearly doubles (to 18 percent). Roughly one in five Black Americans expressed the lowest possible level of institutional commitment to the nation's highest court.

65. For example, Lieberman et al. 2019.
66. Easton 1965.
67. Gibson and Caldeira 1992.

Chapter 2: Cross-institutional Approaches to Institutional Legitimacy: Conceptualization and Measurement

1. I tend to refer to "support for democratic institutions, processes, and values" as the main concept of interest. For brevity's sake, however, I also refer to this as "support for democracy" or "support for democratic values."
2. Dahl 1971. See also the extensive discussion in Gibson and Gouws 2003, especially chapter 3.
3. Gibson 1996, 11. The literature on "false consensus" is vast. See, for example, Coleman 2018; Gill and Rojas 2021; Yousif, Aboody, and Keil 2019.
4. Zakaria 1997; see also Mill 1982.
5. Several scholars operationalize support for democracy with a "satisfaction with democracy" measure. For trenchant criticisms of this approach, see Canache, Mondak, and Seligson 2001; Linde and Ekman 2003. For a review, see Mattes 2018.
6. Gibson 1996.
7. For example, Gibson, Duch, and Tedin 1992; see also Claassen 2019, 2020.
8. For example, Gibson and Gouws 2003.
9. For example, Bartels 2020.
10. One final methodological point requires clarification. This project employs four major surveys, each of which includes some, but not all, of the measures previewed here. The t_3 survey—fielded in February and March 2021 (see the appendix for details)—includes the greatest number of indicators and the largest number of respondents, in part because oversamples of Black Americans and active students are included, and in part because the survey took place after attitudes toward the major events (the presidential election, the insurrection, and the impeachment) had cooled off somewhat. The specific measures I employ at various stages of the analysis may not always be the exact one I discuss in this chapter, but I am always careful to point out when measures deviate (for example, when item wording changed across surveys) and what the consequences might be of that deviation.
11. For example, Bartels and Johnston 2020.
12. Easton 1965.
13. Hannah Werner and Sofie Marien (2022, 431) take a similar approach of focusing on losers, arguing that "finding strategies that can foster" losers' consent is not only an "important undertaking" but perhaps the most important.
14. Easton 1965. Following Gibson and Caldeira (2009), I equate several terms in this book: "institutional legitimacy," "diffuse support," and "institutional loyalty." This

is the same concept that Gregory Caldeira and I refer to as "institutional support" (Caldeira and Gibson 1992). For a full explication of the theoretical foundations of this concept, see the discussion in Caldeira and Gibson (1992, 636–42).

15. Gibson 2011, 2017.

16. Care should be taken here not to focus exclusively on policy outputs as the only basis of performance evaluations. Evaluations can also be based on procedural factors, such as transparency (see, for example, Grimmelikhuijsen and Klijn 2015).

17. Space limitations in the surveys precluded questions about attitudes toward the House of Representatives, although I doubt many people hold distinctive attitudes toward the House and the Senate.

18. See, for example, Gibson, Caldeira, and Baird 1998; Gibson, Caldeira, and Spence 2003a.

19. Nelson and Gibson 2018.

20. An important exception is the pathbreaking work by Andrew Reeves and Jon Rogowski (2015, 2021). However, they focus on what might be called "applied contextualized legitimacy," in much the same way as judicial studies employing experimental vignettes (see, for example, Gibson 2008). This is a somewhat different approach to the generalized sociological legitimacy investigated in this research.

21. For example, Hibbing and Theiss-Morse 1995, 2001. Ironically, one of the earliest studies of institutional legitimacy, G. R. Boynton and Gerhard Loewenberg's (1973) analysis of diffuse support for the German Bundestag, focused on institutional support for a legislature. Follow-ups to that study, however, have been limited.

22. The use of various surveys in this project might become slightly confusing at this point. Readers might expect to see descriptive data reported from the baseline survey (July 2020) in discussing the conceptualizations and operationalizations of key concepts. I have chosen instead to report on the February and March 2021 survey results. That is the survey that included measures of the legitimacy of all three institutions and was fielded after the "heat" from the presidential election had died down to some extent. For descriptive results on the legitimacy of the Supreme Court in mid-2020 (the t_1 survey in this project), see online appendix 2.1 (https://www.russellsage.org/publications/democracys-destruction).

23. An important issue in the use of Likert items (agree/disagree) to measure institutional attitudes is whether to allow respondents an explicit "don't know" (or "neither agree nor disagree") response option. In this research, I tend to present such an option to respondents, under the theory that some people do not devote much thought to political institutions. However, respondents who are semiprofessional survey takers—as they are in all of the NORC AmeriSpeak surveys—may be more motivated to minimize the time and cognitive effort it takes to deliver a conclusion about these questions than to express an opinion about which they have arrived by effortful thought (see Roberts et al. 2019 on "satisficing" behavior in survey research). The availability of a "neither agree nor disagree" response option, while desirable by most criteria, certainly makes satisficing more attractive and easier. Partly in play here is a mode effect—interviewees experience little or no shame in telling a computer that they have

no opinion, whereas telephone interviews with live interviewers may put social desirability pressures on interviewees to formulate substantive answers even when none in fact exists. But also in play is experience: semiprofessional respondents learn how to answer internet-based questions as quickly and easily as possible. Unfortunately, surveys' combination of mode and experience attributes makes it difficult to compare survey results based on different methodologies and samples.

24. The item-set is quite reliable (Cronbach's alpha = 0.85; average inter-item correlation = 0.48) and strongly unidimensional (eigenvalue$_2$ = 0.85). All the items are related to the latent diffuse support construct, with factor loadings ranging from 0.51 to 0.80. (See online appendix 2.1 for a discussion of classical test theory and the measurement methodology used throughout this research.) For a discussion of how to interpret Cronbach's alpha, see the appendix.

25. The index is very strongly correlated with the factor score extracted from the common factor analysis (CFA) of the six items (r = 0.99). This and nearly all variables employed in the analysis are scored to range from 0 to 1.

26. On the "birther" scheme, see, for example, Kelley-Romano and Carew 2018.

27. Cronbach's alpha is 0.89 (mean inter-item correlation = 0.68), and the second factor extracted by CFA has an eigenvalue of only 0.48 (with the smallest factor loading of the items of 0.69). The index is correlated with the factor score from the CFA at 0.99. These findings suggest that the items measuring presidential legitimacy may not be capturing particularly well the entire range of variation in opinions. In essence, it seems that the propositions are roughly redundant—and were perhaps too "easy"—and therefore fail to discriminate adequately among respondents. The main consequence is that there is too much clumping of respondents at the pro-legitimacy end of the index. Future research should certainly work on developing more finely tuned measures of presidential legitimacy.

28. In contrast to attitudes toward individual senators or senators as a collective; see, for example, Mondak et al. 2007.

29. Gibson, Caldeira, and Spence 2005, 195.

30. One item in Boynton and Loewenberg's (1973) measurement of diffuse support for the German Bundestag in the 1950s proposed reducing the parliament's size. On its face, moving from more than two hundred members of parliament (MPs) to just fifty may not seem to threaten legitimacy. But Boynton and Loewenberg argue that such a dramatic decrease in the institution's size would necessarily change its function and that therefore the "reform" should be understood as legitimacy threatening. Structural changes that cause functional changes are often considered to be threats to an institution's legitimacy.

31. Gibson, Caldeira, and Spence 2005.

32. The item-set is weakly reliable (Cronbach's alpha = 0.65; mean inter-item correlation = 0.32) and unidimensional (eigenvalue$_2$ = 0.94), and all items load significantly on the latent factor (minimum loading = 0.41). The index is correlated with the factor score from the CFA at 0.94.

33. The item-set is quite reliable: Cronbach's alpha is 0.78 (mean inter-item correla-

tion = 0.55). CFA confirms that the items are also unidimensional (eigenvalue$_2$ = 0.78), with the strongest factor loading associated with the last statement. The correlation between this index and the factor score from a CFA is 0.97.

34. These findings seem inconsistent with a truism identified by Matthew Graham and Milan Svolik (2020, 392, emphasis added):

> "It is nearly impossible to find an American who says that he is opposed to democracy or favors some alternative. . . . On the contrary, nearly everyone professes to believe that democracy is the best form of government."

> This is how Robert A. Dahl, writing in 1966, summarized contemporary evidence for the support for democracy in the United States (Dahl 1966, 40). *It remains conventional wisdom to this day.*

35. See, for example, Caldeira and Gibson 1992; Sullivan, Pierson, and Marcus 1982.

36. For example, Gibson 2013; Gibson, Claassen, and Barceló 2020; Nelson and Gibson 2017.

37. When the five items are factor-analyzed, a single dominant factor emerges (eigenvalue$_2$ = 0.87). The best indicator of the concept is the last statement (law is not important; what's important is that our government solve society's problems); all indicators load on the first unrotated factor at 0.40 or higher. The item-set is quite reliable, with a Cronbach's alpha of 0.75 and a mean inter-item correlation of 0.38. I have created a measure of support for the rule of law (universalism) that is simply the average response to the five statements. This index correlates with the factor score from the factor analysis at 0.98. For some descriptive purposes, I also use an index indicating the number of pro-liberty responses to the five items. On this measure, 31 percent of respondents gave pro-rule-of-law responses to all five items; 6 percent gave no pro-rule-of-law responses.

38. For example, Gibson 2013; Gibson, Claassen, and Barceló 2020; Nelson and Gibson 2017.

39. When the three items are factor-analyzed, a single dominant factor emerges (eigenvalue$_2$ = 0.69). The best indicator of the concept is the last statement (free speech is just not worth it). The item-set is at least fairly reliable (especially for a scale with only three indicators), with a Cronbach's alpha of 0.64 and a mean inter-item correlation of 0.38. I created a measure of support for minority political liberty that is simply the average response to the three statements. This index correlates with the factor score from the factor analysis at 0.98. For some descriptive purposes, I also use an index indicating the number of pro-liberty responses to the three items. On this measure, 33 percent of respondents gave pro-liberty responses to all three items; 17 percent gave no pro-liberty responses.

40. CFA analysis of the responses to these four items shows a single dominant factor, with an eigenvalue of 2.3. The second extracted factor had an eigenvalue of 0.70. The strongest loading on the first factor was from the item regarding demonstrations by atheists; the weakest was for White nationalists. The item-set is reasonably reliable, with a Cronbach's alpha of 0.74 and a mean inter-item correlation of 0.43. I created a measure

of support for civil liberties that is simply the average response to the four statements. This index correlates with the factor score from the factor analysis at 0.99. For some descriptive purposes, I also use an index indicating the number of tolerant responses to the four items. On this measure, 33 percent gave tolerant responses for all four groups, and 15 percent gave no tolerant responses.

41. See, for example, Gibson 2006, 2013. On dogmatism, see Rokeach 1960.
42. CFA produced a single significant factor (eigenvalue$_2$ = 0.64). The scale is to some considerable degree reliable: Cronbach's alpha = 0.72 (mean inter-item correlation of 0.41). The correlation between the factor scores from this analysis and a simple summated index constructed from the items is 0.99.
43. I reiterate that the estimates for African Americans are more reliable than those for Hispanic people and are considerably more reliable than those for other races.

Chapter 3: Awareness and Assessments of the 2020 Presidential Election Events

1. For challenges to this conclusion, see, for example, Gibson and Caldeira 2009; Lupia 2016.
2. The classic citation is Delli Carpini and Keeter 1996.
3. For a recent paper that assumes that events are exogenous, see Bae and Lee 2021; see also Goldsmith, Horiuchi, and Matush 2021.
4. See Zaller 1992.
5. There is no better example of this than the controversies associated with judging crowd size at events (see, for example, Doig 2021; Phillips and Pohl 2021; Wang 2017).
6. For example, Peffley and Hurwitz 2010.
7. Jefferson, Neuner, and Pasek 2021.
8. As has been documented in surveys conducted by the Pew Research Center and others, Black and White Americans differ profoundly in their perceptions and evaluations of recent police events. "Whites . . . are nearly three times as likely as blacks to express at least a fair amount of confidence in the investigations into the [Ferguson] shootings." Furthermore, "roughly three-quarters of blacks (76%) have little or no confidence in the investigations, with 45% saying they have no confidence at all" (Pew Research Center 2014, 2). A contemporaneous *New York Times*/CBS poll found that a majority of Black people believe that the police are more likely to use deadly force against a Black person; a majority of White people believe that race is not a factor in an officer's decision to use deadly force. In that same survey, 45 percent of Black people said that they had experienced racial discrimination at some point in their lives, while almost no White respondents reported racial discrimination (Vega and Thee-Brenan 2014). In short, polls conducted in the wake of these violent conflicts between African Americans and police have revealed stark racial gulfs in public opinion.

Ferguson is not an aberration—virtually the same findings emerge from evaluations of events ranging all the way from the O. J. Simpson trial in the mid-1990s to the 2012 killing of Trayvon Martin. In a more recent survey, the Pew Research Center (2016) finds that Black Americans are about half as likely as White Americans to believe that police use the right amount of force when the situation demands it, that the police treat racial and ethnic groups equally, and that the police will hold accountable officers accused of misconduct. In short, many Black people have become alienated from the legal system. Indeed, Donald Haider-Markel and Mark Joslyn (2017), studying how people attribute blame for violent confrontations between the police and Black Americans, find stark racial and political differences in public opinion. If men are from Mars and women are from Venus, then White people may be on Earth but many Black people, in their relationship with law enforcement, feel as though they have been expelled to Pluto.

9. Jefferson, Neuner, and Pasek 2021, 1167, table 1. An obvious and relevant example is found in perceptions of the claims about the behavior of Supreme Court nominee Brett Kavanaugh (see Cummings and Jansen 2018).

10. For a definitive analysis of the facts in the case, see the report of Eric Holder's U.S. Department of Justice 2015.

11. Peay and Camarillo 2021.

12. Manekin and Mitts 2022, 176; see also Hipp 2010; Sampson and Raudenbush 2004.

13. Ryan and Aziz 2021.

14. Berlinski et al. 2021. An obvious confirmation of this hypothesis is Vladimir Putin's apparently successful effort through the heavy-handed manipulation of the Russian mass media to convince the Russian people that there is no "war" in Ukraine.

15. For evidence that this is in fact the case, see Nelson and Gibson 2019.

16. Jefferson, Neuner, and Pasek 2021. The authors are careful to use "bias" in an entirely empirical way, without normative judgment, to simply indicate a difference between objective facts and perceptions of those facts.

17. This study is also noteworthy as an example of experimental research that attempts to prime racial identities. Its effort at priming, however, either failed to activate identities or activated innocuous identities that "did not lead respondents to answer summary judgment or belief questions differently" (ibid., 1173).

18. Ibid., 1167.

19. For example, Badrinathan 2021.

20. On Trump's efforts to delegitimize the election's outcome before the election, see Kevin Liptak 2020; Riccardi 2020. In late 2022, Norman Eisen and his colleagues (2021, 7) reported: "Trump's communications with state officials potentially violated state criminal laws on matters of immense state interest. While Trump was president at the time he sought to interfere with the election in Georgia, our constitutional scheme (and its protection of federal interests) poses no barrier to the vindication of Georgia's interests in enforcing its criminal code."

21. I do, however, want to be careful not to simply assume that what tarnishes an individual necessarily tarnishes an institution.

22. Of course, the analyses use the full four-point scale for each of these variables.

23. As it turns out, there is little relationship between awareness of an event and evaluations of it. The strongest correlation is with the Barrett affair, but the correlation coefficient is only –0.06. This finding is no doubt a function of the extremely high salience of the events about which the respondents were questioned, and therefore the results of my analysis might not be entirely generalizable to less salient happenings, should they materialize.

24. I would briefly note here that responses to this item are more closely connected to affect toward Barrett than affect toward the Supreme Court (both measured by 101-point feeling thermometers at t_2). The correlations are 0.67 with the former and 0.30 with the latter.

25. It is worth noting that ideological and partisan self-identifications are not necessarily synonymous: the correlation is only 0.71 (indicating, of course, that about half of their variances are shared). For further discussion of the relationship between these two identities, see the appendix.

26. The relationship in figure 3.2 is an apt reminder of what a statistically significant correlation of 0.14 actually looks like. The relationship is clearly a very weak one.

27. As a mini robustness check, it is noteworthy that institutional support at t_1 does not predict election attitudes, even if it does predict Barrett nomination attitudes.

28. Caution ought to be exercised about assuming that all events are subjected to motivated reasoning. For a contrary example, Christenson and Glick (2019, 647), in their analysis of Supreme Court rulings on the Voting Rights Act and the Defense of Marriage Act, find "no evidence that the effect of these decisions is conditioned by party."

Chapter 4: The Election's Consequences: Did Trump's Canards Undermine the Legitimacy of U.S. Political Institutions?

1. For ease of reference, I refer to the t_2 survey as the December 2020 survey, even though about 15 percent of the interviews were concluded in the first few days of January 2021. This also has the advantage of avoiding confusion with my insurrection survey.

2. For example, Bartels and Johnston 2013.

3. Christenson and Glick 2019, 639, emphasis added.

4. Chapter 2 discusses the conceptualization and operationalization of attitudes toward the national political democratic institutions in great detail. To recap, I developed and validated indices of support for each of these institutions. My analysis revealed that, to a significant degree, these respondents held distinguishable attitudes toward these three institutions. Although support for the Supreme Court and support for the Senate are fairly strongly correlated (r = 0.67, so less than one-half of the variance is shared), neither is very strongly related to support for the Biden presidency (r = 0.22 and 0.27, respectively). It therefore makes sense to analyze the variability in each of these measures individually.

5. Gibson and Nelson 2014a, 215.

6. The item-set is a quite reliable measure of institutional support (Cronbach's alpha = 0.86) and is strongly unidimensional (eigenvalue$_2$ = 0.82), with substantial loadings from each of the six items.
7. Gibson and Caldeira 2009; Krewson 2022.
8. The citizenship variable is the sole exception.
9. On Supreme Court legitimacy, see, for example, Nelson and Gibson 2018.
10. In one limited sense this conclusion is not entirely accurate. Chapter 3 reports the results of an investigation of the predictors of evaluations of the Barrett nomination and confirmation at t_2, largely using attributes of the respondents at t_1. The most important conclusion from that analysis is that perceptions and evaluations of certain events seem to be subject to motivated reasoning and elite leadership, with Republicans and conservatives understanding the events quite differently from Democrats and liberals (for more details, see chapter 3). Still, perceptions of controversies over who gets nominated to the Supreme Court do not necessarily undermine the institution's legitimacy.
11. For example, Christenson and Glick 2019; Zilis 2015; but see Nelson and Tucker 2021.
12. But see, for example, Carrington and French 2021, 2022; Krewson 2022; Krewson and Schroedel 2020, 2023.
13. Note that the panel analysis focuses on a lagged dependent variable, whereas this analysis considers a cross-sectional dependent variable (with, by the way, a considerably larger number of respondents). Accounting for cross-sectional variability is a quite different theoretical and methodological endeavor that stands entirely apart from accounting for change.
14. Gibson and Caldeira 2009; Gibson and Nelson 2018.
15. Reeves and Rogowski 2023.
16. Donovan and Bowler 2019; Hibbing and Theiss-Morse 1995; Kimball and Patterson 1997; Mondak et al. 2007.
17. Caldeira and Gibson 1992.
18. Gibson 2006, 2013.
19. I recognize the possibility that this relationship is to some degree tautological in light of how the legitimacy of the presidency is conceptualized and measured. That is, perceptions that the election was rigged are, to a limited degree, built into the legitimacy measures: the Biden presidency should be denied legitimacy because the election was rigged. With such a potent control variable, it is perhaps remarkable that the other variables in the equation for presidential legitimacy have such significant effects.
20. It is worth reiterating that figure 4.2 shows just how weak the relationship is between Barrett assessments and change in support for the Supreme Court.
21. For example, Gibson 2007, 2017.
22. Bartels and Johnston 2020; see also Armaly and Enders 2022; Hasen 2019; Rogowski and Stone 2021; Zilis and Blandau 2021.
23. I tested for interactive effects between partisan identifications and each of the event assessment variables for each institution. For the Supreme Court and the Senate, no significant interactions are discovered. For the Biden presidency, the interactions as

a group are significant, but the change in explained variance (see Kam and Franzese 2007) from adding the terms to the equation (R^2 change) is a mere 0.008. In general, I conclude that the effects of partisanship are not conditional on assessments of the events.

Slightly stronger relationships are found with the interactions of ideological identification and event assessments, but as with party identification, the addition of the interaction terms to the equation contributes practically no additional explained variance in legitimacy.

24. Gibson and Caldeira 2009. Also note the important finding of Michael Nelson and Patrick Tucker (2021) that in recent years, diffuse support for the Supreme Court has not changed much. From extant literature, it is not clear that even highly controversial fights over confirmations have lasting institutional consequences.

25. Nelson and Gibson 2019.

26. Daniel Cox (2021) reports from a January 2021 survey that 65 percent of the American people believed "that Biden's victory over Trump in the 2020 presidential election was legitimate."

27. Rutenberg et al. 2021.

28. See also Braman 2021.

29. Sniderman 1993.

30. On political tolerance among college students, see, for example, Chong, Citrin and Levy 2022; Naughton 2017.

31. Mondak and Smithey 1997.

Chapter 5: The Riots' Consequences: Did the Attack on the U.S. Capitol Undermine the Legitimacy of U.S. Political Institutions?

1. For methodological details about the survey, see the appendix.

2. In a comparison of data from a survey conducted at the height of the 2001 controversy with survey data dating from 1995 and 1987, Gibson, Caldeira, and Spence (2003b) find no evidence whatsoever that the court's legitimacy fell owing to its decision. Other scholars report similar findings; see Gillman 2001; Kritzer 2001; Nicholson and Howard 2003; Price and Romantan 2004; Yates and Whitford 2002.

3. Gibson and Caldeira 2009.

4. For example, Alon-Barkat and Gilad 2017; Gibson, Lodge, and Woodson 2014; Gibson and Nelson 2018; Nielsen, Robinson, and Smyth 2020.

5. But see Nelson and Tucker 2021 for a similar approach.

6. Benjamin Bishin and his colleagues (2021) demonstrate that backlashes—at least with respect to gay rights—are far less common than ordinarily thought.

7. To explicitly restate my hypothesis-testing standards, these survey databases include a large number of observations. No statistic is more sensitive to sample size than statistical significance. To anticipate my findings in figure 5.2, even a regression coefficient of 0.02 is statistically significant at $p < .01$, and this is for a variable that ranges from 0 to 1 (a dichotomy). Consequently, there is a good chance that in the popula-

tion, the coefficient is distinguishable from zero even if the effect of the variable is entirely trivial, practically speaking. As a consequence, I do not pay much attention to coefficients that are not significant at $p < .001$ at least, and I tend to place the greatest weight on coefficients (not probabilities) of an absolute value of 0.10 or greater. Nevertheless, for readers who want to identify significant but trivial coefficients, I report statistical significance using the traditional system of attaching asterisks to significant coefficients. In the tables that follow, I also indicate whether the variance inflation factor (VIF) for a variable is greater than 5.0. (For no variable is this true.) I do this mainly to address the possibility that the results are excessively clouded by multicollinearity. Conventionally, VIFs between 1 and 5 indicate no more than moderate intercorrelations of the independent variables that are not severe enough to cause worries. VIFs greater than 5.0 are generally considered to indicate potentially severe correlations, resulting in coefficient and p-value estimates that may not be reliable.

8. I decided not to employ a Bonferroni correction for the hypothesis testing reported in this table. Much research employs multiple individual indicators of a single concept, analyzing each indicator individually. In such circumstances, the Bonferroni correction is necessary because exactly the same hypothesis is being tested with each indicator of a single dependent variable. In this case, the dependent variables are institution-specific and are not necessarily measured with the same indicators; I therefore consider the hypothesis testing to be independent.

9. As an example, Bartels, Horowitz, and Kramon (2021) analyze change in support for general judicial power in Kenya. Their table 2 reports R^2 statistics that range from a minimum of 0.06 to a maximum of 0.10.

10. See Caldeira and Gibson 1992. Using a similar but not identical model, Gibson and Nelson (2017, 604) can account for 46 percent of the variance in diffuse support for the Supreme Court.

11. In general, failure to reject the null hypothesis can be the result of either truth or random error. A typical concern about not placing much weight on rejecting the null hypothesis is that failure to reject can be a function of error, especially measurement error. The consequence of random measurement error is to attenuate relationships. In this case, however, each of the dependent variables is measured with a considerable degree of reliability (minimized random error) and with substantial validity as well (minimized systematic error). As for many of the independent variables included in the table—for example, gender—measurement error is unlikely to be of any consequence. For an excellent example of research that assigns an important substantive conclusion to entirely null results, see Lowande and Rogowski 2021.

12. Notably, the two threat variables are correlated only at −0.42 (and as noted, the VIF for both variables is well within acceptable limits).

13. This variable is correlated with a number of party-related indicators (for example, party identification, r = 0.58), although it is correlated with perceptions of Republican threat to democracy at only −0.42.

14. For example, Gibson, Duch, and Tedin 1992.

15. In chapter 2, I hypothesized that these three items are valid and reliable indicators at

t_3 of a latent construct, allegiance to current American democratic institutions, and psychometric analysis supported that hypothesis. For evidence that this measure of support for democratic institutions is not driven by the belief that the current institutional arrangement is antidemocratic (for example, one person/one vote is not uniformly practiced) and that reforms making these institutions more democratic would be appropriate, see the appendix.

16. In table A.10, I also report the bivariate correlation coefficients and indicate whether the VIF for a variable is greater than 5.0. (For no variable is this true.) As before, I do this mainly to address the possibility that the results are excessively clouded by multicollinearity. Because the N for the analysis is large, I pay little attention to coefficients that are significant at $p > .001$; my analysis focuses mainly on regression coefficients that exceed (in absolute value) 0.10.

17. In the equation that includes only awareness and assessments variables, awareness and assessments of the Barrett nomination and confirmation are both significant at $p < .001$ and their regression coefficients exceed 0.10. Respondents who were more knowledgeable and who rated the nomination as appropriate were more likely to extend legitimacy to U.S. political institutions. That these "step 1" results differ from the results in the full equation indicates that awareness and assessments of seemingly exogenous events are associated with people's preexisting attributes.

18. While the awareness and assessments variables are definitely intercorrelated, only a single variable in this group, election unfairness judgments, is correlated at the bivariate level with legitimacy at more than $r = 0.20$. Although we might normally suspect that extreme multicollinearity had a serious effect on the findings, the weak bivariate correlations, coupled with the small VIF scores and no evidence of inflated standard errors, suggest that awareness and assessments are truly not much of a factor in shaping legitimacy judgments.

Chapter 6: Racial Differences in Support for Democratic Institutions

1. See, for example, Gibson and Nelson 2018; Peffley and Hurwitz 2010. For a comprehensive descriptive analysis of interracial differences on attitudes toward the criminal justice system in the United States, see Gramlich 2019.

2. Not a great deal of research has focused on the institutional attitudes of Hispanic people. For an exception, see Pedraza and Ura 2021.

3. Kingzette and Neblo 2021.

4. See, for example, Davis (1995, 1), who concludes: "Black intolerance is a conscious and focused decision that allows Blacks to distinguish between everyday racists and bigots, and the anxiety and fear generated by the Klan."

5. Gibson, Claassen, and Barceló 2020, 65.

6. Gibson and Nelson 2018.

7. Ibid., 33.

8. Ibid., 37–38.

9. Ibid., 39.

10. Ibid., 41.
11. Ibid., 44.
12. Gibson and Caldeira 1992, 1140.
13. Clawson and Waltenburg 2009, 154.
14. The most obvious recent anti-Black court ruling is *Shelby County v. Holder* (2013), a decision that many (if not most) Black people saw as gutting the much-loved Voting Rights Act. The ruling was both extremely salient and widely condemned by Black people, civil rights supporters, the Black mass media, and even President Obama.
15. Overby et al. 2004.
16. Peffley and Hurwitz 2010, 191–92.
17. Ibid., 193.
18. Gibson 2011.
19. Dupree and Hibbing 2023.
20. Monmouth University Polling Institute 2020.
21. See, for example, Pew Research Center 2016; see also Dupree and Hibbing 2023, 405–6.
22. See, for example, Davis 2000; Feagin 2004; Robinson 2001; Torpey and Burkett 2010.
23. Horowitz, Brown, and Cox 2019.
24. Gibson and Nelson 2018, 52; see also Dupree and Hibbing 2023. Of course, policies such as "stop and frisk" have had vastly disproportionate consequences for African Americans (Tyler, Fagan, and Geller 2014).
25. NPR Staff 2021.
26. Summers 2020.
27. Cramer 2021.
28. See, for example, Bucci, Kirk, and Sampson 2022.
29. With a sample of this complexity, the matter of weighting becomes important. For purposes of within-Black analyses, all Black respondents are included, and the subsample is weighted to attributes of the population of African Americans as a whole.
30. Moreover, the questionnaire was presented only in English.
31. Similarly, Dupree and Hibbing (2023, 408) report their inability to examine racial differences among minority groups other than Black people.
32. In light of the findings reported in table A.2, responses to this measure of allegiance to contemporary political institutions unsurprisingly are closely connected to diffuse support for the three national institutions. For Black people, the mean intercorrelation of the four indicators is 0.40; for White people, it is 0.45. Cronbach's alpha for the item-set among Black people is 0.73; for White people it is 0.74. In general, the pattern of intercorrelations is quite similar for Black people and White people. For both groups, the smallest correlations are associated with the legitimacy of the presidency. For Black people, the correlation of general institutional support and Supreme Court support is 0.50; for White people it is 0.57.
33. I report in figure 6.1 an index that is simply the number of items to which the respondent gave pro-democratic responses. This summary measure is more readily interpreted than the mean of the responses to the three items, and therefore I use it for

illustrative purposes. For analytical purposes, however, I always use the mean index as the dependent variable. Of course, the two measures are strongly intercorrelated and always generate the same substantive conclusions.

34. See the appendix for the text of these questions.

35. This has long been the case, as so expertly demonstrated on a variety of legal attitudes by the "separate realities" research of Peffley and Hurwitz (2010).

36. See, for example, Nelson and Gibson 2018. For a study that uses general values to predict attitudes toward democracy, see Bartels 2020.

37. Gibson and Nelson 2018.

38. See, for example, Gibson 2006; Sullivan, Piereson, and Marcus 1982.

39. As methodologists recognize, the coefficients from splitting the data by race are the same as the coefficients in an equation in which race is interacted with each of the independent variables (see Kam and Franzese 2007). I have reported the analysis separately by race so that readers can easily see the results of the tests of the null hypothesis *within* each race. As noted in table A.12, I also indicate when an interaction between race and a predictor is statistically significant in a single integrated equation.

40. This begins, of course, with the pioneering work of Sullivan, Piereson, and Marcus 1982.

41. Gibson 2013.

42. See, for example, Gibson and Nelson 2015, 2017; Nelson and Gibson 2018; Sullivan and Hendriks 2009, 385–86.

43. Although, as table 6.1 documents, this is the awareness item with the greatest amount of variation.

44. I tested for interactive effects of awareness and assessments for each of the event variables, but found a significant effect only for awareness and assessments of the charge that the election was rigged. For both Black people and White people, however, the coefficient was significant only at $p < .05$, signaling quite marginal relationships.

45. Black and White respondents differed greatly in their assessments of the threats. Among White people, the level of perceived democratic threat from Democrats and Republicans was, on average, about the same. Among Black people, the perceived threat from Democrats was low but the perceived threat from Republicans was dramatically higher. For example, while 15 percent of Black respondents saw a substantial threat to democracy from Democrats, fully 77 percent assigned that level of threat to the Republicans. Few Black people seemed to think of Republicans as a viable alternative to Democrats.

46. Although Nathan Kalmoe and Lilliana Mason (2022) do not use the same terms, they make very much the same argument.

47. The interaction term of race and valuation of individual liberty is statistically significant at $p = .055$.

48. But note that neither of these two variables has standard errors that seem bloated.

49. Rokeach 1960.

50. Armaly and Enders 2022; Bartels 2020; Miller and Davis 2021.

51. On the presidency, see, for example, Reeves and Rogowski 2021. On political toler-

ance, see Gibson 2013; Gibson, Claassen, and Barceló 2020. On the Supreme Court, see Gibson and Nelson 2015, 2017.

52. On affective polarization, see Iyengar et al. 2018. On echo chambers, see Jamieson and Cappella 2008. On the persistence of values, see, for example, Tyler and Trinkner 2018. On motivations to assess events, see Lodge and Taber 2013.

53. Graham and Svolik 2020, 394.

54. For example, Gibson and Howard 2007.

55. Dupree and Hibbing 2023.

56. Gibson and Nelson 2018.

Chapter 7: Intra-Black Variability in Legitimacy Attitudes: An Update

1. For example, Gibson and Nelson 2018; Dupree and Hibbing 2023.

2. Dupree and Hibbing 2023, 404–5.

3. Gibson and Nelson 2018.

4. The t_4 item-set also has strong psychometric properties. Cronbach's alpha is 0.76 (mean inter-item correlation = 0.52), and the item-set is strongly unidimensional (eigenvalue$_2$ = 0.58).

5. For the index of institutional support, the relationship is:

$$\text{Support } t_4 = 0.18 + 0.63 * \text{Support } t_3.$$

In terms of the number of pro-democracy replies, most respondents (45.1 percent) endorsed the same number at t_4 that they endorsed at t_3, with 25.9 percent endorsing fewer items and 29.0 percent endorsing more pro-democracy statements.

6. Gibson and Nelson 2018; Peffley and Hurwitz 2010.

7. Peffley and Hurwitz 2010, 41.

8. Gibson and Nelson 2018; Peffley and Hurwitz 2010.

> A vicarious experience is one that is indirect and internalized by the actor, including (1) observations of how the police treat others . . . in public settings, (2) media reporting of incidents involving police officers (for example, Rodney King, Abner Louima, Sean Bell), and (3) communications from others about their personal experiences. (Brunson and Weitzer 2011, 428–29; see also Mondak et al. 2017)

9. Gibson and Nelson 2018.

10. McClain et al. 2009.

11. See, for example, Tajfel 1981.

12. McClain et al. 2009, 476.

13. Ibid., 477; see also Dawson 1994.

14. Owing to the skewed measure of in-group attachment (70.8 percent of respondents said that it was very important to think of themselves as Black; only 2.7 percent said that Black identity was not important at all; skewness = 1.8), the correlations with the other two indicators are depressed somewhat. Nevertheless, Cronbach's alpha for the

three-item-set is still 0.59 (based on an average inter-item correlation of 0.33). An attempted CFA of this item-set produced a commonality of an item exceeding 1.0. A maximum-likelihood CFA identified only a single significant factor, but the loading of the identity importance indicator was only 0.33. Clearly, the skewness of the identity importance measure is unsettling these psychometric results.

15. I should note that these findings differ rather dramatically from those reported by Gibson and Nelson (2018): every indicator of in-group attachments registers much larger percentages than in their 2014 survey.

16. These findings differ dramatically from those of Gabriel Sanchez and Edward Vargas (2016), whose findings were based on a 2004 national survey of Black people:

> Substantively, what these findings suggest is that for blacks: collective action, commonality, perceived discrimination, and linked fate are all tapping into the same general construct (i.e., group identity). . . . The three dimensions of group consciousness typically used by researchers using a multidimensional approach with measurement load onto one factor for both Latinos and African Americans. This implies that creating a single measure based on these dimensions to capture group consciousness is justifiable for these two groups, less so for Asian Americans or whites. (Sanchez and Vargas 2016, 171).

Throughout this book, I develop a hypothesis positing that linked fate is determined more by external environmental forces than by internal individual psychology and is therefore more malleable than some researchers seem to assume.

17. Tajfel and Turner 1979.

18. Chong, Citrin, and Levy 2022.

19. Recall that the correlation of the two dependent variables at t_3 is 0.52; at t_4, it is 0.39.

20. Gibson and Nelson 2018.

21. I do find a hint of an interactive relationship between vicarious perceptions and group attachments. When group attachments are at their highest level (quite common), the coefficient linking vicarious perceptions and Supreme Court support is 0.17; respondents who saw more unfair treatment of Black people were *more* supportive of the court. When group attachments are at their lowest score (not very common), the relationship turns negative: b = −0.13 (those who saw more unfair treatment of Black people were *less* supportive of the Court). The interactive relationship is weak at best, however, and pertains only to vicarious perceptions and group identities, not to vicarious perceptions and senses of linked fates.

22. Notably, the multivariate results reported earlier (which include a control for support at t_3) can be added to this table for the measure of support at t_4. With the exception of open-mindedness, which I have discussed in some detail, the multivariate coefficients for democratic values and support at t_4 are indistinguishable from zero. For attitudes toward the Supreme Court, support for the rule of law is not related to support at t_4 controlling for support at t_3, while support for the rule of law is significantly related (negatively) to change in support.

23. I note with interest that the correlation of support for the rule of law and the institu-

tional attitudes decreases at t_4 in comparison to t_3. Some might have expected the correlation to increase because the two variables were measured at the same point in time. While it is beyond the scope of this analysis to consider this changing relationship in greater detail, one simple understanding of the diminished relationship is that change moved institutional attitudes away from their grounding in democratic values. The correlations show that respondents more supportive of the rule of law at t_3 were somewhat more likely to withdraw support from the institutions (negative correlations); this change, of course, would tend to weaken the contemporaneous correlations at t_4.

24. Jessee, Malhotra, and Sen 2022.

Chapter 8: Destroying Democracy?

1. For example, on December 26, 2020, Trump tweeted:

   The U.S. Supreme Court has been totally incompetent and weak on the massive Election Fraud that took place in the 2020 Presidential Election. We have absolute PROOF, but they don't want to see it—No "standing," they say. If we have corrupt elections, we have no country! (Brendan Brown, Trump Twitter Archive, https://www.thetrumparchive.com/ [accessed December 15, 2022])

2. According to the *Washington Post*, eighty-six judges rejected post-election lawsuits. Moreover, "According to a review by The Washington Post in mid-December 2020— shortly before the electoral college certified Joe Biden's win—38 of 86 judges who rejected at least one post-election lawsuit were Republican appointees" (Blake 2022).

3. Nelson and Gibson 2019; Kalmoe and Mason 2022, 158.

4. We must be careful about the arithmetic: while it may be true that more than half of Republicans believe that the election was rigged, Republicans are a minority of the American people; thus, using a full denominator, the percentage of Americans who believe that the election was rigged is actually smaller than might be assumed at first glance.

5. Bishin et al. 2022.

6. Duch and Gibson 1992.

7. See "Select Committee to Investigate the January 6th Attack on the United States Capitol," GovInfo, https://www.govinfo.gov/committee/house-january6th?path= /browsecommittee/chamber/house/committee/january6th/collection/CRPT (accessed December 21, 2023).

8. Although I certainly do not claim that other subgroups are unimportant for understanding the health of democracy in the United States, the heterogeneity of some groups makes surveying them quite expensive (for example, some surveys of Hispanics create multiple and distinct versions of their Spanish-language questionnaire); thus, sub-subgroup analysis (such as treating all Americans of Asian origin as in any meaningful sense a single subgroup) may be useful but exceedingly difficult. In fact,

I sought resources for this project for an enhanced Hispanic subsample but failed to find adequate support.

9. Meaney 2022.
10. See, for example, Gibson and Caldeira 1992.
11. Ahmed 2022, 1.
12. Ibid., 5.
13. Normative judgments inevitably depend on whether one prefers the consequences of that legitimacy—is it good or bad that people accept decisions that they oppose? Whether obedience is desirable often depends on value judgments that may differ across individuals (and even across scholars).
14. See, for example, Gibson and Bingham 1985.
15. Gibson and Howard 2007.
16. Although I must acknowledge the general finding that the majority does indeed usually get the state-level public policies it prefers.
17. For a recent review of these meta-analyses, see Marcinkowski and Reid 2019.
18. Contrarians most often cite evidence that denominational prayers in public school are an everyday practice in some parts of the country (largely rural areas) despite rulings to the contrary by the Supreme Court. That some people may violate the law of the land does not stand as compelling evidence of the overall impotence of institutional legitimacy.
19. Gibson 2024a.
20. But see Gibson 2024c.
21. Elliot Aronson and his colleagues (1990) distinguish between "experimental realism" (the content of an experiment being realistic to the subjects so that they take the task seriously) and "mundane realism" (the similarity of the experimental context and stimuli to events likely to occur in the real world—in short, verisimilitude).
22. Dickson, Gordon, and Huber (2022, 10) explain why they assigned greater value to establishing internal than external validity:

> While it is tempting to add additional features [to their experiment] that capture the complexity of "real-world" citizen-authority interactions, doing so would imperil our ability to make progress in understanding the causal role of legitimacy. It is precisely because the wealth of evidence drawn from observations of actual citizen-authority interactions is compatible with multiple theoretical explanations that more credible evidence is needed. Skeptics of legitimacy-based accounts . . . have pointed to this empirical ambiguity as a reason to discard legitimacy-based explanations altogether. In this case, while abstraction removes some of the texture and complexity of real life, the advantages in terms of theory testing are real and substantial.

23. For an example, see Gibson 2009a.
24. I also note that if a measure is packed with random measurement error, that measure is unlikely to correlate with anything, not just the hypothesized variables. My intu-

ition is that my measure of authoritarianism—even though based on the latest thinking about how to measure the concept—is the variable most contaminated with
random measurement error.

25. About a decade ago, a task force of the American Association of Public Opinion
Research produced a report sharply critical of opt-in samples (Baker et al. 2010).

26. In a recent article on legitimacy, Eric Dickson, Sanford Gordon, and Gregory Huber
(2022) focus strongly on establishing internal validity for their favored hypotheses.
Their analysis, which is incredibly well thought out, investigates in detail the mechanisms linking legitimacy with obedience to authority, and their findings essentially
corroborate years of non-experimental research from the same hypothesis.

The external validity of their findings, however, is worrisome. First, I put aside for
the moment whether findings from Yale and NYU undergraduates generalize to the
American population as a whole. (Perhaps undergraduates are an example of the
heterogeneity of effects that I referenced earlier.) More important, the undergraduates
play an interactive computer game that has fairly complicated rules and is quite difficult to understand. The game centers on the exchange of tokens between an authority and its constituents. (The undergraduates perform both roles in up to twenty it-
erations of the game.) These tokens are worth one-thirtieth of a U.S. dollar, a unit
with no physical representation in American currency. Across two experiments, the
payments to the subjects ranged from a low of \$12.47 to a high of \$30.07. (Whether
these figures include the \$7.00 payment for merely showing up for the task is unclear.)
Tuition and boarding costs for students at both Yale and NYU exceed \$60,000 a year.

I do not dismiss the contributions to legitimacy theory from research such as that
reported by Dickson, Gordon, and Huber. They have quite consciously and deliber-
ately placed all their marbles (tokens) on producing research with strong certainty
about causal relationships. I am sure the authors recognize that the external validity
of their research is low, perhaps just as low as the internal validity of some portions
of my research.

27. Gibson and Nelson 2018.

28. Gibson and Duch 1993.

29. Jeffers 2003.

30. Mitchell, Joni. 1970. "Big Yellow Taxi." Reprise Records.

Appendix

1. The interview was divided into two modules, with the Freedom and Tolerance Surveys
questions asked first. The median (twenty-nine minutes) was the total length of the
interview.

2. Reeves and Rogowski 2021, 35.

3. Gibson, Caldeira, and Spence 2005.

4. When the four indices are subjected to CFA, a single significant factor is extracted
(eigenvalue$_2$ = 0.86). However, the loading for presidential legitimacy is only 0.36. At

the same time, Cronbach's alpha for the four-item set is 0.73. One of the advantages of the measure of support for U.S. democratic institutions is that it can stand as a summary of a willingness to extend legitimacy to the established institutions of America's democracy.

5. See Gallup, "Supreme Court," https://news.gallup.com/poll/4732/supreme-court.aspx (accessed December 2, 2019).

6. Following convention, I asked the respondents not to look up the answers to these knowledge questions on the internet by asking for a yes-or-no answer to this question: "Next, we are going to ask you some additional questions about American political institutions. It is important to us that you do not use outside sources like the internet to search for the correct answers. We are trying to understand what people know about public affairs, not what they can look up. Do you agree to answer the following questions without help from outside sources?" Nearly all of the respondents (99.5 percent) answered yes.

7. See, for example, Gibson 2013; Gibson, Claassen, and Barceló 2020.

8. Since there is no known sampling distribution for Cronbach's alpha, we are left with rules of thumb and conventions for interpreting the coefficient. I am typically guided in this research by the following:

> Nunnally (1978) suggests a value of .70 as a lower acceptable bound for alpha. It is not unusual to see published scales with lower alphas. Different methodologists and investigators begin to squirm at different levels of alpha. My personal comfort ranges for research scales are as follows: below .60, unacceptable; between .60 and .65, undesirable; between .65 and .70, minimally acceptable; between .70 and .80, respectable; between .80 and .90, very good; much above .90, one should consider shortening the scale. (DeVellis 2003, 95–96)

> Similarly, I agree with Bear Braumoeller's (2008, 90) statement of the standards for evaluating alpha: "Cronbach's alpha is a worthwhile measure of intercoder reliability, with values below 0.60 considered clearly problematic, those in the 0.60–0.69 range borderline (acceptable by some scholars but not others), 0.70–0.79 acceptable, and 0.80 and above very strong." Of course, even this rule of thumb can be misleading because alpha is extraordinarily sensitive to the number of items in the index. Moreover, very large alphas are often indicative of indicators that are *too strongly* intercorrelated (and therefore duplicative), resulting in indices that may not capture the full range of variability in the opinions that people hold.

9. Adam Liptak 2020.

10. Blake 2020.

11. See Order List: 592 U.S., January 11, 2021, https://www.supremecourt.gov/orders/co urtorders/011121zor_5he6.pdf (accessed February 4, 2021).

12. Some observers might have concerns about the use of the term "riot" in this question. I am not alone in using the term; Pew Research Center (2021), for instance, reports on "views on the rioting at the U.S. Capitol." One question reads:

How much, if anything, have you read or heard about rioting at the U.S. Capitol in Washington DC on January 6, when, following a protest earlier in the day, supporters of Donald Trump broke into the Capitol building while the Senate and House were in the process of certifying Electoral College votes?

This was followed by an open-ended request that the respondent "describe, in a few words, your reaction to rioting at the Capitol."

13. For guidance on measuring authoritarianism, I relied on Engelhardt, Feldman, and Hetherington 2021.

REFERENCES

Abbott, Philip, Lyke Thompson, and Marjorie Sarbaugh-Thompson. 2002. "The Social Construction of a Legitimate President." *Studies in American Political Development* 16(2): 208–30.

Ahmed, Amel. 2022. "Is the American Public Really Turning Away from Democracy? Backsliding and the Conceptual Challenges of Understanding Public Attitudes." *Perspectives on Politics* 21(3): 967–78.

Alon-Barkat, Saar, and Sharon Gilad. 2017. "Compensating for Poor Performance with Promotional Symbols: Evidence from a Survey Experiment." *Journal of Public Administration Research and Theory* 27(4): 661–75.

Althaus, Scott, Nathaniel Swigger, Svitlana Chernykh, David Hendry, Sergio Wals, and Christopher Tiwald. 2011. "Assumed Transmission in Political Science: A Call for Bringing Description Back In." *Journal of Politics* 73(4): 1065–80.

Armaly, Miles T. 2018. "Extra-Judicial Actor Induced Change in Supreme Court Legitimacy." *Political Research Quarterly* 71(3): 600–613.

Armaly, Miles T., and Adam M. Enders. 2022. "Affective Polarization and Support for the U.S. Supreme Court." *Political Research Quarterly* 75(2): 409–24.

Aronson, Elliot, Phoebe C. Ellsworth, J. Merrill Carlsmith, and Marti Hope Gonzales. 1990. *Methods of Research in Social Psychology*, 2nd ed. New York: McGraw-Hill.

Badrinathan, Sumitra. 2021. "Educative Interventions to Combat Misinformation: Evidence from a Field Experiment in India." *American Political Science Review* 115(4): 1325–41.

Bae, Joonbum, and YuJung Julia Lee. 2021. "Gender, Events, and Elite Messages in Mass Opinion on Foreign Relations." *Journal of Global Security Studies* 6(2): 1–16.

Baker, Reg, Stephen J. Blumberg, J. Michael Brick, Mick P. Couper, Melanie Courtright, J. Michael Dennis, Don Dillman, Martin R. Frankel, Philip Garland, Robert M. Groves, Courtney Kennedy, Jon Krosnick, Paul J. Lavrakas, Sunghee Lee, Michael Link, Linda Piekarski, Kumar Rao, Randall K. Thomas, and Dan Zahs. 2010. "AAPOR Report on Online Panels." *Public Opinion Quarterly* 74(4): 711–81.

Bartels, Brandon L., and Christopher D. Johnston. 2013. "On the Ideological Foundations of Supreme Court Legitimacy in the American Public." *American Journal of Political Science* 57(1): 184–99.

———. 2020. *Curbing the Court: Why the Public Constrains Judicial Independence.* New York: Cambridge University Press.

Bartels, Brandon L., Jeremy Horowitz, and Eric Kramon. 2021. "Can Democratic Principles Protect High Courts from Partisan Backlash? Public Reactions to the Kenyan Supreme Court's Role in the 2017 Election Crisis." *American Journal of Political Science* 67(3): 790–807.

Bartels, Larry M. 2020. "Ethnic Antagonism Erodes Republicans' Commitment to Democracy." *Proceedings of the National Academy of Science* 117(37): 22752–59.

Berlinski, Nicolas, Margaret Doyle, Andrew M. Guess, Gabrielle Levy, Benjamin Lyons, Jacob M. Montgomery, Brendan Nyhan, and Jason Reifler. 2021. "The Effects of Unsubstantiated Claims of Voter Fraud on Confidence in Elections." *Journal of Experimental Political Science* 10(1): 1–16.

Bishin, Benjamin G., Thomas J. Hayes, Matthew B. Incantalupo, and Charles Anthony Smith. 2021. "Immigration and Public Opinion: Will Backlash Impede Immigrants' Policy Progress?" *Social Science Quarterly* 102(6): 3036–49.

———. 2022. "Response to Michael J. Nelson and James L. Gibson's Review of Elite-Led Mobilization and Gay Rights: Dispelling the Myth of Mass Opinion Backlash." *Perspectives on Politics* 20(2): 675–76.

Blake, Aaron. 2020. "Trump's Spin on His Big Supreme Court Failure Is as Bad as His Legal Case." *Washington Post*, December 12, 2020. https://www.washingtonpost.com/politics/2020/12/12/trumps-spin-his-big-supreme-court-failure-is-bad-his-legal-case/.

———. 2022. "Trump-Appointed Judges Keep Ruling against Trump and Co. on Jan. 6." *Washington Post*, July 13, 2022. https://www.washingtonpost.com/politics/2022/07/13/trump-appointed-judges-keep-ruling-against-trump-co-on-jan-6/.

Bloomberg. 2020. "We Won the Election, Elections Have Consequences: Trump." September 29, 2020. https://www.youtube.com/watch?v=MTzICCwUUSY.

Boynton, G. R., and Gerhard Loewenberg. 1973. "The Development of Public Support for Parliament in Germany, 1951–59." *British Journal of Political Science* 3(2): 169–89.

Braman, Eileen. 2021. "Thinking about Government Authority: Constitutional Rules and Political Context in Citizens' Assessments of Judicial, Legislative, and Executive Action." *American Journal of Political Science* 65(2): 389–404.

Braumoeller, Bear F. 2008. "Systemic Politics and the Origins of Great Power Conflict." *American Political Science Review* 102(1): 77–93.

Brunson, Rod K., and Ronald Weitzer. 2011. "Negotiating Unwelcome Police Encounters: The Intergenerational Transmission of Conduct Norms." *Journal of Contemporary Ethnography* 40(4): 425–56.

Bucci, Rebecca, David S. Kirk, and Robert J. Sampson. 2022. "Visualizing How Race, Support for Black Lives Matter, and Gun Ownership Shape Views of the U.S. Capitol Insurrection of January 6, 2021." *Socius: Sociological Research in a Dynamic World* 8: 1–4.

Bullock, John G. 2011. "Elite Influence on Public Opinion in an Informed Electorate." *American Political Science Review* 105(3): 496–515.

Caldeira, Gregory A., and James L. Gibson. 1992. "The Etiology of Public Support for the Supreme Court." *American Journal of Political Science* 36(3): 635–64.

Canache, Damarys, Jeffery J. Mondak, and Mitchell A. Seligson. 2001. "Meaning and Measurement in Cross-National Research on Satisfaction with Democracy." *Public Opinion Quarterly* 65(4): 506–28.

Cann, Damon M., and Jeff Yates. 2016. *These Estimable Courts: Understanding Public Perceptions of State Judicial Institutions and Legal Policy-Making.* New York: Oxford University Press.

Cantor, Eric. 2017. "What the Obama Presidency Looked Like to the Opposition." *New York Times*, January 14, 2017. https://www.nytimes.com/2017/01/14/opinion/sunday/eric-cantor-what-the-obama-presidency-looked-like-to-the-opposition.html.

Carey, John M., Gretchen Helmke, Brendan Nyhan, Mitchell Sanders, and Susan Stokes. 2019. "Searching for Bright Lines in the Trump Presidency." *Perspectives on Politics* 17(3): 699–718.

Carrington, Nathan T., and Colin French. 2021. "One Bad Apple Spoils the Bunch: Kavanaugh and Change in Institutional Support for the Supreme Court." *Social Science Quarterly* 102(4): 1484–95.

———. 2022. "Mechanisms, Measurements, and Manifestations in Evaluating the Effects of Confirmation Hearings on Supreme Court Legitimacy." *Social Science Quarterly* 103(5): 1290–94.

Chapman, Terrence L. 2007. "International Security Institutions, Domestic Politics, and Institutional Legitimacy." *Journal of Conflict Resolution* 51(1): 134–66.

Chatagnier, J. Tyson. 2012. "The Effect of Trust in Government on Rallies 'Round the Flag.'" *Journal of Peace Research* 49(5): 631–45.

Chong, Dennis, Jack Citrin, and Morris Levy. 2022. "The Realignment of Political Tolerance in the United States." *Perspectives on Politics* (October 18, 2022): 1–22.

Christenson, Dino P., and David M. Glick. 2019. "Reassessing the Supreme Court: How Decisions and Negativity Bias Affect Legitimacy." *Political Research Quarterly* 72(3): 637–52.

Claassen, Christopher. 2019. "Does Public Support Help Democracy Survive?" *American Journal of Political Science* 64(1): 118–34.

———. 2020. "In the Mood for Democracy? Democratic Support as Thermostatic Opinion." *American Political Science Review* 114(1): 36–53.

Clawson, Rosalee A., and Eric N. Waltenburg. 2009. *Legacy and Legitimacy: Black Americans and the Supreme Court.* Philadelphia: Temple University Press.

Coleman, Martin D. 2018. "Emotion and the False Consensus Effect." *Current Psychology* 37(1): 58–64.

Cox, Daniel A. 2021. "After the Ballots Are Counted: Conspiracies, Political Violence, and American Exceptionalism: Findings from the January 2021 American Perspectives Survey." Survey Center on American Life, February 11, 2021. https://www.americansurveycenter.org/research/after-the-ballots-are-counted-conspiracies-political-violence-and-american-exceptionalism/.

Cramer, Maria. 2021. "Confederate Flag an Unnerving Sight in Capitol." *New York Times*,

January 14, 2021. https://www.nytimes.com/2021/01/09/us/politics/confederate-flag -capitol.html.

Cummings, William, and Bart Jansen. 2018. "'No Evidence to Substantiate Any of the Claims': Takeaways from Report on Kavanaugh Allegations." *USA Today*, November 5, 2018. https://www.usatoday.com/story/news/politics/2018/11/05/brett-kavanaugh-alleg ations-report/1889770002/.

Dahl, Robert A. 1966. *Political Oppositions in Western Democracies*. New Haven, Conn.: Yale University Press.

———. 1971. *Polyarchy: Participation and Opposition*. New Haven, Conn.: Yale University Press.

Davis, Adrienne D. 2000. "The Case for United States Reparations to African Americans." *Human Rights Brief* 7(3): 3–5, 11.

Davis, Darren W. 1995. "Exploring Black Political Intolerance." *Political Behavior* 17(1): 1–22.

Davis, Darren W., and David C. Wilson. 2022. *Racial Resentment in the Political Mind*. Chicago: University of Chicago Press.

Dawson, Michael C. 1994. *Behind the Mule: Race and Class in African-American Politics*. Princeton, N.J.: Princeton University Press.

Delli Carpini, Michael X., and Scott Keeter. 1996. *What Americans Know about Politics and Why It Matters*. New Haven, Conn.: Yale University Press.

DeVellis, Robert F. 2003. *Scale Development: Theory and Applications*, 2nd ed. Thousand Oaks, Calif.: Sage Publications.

Diamond, Larry. 1999. *Developing Democracy: Toward Consolidation*. Baltimore: Johns Hopkins University Press.

Dickson, Eric S., Sanford C. Gordon, and Gregory A. Huber. 2022. "Identifying Legitimacy: Experimental Evidence on Compliance with Authority." *Science Advances* 8(7): eabj7377.

Dietsch, Peter. 2019. "Independent Agencies, Distribution, and Legitimacy: The Case of Central Banks." *American Political Science Review* 114(2): 591–95.

Doherty, David, and Jennifer Wolak. 2012. "When Do the Ends Justify the Means? Evaluating Procedural Fairness." *Political Behavior* 34(2): 301–23.

Doig, Steve. 2021. "It Is Difficult, If Not Impossible, to Estimate the Size of the Crowd That Stormed Capitol Hill." Conversation, January 8, 2021. https://theconversation.com /it-is-difficult-if-not-impossible-to-estimate-the-size-of-the-crowd-that-stormed -capitol-hill-152889.

Donovan, Todd, and Shaun Bowler. 2019. "To Know It Is to Loath It: Perceptions of Campaign Finance and Attitudes about Congress." *American Politics Research* 47(5): 951–69.

Duch, Raymond M., and James L. Gibson. 1992. "'Putting Up with' Fascists in Western Europe: A Comparative, Cross-Level Analysis of Political Tolerance." *Western Political Quarterly* 45(1): 237–73.

Dupree, Ernest, III, and John R. Hibbing. 2023. "Black Trust in U.S. Legislatures." *Legislative Studies Quarterly* 48(2): 399–424.

Easton, David. 1965. *A Systems Analysis of Political Life*. New York: John Wiley & Sons.

———. 1975. "A Re-assessment of the Concept of Political Support." *British Journal of Political Science* 5(4): 435–57.

Eisen, Norman, Joshua Matz, Donald Ayer, Gwen Keyes Fleming, Colby Galliher, Jason Harrow, and Raymond P. Tolentino. 2021. *Fulton County, Georgia's Trump Investigation: An Analysis of the Reported Facts and Applicable Law.* Brookings Institute, October 4, 2021. https://www.brookings.edu/wp-content/uploads/2021/10/Fulton-County-Trump -Investigation_Brookings-Report_October2021.pdf.

Engelhardt, Andrew M., Stanley Feldman, and Marc J. Hetherington. 2021. "Advancing the Measurement of Authoritarianism." *Political Behavior* 45(2): 537–60.

Fallon, Richard H. 2018. *Law and Legitimacy in the Supreme Court.* Cambridge, Mass.: Harvard University Press.

Farganis, Dion. 2012. "Do Reasons Matter? The Impact of Opinion Content on Supreme Court Legitimacy." *Political Research Quarterly* 65(1): 206–16.

Feagin, Joe R. 2004. "Documenting the Costs of Slavery, Segregation, and Contemporary Racism: Why Reparations Are in Order for African Americans." *Harvard BlackLetter Law Journal* 20(September): 49–81.

Friedman, Lawrence M. 1977. *Law and Society: An Introduction.* Englewood Cliffs, N.J.: Prentice-Hall.

Gerstein, Josh. 2022. "Kagan Repeats Warning That Supreme Court Is Damaging Its Legitimacy." *Politico*, September 14, 2022. https://www.politico.com/news/2022/09/14/kagan -supreme-court-legitimacy-00056766.

Gibson, James L. 1989. "Understandings of Justice: Institutional Legitimacy, Procedural Justice, and Political Tolerance." *Law and Society Review* 23(3): 469–96.

———. 1996. "A Mile Wide but an Inch Deep(?): The Structure of Democratic Commitments in the Former USSR." *American Journal of Political Science* 40(2): 396–420.

———. 1997. "The Struggle between Order and Liberty in Contemporary Russian Political Culture." *Australian Journal of Political Science* 32(2): 271–90.

———. 1998. "A Sober Second Thought: An Experiment in Persuading Russians to Tolerate." *American Journal of Political Science* 42(3): 819–50.

———. 2004. *Overcoming Apartheid: Can Truth Reconcile a Divided Nation?* New York: Russell Sage Foundation.

———. 2006. "Enigmas of Intolerance: Fifty Years after Stouffer's Communism, Conformity, and Civil Liberties." *Perspectives on Politics* 4(1): 21–34.

———. 2007. "The Legitimacy of the U.S. Supreme Court in a Polarized Polity." *Journal of Empirical Legal Studies* 4(3): 507–38.

———. 2008. "Group Identities and Theories of Justice: An Experimental Investigation into the Justice and Injustice of Land Squatting in South Africa." *Journal of Politics* 70(3): 700–716.

———. 2009a. *Overcoming Historical Injustices: Land Reconciliation in South Africa.* New York: Cambridge University Press.

———. 2009b. "Political Intolerance in the Context of Democratic Theory." In *The Oxford Handbook of Political Science*, edited by Robert E. Goodwin. New York: Oxford University Press.

———. 2011. "A Note of Caution about the Meaning of 'The Supreme Court Can Usually

Be Trusted . . . .'" *Law and Courts: Newsletter of the Law and Courts Section of the American Political Science Association* 2(3): 10–16.

———. 2012. *Electing Judges: The Surprising Effects of Campaigning on Judicial Legitimacy.* Chicago: University of Chicago Press.

———. 2013. "Measuring Political Tolerance and General Support for Pro–Civil Liberties Policies: Notes, Evidence, and Cautions." *Public Opinion Quarterly* 77(special issue): 45–68.

———. 2015. "Legitimacy Is for Losers: The Interconnections of Institutional Legitimacy, Performance Evaluations, and the Symbols of Judicial Authority." In *Motivating Cooperation and Compliance with Authority: The Role of Institutional Trust*, edited by Brian H. Bornstein and Alan J. Tomkins. New York: Springer.

———. 2016. "Reassessing the Institutional Legitimacy of the South African Constitutional Court: New Evidence, Revised Theory." *Politikon* 43(1): 53–77.

———. 2017. "Performance Evaluations Are Not Legitimacy Judgments: A Caution about Interpreting Public Opinions toward the U.S. Supreme Court." *Washington University Journal of Law and Policy* 54: 71–88.

———. 2024a. "Losing Legitimacy: The Challenges of the *Dobbs* Ruling to Conventional Legitimacy Theory." *American Journal of Political Science*, February 6. https://doi.org/10.1111/ajps.12834.

———. 2024b. "African Americans' Willingness to Extend Legitimacy to the Police: Connections to Identities and Experiences in the Post-George Floyd Era." *Journal of Law and Courts.* https://doi.org/10.1017/jlc.2023.20.

———. 2024c. "Do the Effects of Unpopular Supreme Court Rulings Linger? The *Dobbs* Decision Rescinding Abortion Rights." *American Political Science Review.* https://doi.org/10.1017/S0003055424000169.

Gibson, James L., and Richard D. Bingham. 1982. "On the Conceptualization and Measurement of Political Tolerance." *American Political Science Review* 76(3): 603–20.

———. 1985. *Civil Liberties and Nazis: The Skokie Free-Speech Controversy.* New York: Praeger.

Gibson, James L., and Gregory A. Caldeira. 1992. "Black People and the United States Supreme Court: Models of Diffuse Support." *Journal of Politics* 54(4): 1120–45.

———. 2009. *Citizens, Courts, and Confirmations: Positivity Theory and the Judgments of the American People.* Princeton, N.J.: Princeton University Press.

———. 2011. "Has Legal Realism Damaged the Legitimacy of the U.S. Supreme Court?" *Law and Society Review* 45(1): 195–219.

Gibson, James L., Gregory A. Caldeira, and Vanessa Baird. 1998. "On the Legitimacy of National High Courts." *American Political Science Review* 92(2): 343–58.

Gibson, James L., Gregory A. Caldeira, and Lester Kenyatta Spence. 2003a. "Measuring Attitudes toward the United States Supreme Court." *American Journal of Political Science* 47 (2): 354–67.

———. 2003b. "The Supreme Court and the U.S. Presidential Election of 2000: Wounds, Self-Inflicted or Otherwise?" *British Journal of Political Science* 33(4): 535–56.

———. 2005. "Why Do People Accept Public Policies They Oppose? Testing Legitimacy Theory with a Survey-Based Experiment." *Political Research Quarterly* 58(2): 187–201.

Gibson, James L., Christopher Claassen, and Joan Barceló. 2020. "Putting Groups Back into the Study of Political Intolerance." In *At the Forefront of Political Psychology: Essays in Honor of John L. Sullivan*, edited by Eugene Borgida, Christopher M. Federico, and Joanne M. Miller. New York: Routledge.

Gibson, James L., and Raymond M. Duch. 1993. "Emerging Democratic Values in Soviet Political Culture." In *Public Opinion and Regime Change: The New Politics of Post-Soviet Societies*, edited by Arthur H. Miller, William M. Reisinger, and Vicki L. Hesli. Boulder, Colo.: Westview Press.

Gibson, James L., Raymond M. Duch, and Kent L. Tedin. 1992. "Democratic Values and the Transformation of the Soviet Union." *Journal of Politics* 54(2): 329–71.

Gibson, James L., and Amanda Gouws. 2001. "Making Tolerance Judgments: The Effects of Context, Local and National." *Journal of Politics* 63(4): 1067–90.

———. 2003. *Overcoming Intolerance in South Africa: Experiments in Democratic Persuasion.* New York: Cambridge University Press.

Gibson, James L., and Marc Morjé Howard. 2007. "Russian Anti-Semitism and the Scapegoating of Jews." *British Journal of Political Science* 37(2): 193–223.

Gibson, James L., Milton Lodge, and Benjamin Woodson. 2014. "Losing, but Accepting: Legitimacy, Positivity Theory, and the Symbols of Judicial Authority." *Law and Society Review* 48(4): 837–66.

Gibson, James L., and Michael J. Nelson. 2014a. "The Legitimacy of the U.S. Supreme Court: Conventional Wisdoms and Recent Challenges Thereto." *Annual Review of Law and Social Science* 10(November): 201–19.

———. 2014b. "Can the U.S. Supreme Court Have Too Much Legitimacy?" In *Making Law and Courts Research Relevant: The Normative Implications of Empirical Research*, edited by Brandon L. Bartels and Chris W. Bonneau. New York: Routledge.

———. 2015. "Is the U.S. Supreme Court's Legitimacy Grounded in Performance Satisfaction and Ideology?" *American Journal of Political Science* 59(1): 162–74.

———. 2017. "Reconsidering Positivity Theory: What Roles Do Politicization, Ideological Disagreement, and Legal Realism Play in Shaping U.S. Supreme Court Legitimacy?" *Journal of Empirical Legal Studies* 14(3): 592–617.

———. 2018. *Black and Blue: How and Why African Americans Judge the American Legal System.* New York: Oxford University Press.

———. 2019. "The Least Accountable Branch." *Court Review* 55(1): 30–35.

Gibson, James L., and Kent L. Tedin. 1988. "The Etiology of Intolerance of Homosexual Politics." *Social Science Quarterly* 69(3): 587–604.

Gill, Hyungjin, and Hernando Rojas. 2021. "Perceiving Immigrants as a Threat: A Motivational Approach to False Consensus." *Communication Research* 49(8): 1–28.

Gillman, Howard. 2001. *The Votes That Counted: How the Court Decided the 2000 Presidential Election.* Chicago: University of Chicago Press.

Goldsmith, Benjamin E., Yusaku Horiuchi, and Kelly Matush. 2021. "Does Public Diplomacy Sway Foreign Public Opinion? Identifying the Effect of High-Level Visits." *American Political Science Review* 115(4): 1342–57.

Graham, Matthew H., and Milan W. Svolik. 2020. "Democracy in America? Partisanship, Polarization, and the Robustness of Support for Democracy in the United States." *American Political Science Review* 114(2): 392–409.

Gordon, Sanford C., and Gregory A. Huber. 2019. "The Empirical Study of Legitimate Authority: Normative Guidance for Positive Analysis." In *Political Legitimacy: NOMOS LXI*, edited by Jack Knight and Melissa Schwartzberg. New York: New York University Press.

Gramlich, John. 2019. "From Police to Parole, Black and White Americans Differ Widely in Their Views of Criminal Justice System." Pew Research Center, May 21, 2019. https://www.pewresearch.org/short-reads/2019/05/21/from-police-to-parole-black-and-white-americans-differ-widely-in-their-views-of-criminal-justice-system/.

———. 2020. "What the 2020 Electorate Looks Like by Party, Race and Ethnicity, Age, Education and Religion." Pew Research Center, October 26, 2020. https://www.pewresearch.org/fact-tank/2020/10/26/what-the-2020-electorate-looks-like-by-party-race-and-ethnicity-age-education-and-religion/.

Grimmelikhuijsen, Stephan, and Albert Klijn. 2015. "The Effects of Judicial Transparency on Public Trust: Evidence from a Field Experiment." *Public Administration* 93(4): 995–1011.

Groeling, Tim, and Matthew A. Baum. 2008. "Crossing the Water's Edge: Elite Rhetoric, Media Coverage, and the Rally-Round-the-Flag Phenomenon." *Journal of Politics* 70(4): 1065–85.

Haglin, Kathryn, Soren Jordan, Alison Higgins Merrill, and Joseph Daniel Ura. 2021. "Ideology and Specific Support for the Supreme Court." *Political Research Quarterly* 74(4): 955–69.

Haider-Markel, Donald P., and Mark R. Joslyn. 2017. "Bad Apples? Attributions of Police Treatment of African Americans." *Analyses of Social Issues and Public Policy* 17(1): 358–78.

Harell, Allison, Robert Hinckley, and Jordan Mansell. 2021. "Valuing Liberty or Equality? Empathetic Personality and Political Intolerance of Harmful Speech." *Frontiers of Political Science* 3(June 17, 2021): 663858.

Hasen, Richard L. 2019. "Polarization and the Judiciary." *Annual Review of Political Science* 22(1): 261–76.

Hetherington, Marc J., and Michael Nelson. 2003. "Anatomy of a Rally Effect: George W. Bush and the War on Terrorism." *Political Science and Politics* 36(1): 37–42.

Hibbing, John R., and Elizabeth Theiss-Morse. 1995. *Congress as Public Enemy.* New York: Cambridge University Press.

———. 2001. *What Is It about Government That Americans Dislike?* New York: Cambridge University Press.

Hill, Fiona. 2021. "Yes, It Was a Coup Attempt. Here's Why." *Politico*, January 11, 2021. https://www.politico.com/news/magazine/2021/01/11/capitol-riot-self-coup-trump-fiona-hill-457549.

Hipp, John R. 2010. "Resident Perceptions of Crime and Disorder: How Much Is 'Bias,' and How Much Is Social Environment Differences?" *Criminology* 48(2): 475–508.

Hitt, Matthew P., Kyle L. Saunders, and Kevin M. Scott. 2019. "Justice Speaks, but Who's Listening? Mass Public Awareness of U.S. Supreme Court Cases." *Journal of Law and Courts* 7(1): 29–52.

Hong, Nicole, William K. Rashbaum, and Ben Protess. 2021. "Court Suspends Giuliani's Law License, Citing Trump Election Lies." *New York Times*, June 24, 2021. https://www.nytimes.com/2021/06/24/nyregion/giuliani-law-license-suspended-trump.html.

Horowitz, Juliana Menasce, Anna Brown, and Kiana Cox. 2019. "Race in America 2019." Policy Commons, April 9, 2019. https://policycommons.net/artifacts/616872/race-in-america-2019/1597597/.

Hurley, Lawrence. 2022. "Justices Join Debate on Supreme Court's Legitimacy after Abortion Ruling." NBC News, September 18, 2022. https://www.nbcnews.com/politics/supreme-court/justices-join-debate-supreme-courts-legitimacy-abortion-ruling-rcna47795.

Iyengar, Shanto, Yphtach Lelkes, Matthew Levendusky, Neil Malhotra, and Sean J. Westwood. 2018. "The Origins and Consequences of Affective Polarization in the United States." *Annual Review of Political Science* 22(1): 129–46.

Jamieson, Kathleen Hall, and Joseph N. Cappella. 2008. *Echo Chamber: Rush Limbaugh and the Conservative Media Establishment.* New York: Oxford University Press.

Jeffers, Harry Paul. 2003. *The 100 Greatest Heroes.* New York: Citadel Press.

Jefferson, Hakeem, Fabian G. Neuner, and Josh Pasek. 2021. "Seeing Blue in Black and White: Race and Perceptions of Officer-Involved Shootings." *Perspectives on Politics* 19(4): 1165–83.

Jessee, Stephen, Neil Malhotra, and Maya Sen. 2022. "A Decade-Long Longitudinal Survey Shows That the Supreme Court Is Now Much More Conservative than the Public." *Proceedings of the National Academy of Sciences* 119(24): 1–7.

Jones, RonNell Andersen, and Lisa Grow Sun. 2017. "Enemy Construction and the Press." *Utah Law Faculty Scholarship* 17. April 27, 2017. https://dc.law.utah.edu/scholarship/17.

Kalmoe, Nathan P., and Lilliana Mason. 2022. *Radical American Partisanship: Mapping Extreme Hostility, Its Causes, and the Consequences for Democracy.* Chicago: University of Chicago Press.

Kam, Cindy, and Robert Franzese Jr. 2007. *Modeling and Interpreting Interactive Hypotheses in Regression Analysis.* Ann Arbor: University of Michigan Press.

Kelley-Romano, Stephanie, and Kathryn L. Carew. 2018. "Make America Hate Again: Donald Trump and the Birther Conspiracy." *Journal of Hate Studies* 14(1): 33–52.

Kimball, David C., and Samuel C. Patterson. 1997. "Living Up to Expectations: Public Attitudes toward Congress." *Journal of Politics* 59(3): 701–28.

Kingzette, Jon, and Michael A. Neblo. 2021. "The Civil Culture(s): Groups, Norms, and the Health of Democracy." *Journal of Race, Ethnicity, and Politics* 6(1): 144–56.

Knight, Jack, and Melissa Schwartzberg, eds. 2019. *Political Legitimacy: NOMOS LXI.* New York: New York University Press.

Krewson, Christopher N. 2022. "Political Hearings Reinforce Legal Norms: Confirmation

Hearings and Views of the United States Supreme Court." *Political Research Quarterly* 76(1): 418–31.

Krewson, Christopher N., and Jean R. Schroedel. 2020. "Public Views of the U.S. Supreme Court in the Aftermath of the Kavanaugh Confirmation." *Social Science Quarterly* 101(4): 1430–41.

———. 2023. "Modern Judicial Confirmation Hearings and Institutional Support for the Supreme Court." *Social Science Quarterly* 104(3): 364–69.

Kritzer, Herbert M. 2001. "The Impact of *Bush v. Gore* on Public Perceptions and Knowledge of the Supreme Court." *Judicature* 85(1): 32–38.

Kromphardt, Christopher D., and Michael F. Salamone. 2021. "'Unpresidented!' Or: What Happens When the President Attacks the Federal Judiciary on Twitter." *Journal of Information Technology and Politics* 18(1): 84–100.

Lanis, Roman, and Grant Richardson. 2012. "Corporate Social Responsibility and Tax Aggressiveness: A Test of Legitimacy Theory." *Accounting, Auditing, and Accountability Journal* 26(1): 75–100.

Levi, Margaret. 2019. "Trustworthy Government and Legitimating Beliefs." In *Political Legitimacy: NOMOS LXI*, edited by Jack Knight and Melissa Schwartzberg. New York: New York University Press.

Levitsky, Steven, and Daniel Ziblatt. 2018. *How Democracies Die.* New York: Penguin Books.

Lieberman, Robert C., Suzanne Mettler, Thomas B. Pepinsky, Kenneth M. Roberts, and Richard Valelly. 2019. "The Trump Presidency and American Democracy: A Historical and Comparative Analysis." *Perspectives on Politics* 17(2): 470–79.

Linde, Jonas, and Joakim Ekman. 2003. "Satisfaction with Democracy: A Note on a Frequently Used Indicator in Comparative Politics." *European Journal of Political Research* 42(3): 391–408.

Liptak, Adam. 2020. "Supreme Court Rejects Republican Challenge to Pennsylvania Vote." *New York Times*, December 10, 2020. https://www.nytimes.com/2020/12/08/us/supreme -court-republican-challenge-pennsylvania-vote.html.

Liptak, Kevin. 2020. "A List of the Times Trump Has Said He Won't Accept the Election Results or Leave Office If He Loses." CNN, September 24, 2020. https://www.cnn.com /2020/09/24/politics/trump-election-warnings-leaving-office/index.html.

Lodge, Milton, and Charles S. Taber. 2013. *The Rationalizing Voter: Experiments on Motivated Political Reasoning.* New York: Cambridge University Press.

Lowande, Kenneth, and Jon C. Rogowski. 2021. "Presidential Unilateral Power." *Annual Review of Political Science* 24(1): 21–43.

Lupia, Arthur. 2016. *Uninformed: Why People Know So Little about Politics and What We Can Do about It.* New York: Oxford University Press.

Malhotra, Neil, and Stephen A. Jessee. 2014. "Ideological Proximity and Support for the Supreme Court." *Political Behavior* 36(4): 817–46.

Manekin, Devorah, and Tamar Mitts. 2022. "Effective for Whom? Ethnic Identity and Nonviolent Resistance." *American Political Science Review* 116(1): 161–80.

Marcinkowski, Tom, and Alan Reid. 2019. "Reviews of Research on the Attitude-Behavior

Relationship and Their Implications for Future Environmental Education Research." *Environmental Education Research* 25(4): 459–71.

Martin, Kirsten, and Ari Waldman. 2022. "Are Algorithmic Decisions Legitimate? The Effect of Process and Outcomes on Perceptions of Legitimacy of AI Decisions." *Journal of Business Ethics* 183: 653–70.

Mattes, Robert. 2018. "Support for Democracy." In *Oxford Research Encyclopedia in Politics*, edited by William R. Thompson. New York: Oxford University Press.

McClain, Paula D., Jessica D. Johnson Carew, Eugene Walton Jr., and Candis S. Watts. 2009. "Group Membership, Group Identity, and Group Consciousness: Measures of Racial Identity in American Politics?" *Annual Review of Political Science* 12(1): 471–85.

McIntire, Mike, and Michael H. Keller. 2021. "The Demand for Money behind Many Police Traffic Stops." *New York Times*, November 1, 2021. https://www.nytimes.com/2021/10/31/us/police-ticket-quotas-money-funding.html.

Meaney, Thomas. 2022. "When America Was Awash in Patriotic Frenzy and Political Repression." *New York Times*, October 3, 2022. https://www.nytimes.com/2022/10/03/books/review/american-midnight-adam-hochschild.html.

Michaels, Jon D. 2018. "The American Deep State." *Notre Dame Law Review* 93(4): 1653–70.

Mill, John Stuart. 1982. *On Liberty.* London: Penguin Classics. Originally published in 1859.

Miller, Steven V., and Nicholas T. Davis. 2021. "The Effect of White Social Prejudice on Support for American Democracy." *Journal of Race, Ethnicity, and Politics* 6(2): 334–51.

Mondak, Jeffery J., Edward G. Carmines, Robert Huckfeldt, Dona-Gene Mitchell, and Scot Schraufnagel. 2007. "Does Familiarity Breed Contempt? The Impact of Information on Mass Attitudes toward Congress." *American Journal of Political Science* 51(1): 34–48.

Mondak, Jeffrey J., Jon Hurwitz, Mark Peffley, and Paul Testa. 2017. "The Vicarious Bases of Perceived Injustice." *American Journal of Political Science* 61(4): 804–19.

Mondak, Jeffery J., and Shannon Ishiyama Smithey. 1997. "The Dynamics of Public Support for the Supreme Court." *Journal of Politics* 59(4): 1114–42.

Monmouth University Polling Institute. 2020. "Protestors' Anger Justified Even If Actions May Not Be." Monmouth University, June 2, 2020. https://www.monmouth.edu/polling-institute/reports/monmouthpoll_us_060220/.

Mutz, Diana C., and Jeffery J. Mondak. 1997. "Dimensions of Sociotropic Behavior: Group-Based Judgments of Fairness and Well-being." *American Journal of Political Science* 41(1): 284–308.

Naughton, Kelsey A. 2017. *Speaking Freely: What Students Think about Expression at American Colleges.* Philadelphia: Foundation for Individual Rights in Education.

Nelson, Michael J., and James L. Gibson. 2017. "U.S. Supreme Court Legitimacy: Unanswered Questions and an Agenda for Future Research." In *Routledge Handbook of Judicial Behavior*, edited by Robert M. Howard and Kirk A. Randazzo. New York: Routledge.

———. 2018. "Has Trump Trumped the Courts?" *New York University Law Review Online* 93(April): 32–40.

———. 2019. "How Does Hyperpoliticized Rhetoric Affect the US Supreme Court's Legitimacy?" *Journal of Politics* 81(4): 1512–16.

Nelson, Michael J., and Patrick D. Tucker. 2021. "The Stability and Durability of the US Supreme Court's Legitimacy." *Journal of Politics* 83(2): 767–71.

Neumeister, Larry, Tom Hays, and Eric Tucker. 2022. "Prosecutors: No Criminal Charges Expected from Giuliani Raid." AP News, November 14, 2022. https://apnews.com/article/europe-new-york-8a4bdf8e00494dc11ed972378d9028bf.

Nicholson, Stephen P., and Robert M. Howard. 2003. "Framing Support for the Supreme Court in the Aftermath of *Bush v. Gore*." *Journal of Politics* 65(3): 676–95.

Nielsen, Ingrid, Zoe Robinson, and Russell Smyth. 2020. "Keep Your (Horse) Hair On? Experimental Evidence on the Effect of Exposure to Legitimising Symbols on Diffuse Support for the High Court." *Federal Law Review* 48(3): 382–400.

NPR Staff. 2021. "Understanding the 2020 Electorate: AP VoteCast Survey." NPR, March 16, 2021. https://www.npr.org/2020/11/03/929478378/understanding-the-2020-electorate-ap-votecast-survey.

Nunnally, Jum C. 1978. "An Overview of Psychological Measurement." In *Clinical Diagnosis of Mental Disorders: A Handbook*, edited by Benjamin B. Wolman. Boston: Springer.

Overby, L. Marvin, Robert D. Brown, John M. Bruce, Charles E. Smith Jr., and John W. Winkle III. 2004. "Justice in Black and White: Race, Perceptions of Fairness, and Diffuse Support for the Judicial System in a Southern State." *Justice System Journal* 25(2): 159–81.

Peay, Periloux C., and Tyler Camarillo. 2021. "No Justice! Black Protests? No Peace: The Racial Nature of Threat Evaluations of Nonviolent #BlackLivesMatter Protests." *Social Science Quarterly* 102(1): 198–208.

Pedraza, Francisco I., and Joseph Daniel Ura. 2021. "Latinos' Knowledge of the Supreme Court." *Journal of Law and Courts* 9(1): 27–48.

Peffley, Mark, and Jon Hurwitz. 2010. *Justice in America: The Separate Realities of Black People and White People*. Cambridge: Cambridge University Press.

Pew Research Center. 2014. "Stark Racial Divisions in Reactions to Ferguson Police Shooting." August 18, 2014. https://assets.pewresearch.org/wp-content/uploads/sites/5/2014/08/8-18-14-Ferguson-Release.pdf.

———. 2016. "On Views of Race and Inequality, Blacks and Whites Are Worlds Apart." June 27, 2016. https://www.pewresearch.org/social-trends/2016/06/27/on-views-of-race-and-inequality-blacks-and-whites-are-worlds-apart/.

———. 2021. "Biden Begins Presidency with Positive Ratings; Trump Departs with Lowest-Ever Job Mark." January 15, 2021. https://www.pewresearch.org/politics/2021/01/15/biden-begins-presidency-with-positive-ratings-trump-departs-with-lowest-ever-job-mark/.

Phillips, Kristine. 2017. "Analysis: All the Times Trump Personally Attacked Judges—and Why His Tirades Are 'Worse than Wrong.'" *Washington Post*, April 26, 2017. https://www.washingtonpost.com/news/the-fix/wp/2017/04/26/all-the-times-trump-personally-attacked-judges-and-why-his-tirades-are-worse-than-wrong/.

Phillips, Peter J., and Gabriela Pohl. 2021. "Crowd Counting: A Behavioural Economics Perspective." *Quality and Quantity* 55(6): 2253–70.

Price, Vincent, and Anca Romantan. 2004. "Confidence in Institutions before, during, and after 'Indecision 2000.'" *Journal of Politics* 66(3): 939–56.

Reeves, Andrew, and Jon C. Rogowski. 2015. "Public Opinion toward Presidential Power." *Presidential Studies Quarterly* 45(4): 742–59.

———. 2021. *No Blank Check: Why the Public Dislikes Presidential Power and What It Means for Governing.* New York: Cambridge University Press.

———. 2023. "Democratic Values and Support for Executive Power." *Presidential Studies Quarterly* 53(2): 293–312.

Revesz, Rachael. 2017. "Donald Trump Says Federal Judges Ruling against His 'Muslim Ban' Are Political." *Independent,* February 8, 2017. https://www.independent.co.uk/news /world/americas/donald-trump-muslim-ban-federal-judges-political-ruling-immigration -travel-restrictions-a7569341.html.

Riccardi, Nicholas. 2020. "Here's the Reality behind Trump's Claims about Mail Voting." AP News, September 30, 2020. https://apnews.com/article/virus-outbreak-joe-biden-el ection-2020-donald-trump-elections-3e8170c3348ce3719d4bc7182146b582.

Roberts, Caroline, Emily Gilbert, Nick Allum, and Léïla Eisner. 2019. "Satisficing in Surveys: A Systematic Review of the Literature." *Public Opinion Quarterly* 83(3): 598–626.

Robinson, Randall. 2001. *The Debt: What America Owes to Black People.* New York: Plume.

Rogowski, Jon C., and Andrew R. Stone. 2021. "How Political Contestation over Judicial Nominations Polarizes Americans' Attitudes toward the Supreme Court." *British Journal of Political Science* 51(3): 1251–69.

Rokeach, Milton. 1960. *The Open and Closed Mind.* New York: Basic Books.

Roose, Josh. 2021. "'It's Almost Like Grooming': How Anti-Vaxxers, Conspiracy Theorists, and the Far-Right Came Together over COVID." Conversation, September 21, 2021. https://theconversation.com/its-almost-like-grooming-how-anti-vaxxers-conspiracy -theorists-and-the-far-right-came-together-over-covid-168383.

Roosma, Femke, Wim van Oorschot, and John Gelissen. 2014. "The Preferred Role and Perceived Performance of the Welfare State: European Welfare Attitudes from a Multidimensional Perspective." *Social Science Research* 44(March): 200–210.

Rutenberg, Jim, Jo Becker, Eric Lipton, Maggie Haberman, Jonathan Martin, Matthew Rosenberg, and Michael S. Schmidt. 2021. "77 Days: Trump's Campaign to Subvert the Election." *New York Times,* January 31, 2021. https://www.nytimes.com/2021/01/31/us /trump-election-lie.html.

Ryan, Timothy J., and Amanda R. Aziz. 2021. "Is the Political Right More Credulous? Experimental Evidence against Asymmetric Motivations to Believe False Political Information." *Journal of Politics* 83(3): 1168–72.

Sampson, Robert J., and Stephen W. Raudenbush. 2004. "Seeing Disorder: Neighborhood Stigma and the Social Construction of 'Broken Windows.'" *Social Psychology Quarterly* 67(4): 319–42.

Sanchez, Gabriel R., and Edward D. Vargas. 2016. "Taking a Closer Look at Group Identity: The Link between Theory and Measurement of Group Consciousness and Linked Fate." *Political Research Quarterly* 69(1): 160–74.

Smith, Rogers M., and Desmond King. 2021. "White Protectionism in America." *Perspectives on Politics* 19(2): 460–78.

Smyth, Russell. 2021. "Public Opinion and Legitimacy." In *The Oxford Handbook of Comparative Judicial Behavior*, edited by Lee Epstein, Gunnar Grendstad, Urksa Sadl, and Keren Weinshall. New York: Oxford University Press.

Sniderman, Paul. 1993. "The New Look in Public Opinion Research." In *Political Science: The State of the Discipline II*, edited by Ada Finifter. Washington, D.C.: American Political Science Association.

Sullivan, John L., and Henriët Hendriks. 2009. "Public Support for Civil Liberties Pre- and Post-9/11." *Annual Review of Law and Social Science* 5(1): 375–91.

Sullivan, John L., James E. Piereson, and George E. Marcus. 1982. *Political Tolerance and American Democracy*. Chicago: University of Chicago Press.

Summers, Juana. 2020. "Trump Push to Invalidate Votes in Heavily Black Cities Alarms Civil Rights Groups." NPR, November 24, 2020. https://www.npr.org/2020/11/24/938187233/trump-push-to-invalidate-votes-in-heavily-black-cities-alarms-civil-rights-group.

Tajfel, Henri. 1981. *Human Groups and Social Categories*. New York: Cambridge University Press.

Tajfel, Henri, and John C. Turner. 1979. "An Integrative Theory of Intergroup Conflict." In *The Social Psychology of Intergroup Relations*, edited by William G. Austin and Stephen Worchel. Monterey, Calif.: Brooks/Cole.

Tankebe, Justice. 2013. "Viewing Things Differently: The Dimensions of Public Perceptions of Police Legitimacy." *Criminology* 51(1): 103–35.

Tobias, Carl. 2019. "President Donald Trump's War on Federal Judicial Diversity." *Wake Forest Law Review* 54(2): 531–74.

Toikko, Timo, and Teemu Rantanen. 2017. "How Does the Welfare State Model Influence Social Political Attitudes? An Analysis of Citizens' Concrete and Abstract Attitudes toward Poverty." *Journal of International and Comparative Social Policy* 33(3): 201–24.

Torpey, John, and Maxine Burkett. 2010. "The Debate over African American Reparations." *Annual Review of Law and Social Science* 6(1): 449–67.

Tyler, Tom R. 2006. "Psychological Perspectives on Legitimacy and Legitimation." *Annual Review of Psychology* 57(January): 375–400.

Tyler, Tom R., Jeffrey Fagan, and Amanda Geller. 2014. "Street Stops and Police Legitimacy: Teachable Moments in Young Urban Men's Legal Socialization." *Journal of Empirical Legal Studies* 11(4): 751–85.

Tyler, Tom R., and Rick Trinkner. 2018. *Why Children Follow Rules: Legal Socialization and the Development of Legitimacy*. New York: Oxford University Press.

Unger, Michael A. 2008. "After the Supreme Word: The Effect of *McCreary County v. ACLU* (2005) and *Van Orden v. Perry* (2005) on Support for Public Displays of the Ten Commandments." *American Politics Research* 36(5): 750–75.

Ura, Joseph Daniel, and Matthew Hall. 2022. "When the Supreme Court Loses Americans' Loyalty, Chaos—Even Violence—Can Follow." Conversation, November 2, 2022. https://today.tamu.edu/2022/11/02/when-the-supreme-court-loses-americans-loyalty-chaos-even-violence-can-follow/.

U.S. Department of Justice. 2015. *Department of Justice Report Regarding the Criminal Investigation into the Shooting Death of Michael Brown by Ferguson, Missouri Police Officer Darren Wilson*, March 4, 2015. https://www.justice.gov/sites/default/files/opa/press-releases/attachments/2015/03/04/doj_report_on_shooting_of_michael_brown_1.pdf.

Vega, Tanzina, and Megan Thee-Brenan. 2014. "Poll Shows Broad Divisions amid Missouri Turmoil." *New York Times*, August 21, 2014. https://www.nytimes.com/2014/08/22/us/on-ferguson-unrest-poll-shows-sharp-racial-divide.html.

Wang, Amy B. 2017. "It's Usually Difficult for People to Agree on a Crowd's Size. Here's Why." *Washington Post*, January 22, 2017. https://www.washingtonpost.com/news/wonk/wp/2017/01/22/its-usually-difficult-for-people-to-agree-on-a-crowds-size-heres-why/.

Wells, Michael L. 2007. "Sociological Legitimacy in Supreme Court Opinions." *Washington and Lee Law Review* 64(3): 1011–70.

Werner, Hannah, and Sofie Marien. 2022. "Process vs. Outcome? How to Evaluate the Effects of Participatory Processes on Legitimacy Perceptions." *British Journal of Political Science* 52(1): 429–36.

Woodruff, Judy. 2017. "Do Trump's Attacks on Judicial Legitimacy Go Too Far?" *PBS News Hour*, February 9, 2017. https://www.pbs.org/newshour/show/trumps-attacks-judicial-legitimacy-go-far.

Yates, Jeffrey L., and Andrew B. Whitford. 2002. "The Presidency and the Supreme Court after *Bush v. Gore*: Implications for Legitimacy and Effectiveness." *Stanford Law and Policy Review* 13(1): 101–18.

Yousif, Sami R., Rosie Aboody, and Frank C. Keil. 2019. "The Illusion of Consensus: A Failure to Distinguish between True and False Consensus." *Psychological Science* 30(8): 1195–1204.

Zakaria, Fareed. 1997. "The Rise of Illiberal Democracy." *Foreign Affairs* 76(November/December): 22–43.

Zaller, John R. 1992. *The Nature and Origins of Mass Opinion*. Cambridge: Cambridge University Press.

Zilis, Michael A. 2015. *The Limits of Legitimacy: Dissenting Opinions, Media Coverage, and Public Responses to Supreme Court Decisions*. Ann Arbor: University of Michigan Press.

Zilis, Michael A., and Rachel Blandau. 2021. "Judicial Legitimacy, Political Polarization, and How the Public Views the Supreme Court." In *Oxford Research Encyclopedia in Politics Online* (March 25). https://oxfordre.com/politics/display/10.1093/acrefore/9780190228637.001.0001/acrefore-9780190228637-e-1781;jsessionid=2E6875A319BEB0DB1179322930B0033C.

INDEX

Tables and figures are listed in **boldface**.

research design: causality and, 54, 205n4; limitations of, 70–71, 77, 119, 143–55, **149** (*see also* unanswered questions and challenges); racial differences in legitimacy attitudes and, 103, 210nn29–31; surveys, 12–14, 54, 69–70, 146–48, 157–63, **158**, **161**, 199n10, 200–201nn22–23

rigged election perceptions: insurrection and, 86–88, **87**, **89**, 91, **92–93**; racial differences in, 105–14, **106**, **110–11**, **114**

riots. *See also* insurrection at U.S. capitol and impeachment of Trump; political violence

Rogowski, Jon, 200n20

Rosenstiel, Tom, 36

rule of law, support for: conceptualizing, 31, 202n37; election events, awareness and assessment of, **48–50**, 51, 52; intra-Black variability in Supreme Court support, 137–38, **137**, 213–14–nn22–23; measures of, 177, 217n8; predictors of support for democratic institutions following insurrection, **92**, 94; predictors of support for institutional legitimacy, 62, **63–65**; racial differences in, 100, 107, 109, **110–11**, 116; Supreme Court legitimacy and, **81**, 85, 90

Ryan, Timothy, 38–39

Sanchez, Gabriel, 213n16

Saunders, Kyle, 198n54

Scott, Kevin, 198n54

Selby County v. Holder (2013), 210n14

Senate legitimacy: Barrett confirmation vote and, 60; cross-sectional analysis of attitudes on, 61–67, **63–65**; insurrection and, 75–76, **75**, **82**, 85–86, 88–90, **89**; measuring, 27–29, **28**, 166–67, **166–67**, 201n32; predictors of support for, **182–84**, **187–91**; racial differences in support for, 33, **34**; resilience of, 68–69; rigged election perceptions and, 86–88, **87**

Smith, Rogers, 198n63

social identity theory, 39–40, 125, 204n17

Spence, Lester Kenyatta, 27, 207n2

Supreme Court decisions: *Dobbs* ruling undermining legitimacy, 148–50, **149**;

2000 presidential election, deciding, 68, 74, 148, 207n2; 2020 presidential election, rulings on fraud during, 60–61, 181–82

Supreme Court justices: legitimacy, use of term in opinions of, 9; politicization of nominations, 10, 13; Senate confirmations of, 22, 60; Trump appointees, 2, 5, 13, 204n20. *See also* Barrett, Amy Coney, nomination and confirmation of

Supreme Court legitimacy: African Americans and declining support for, 9–10, 198–99n64; Barrett nomination and, 45–46, **45**, **57**, 58–60, **59**, 67–68, 148–50, 206n10; change in support for, 55–61, **56–57**, **59**, 207n24; cross-sectional analysis of attitudes on, 61–67, **63–65**; insurrection and, 74–75, **75**, **81**, 84–85, 88–90, **89**; intra-Black variability in attitudes on, **121**, 122, 133–38, **134–35**, **137**, 213n21, 213–14–nn22–23; measuring, 8–10, 22, 23–25, **24**, 148, 167–69, **167**, **169**, 200–201nn23–25; partisan and ideological differences in support for, 45–47, **46**, **57**, 58–60; polarized opinions on, 67; predictors of support for, **179–84**, **187–91**; public attitudes toward, measuring, 12, 198nn53–54; racial differences in support for, 15, 33, **34**, 99–103, 210n14; resilience of, 67–68; rigged election perceptions and of, 86, **87**

Svolik, Milan, 116, 145, 202n34

Tajfel, Henri, 129

Theiss-Morse, Elizabeth, 23

Trump, Donald: African American voters and, 15, 103, 198n61; Biden presidency, verbal attacks on, 68; democracy, undermining, 141; efforts to overturn 2020 election, 41–42, **42**, **49**, 51, **92**, 94; Georgia election interference, 198n56, 204n20; on legitimacy of 2020 presidential election, 2, 10, 13, 41–42, **42**, **50**, 51, 53, 103, 195n6, 198n56, 214n1; on legitimacy of federal courts, 3, 68, 141, 196n11, 214n1; racism of, 115; White Protectionism and, 198n63. *See also* institutional le-

gitimacy, Trump undermining; insurrection at U.S. capitol and impeachment of Trump
Tucker, Patrick, 207n24
Turner, John, 129
Tyler, Tom, 6

unanswered questions and challenges, 143–55; African Americans and legitimacy of democratic institutions, 153–54; empirical analysis and causal structures of attitudes, 150–53, 215–16n24, 215nn21–22, 216n26; future threats to democratic institutions and, 154–55; institutional support measures and effect of 2020 election and insurrection, 148–50, **149**; other observers' conclusions on, 144–46; survey responses, reliability of, 146–47, 215n13; survey responses, truth of, 147–48, 215n18
Unger, Michael, 198n54

values. *See* democratic values
Vargas, Edward, 213n16
vicarious experiences: defined, 212n8; institutional legitimacy and, 143; intra-Black variability in legitimacy attitudes, **131**, 133, 138
violence. *See* political violence
Voting Rights Act (1965), 210n14

Waltenburg, Eric, 101
Warren, Earl, 100
Weber, Max, 7
Werner, Hannah, 199n13
White Americans, 38, 203–4n8. *See also* racial differences in support for democratic institutions
White House. *See* insurrection at U.S. capitol and impeachment of Trump
White nationalism and protectionism, 15, 103, 115, 198n63
Wilson, Darren, 38